Beyond the Court

A Lawyer's Guide to Campaigning

WITHDRAWN

Katie Ghose is a barrister and Director of the British Institute for Human Rights. She practised from 1 Pump Court chambers (1997-99). Katie has extensive campaigns and political experience, having worked in campaigns and public affairs at Age Concern England (2001-05), as an MP's researcher (1992-94), for Citizens Advice as their parliamentary adviser (1994-95) and as Campaign Manager for the Child Accident Prevention Trust (1999-2000). She has also worked as a freelance consultant, providing lectures and training to City law firms and charities on parliamentary procedures and lobbying techniques. Katie was a member of the Taskforce which advised the Government on the establishment of the Commission for Equality and Human Rights.

She is a trustee of Stonewall and Bail for Immigration Detainees (BID). From 1997-99 she was Chair of Asylum Aid and was Chair of BID from 2002-04.

The Legal Action Group wishes to thank Irwin Mitchell solicitors for generously supporting this book.

The Legal Action Group is a national, independent charity which campaigns for equal access to justice for all members of society.
Legal Action Group:
- provides support to the practice of lawyers and advisers
- inspires developments in that practice
- campaigns for improvements in the law and the administration of justice
- stimulates debate on how services should be delivered.

Beyond the Courtroom

A Lawyer's Guide to Campaigning

Katie Ghose

 Legal Action Group
2005

This edition published in Great Britain 2005
by LAG Education and Service Trust Limited
242 Pentonville Road, London N1 9UN
www.lag.org.uk

While every effort has been made to ensure that the details in this text are correct, readers must be aware that the law changes and that the accuracy of the material cannot be guaranteed and the author and the publisher accept no responsibility for any losses or damage sustained.

The rights of the author to be identified as the author of this work has been asserted in accordance with the Copyright, Designs and Patents Act 1988.

British Library Cataloguing in Publication Data
a CIP catalogue record for this book is available from the British Library.

Crown copyright material is produced with the permission of the Controller of HMSO and the Queen's Printer for Scotland.

ISBN-10 1 903307 35 X
ISBN-13 978 1 903307 35 9

Typeset and printed by Hobbs the Printers, Totton, Hampshire

For my parents, Daphne and Toon

Foreword

As practitioners we tend to think of campaigning activities as a desirable adjunct to an important test case. The point, then, is to propagate to the world beyond the parties and specialist lawyers the nature of the wrong and the argument for it to be righted. Such strategic test cases can have great impact.

A good example was the appeal of Emma Humphries, who I represented, in 1994. She overturned her conviction for the murder, when aged sixteen, of a violent pimp into whose clutches she had fallen as an already dysfunctional child. The judge had failed to tell the jury to add in her dysfunctional personality when balancing whether the victim's conduct provoked her and had ignored a background of seriously oppressive treatment of this girl, by the victim. Emma was really guilty only of manslaughter. The judgment had a major impact on the law of provocation and in a recently announced government review of murder law Emma will again play a role in pointing to the iniquity that women who kill in fear after a history of cruel treatment can be convicted of murder, whilst men who kill in anger are usually convicted only of manslaughter.

None of that law is likely to have been made if the case had not been accompanied by a quite superb press and publicity campaign from Justice for Women, headed by Harriet Wistrich, the lawyer who now acts for the family of Jean Charles de Menezes. The clarity with which J for W's campaign set out the dire position of women, battered in their own homes and unable to escape until a final desperate strike, undoubtedly moulded the framework for the Court of Appeal's sympathetic reasoning.

However, test cases are not enough. They depend on the infrequent coincidence of a client with the courage, time and money to take a case through the courts and a strong point of legal principle recognised and pursued by the most competent lawyers. When determined, such a case may often only impact on the parties and those who subsequently have the benefit of legal advice on the point. It is unusual for the decision to become so well known that a single case changes people's behaviour so as to prevent the injustice occurring again. To do that it is necessary to change the culture underpinning the injustice and this requires a steadfast publicity campaign, parliamentary debate and very public advocacy culminating in fresh policy or legislative change.

In taking cases, lawyers work 'downstream' in the sense that they are recipients of the law and have to rescue their client from its impact. Campaigning for change in an unjust law or to lay a fairer framework is upstream of that. Lawyers are good people to be swimming in that direction. Specialising, as most now do, in one branch of the law, they repeatedly encounter the same injustices, causing the same problems for clients and have to right them individually before a court, when their experience really points to the need for a change in the law. Having clients has a two-fold effect on the value of lawyers as campaigners. Firstly, they are real life, not theoretical examples, of laws being wrong. In addition they are individuals with families, histories and stories to tell. They are human interest to the journalist. They are constituency interest to the MP – for what is going wrong for a client in London is bound to be going wrong too for a voter somewhere in Rowley Regis or Blyth. Lawyers' clients are simultaneously the point of the story and the means by which its telling arouses public response.

In addition, lawyers are used to dealing with institutions of state, albeit usually the courts. They can adapt so as to become equally adept at working within legislative procedures and are ideally qualified, if anyone is, to work out the curious interactions of the maze that is Whitehall and the executive.

There have been some notable examples of successful lawyer activism recently, in particular the removal of the 'ouster clause' from the Asylum and Immigration (Treatment of Claimants etc) Bill. The future of jury trial is about to re-emerge on the parliamentary stage and there will be many more injustices and challenges for lawyers to get their teeth into, in and out of the courtroom. This book provides a comprehensive, detailed and accurate road map for the new starter to campaigning, and a handy reference book for all. Read it quickly.

Vera Baird QC MP

Preface

Say the words 'legal campaigning' and most lawyers start talking about test cases. 'Strategic litigation', or test cases, are an important way to publicise injustices, mobilise support and sometimes even change the law! But they are only one way to effect lasting social change, and on their own are rarely enough. A case may never get to court, either because the right point or client never emerges or because the authorities settle, so as to avoid having to commit to broader change. A case may reach court but see any prospect of policy change stumped by hostile judges. Or a lawyer may win, only to have the government use its parliamentary majority to overturn a court's decision.

Throughout history lawyers have been at the forefront of major social reforms, but have often found that the 'legal route' is not enough on its own. The suffragettes, campaigning in the late nineteenth and early twentieth century to secure votes for women, had to 'fight on all fronts'. National and local suffrage organisations sprang up, seeking public support; liberal MPs led the movement from within Parliament; and campaigners turned to the courts, to be given short shrift. Many turned to direct action – most famously Emily Davison who died when she stepped out in front of the King's horse at the 1913 Derby. Women's work during World War I finally made reform inevitable.[1]

Nearly a hundred years later, the limits of legal challenges alone are illustrated by the experiences of thousands of Gypsies and Travellers, who have suffered intolerance and major barriers to living their chosen way of life. In 1994 local authorities' legal obligation to provide adequate accommodation (under the Caravan Sites Act 1968) was repealed, making it increasingly difficult over the subsequent years for Travellers to access basic services like health and education. Solicitor Luke Clements has been representing Gypsies and Travellers for more than twenty years. Domestic courts were unsympathetic when actions were taken against local authorities who were decreasing the places available (or rendering them unsuitable). Clements then started to make applications to the European Court and Commission of Human Rights. Despite being more sympathetic, the complaints were rejected. At this

---

1 The Representation of the Peoples Act 1918 granted women over 30 the right to vote.

point Clements and others questioned the wisdom of continuing with a litigation strategy – especially when a client pointed out that he was facing eviction yet again whilst his lawyer was driving a new car!

A new stage in the battle for the right to live a nomadic way of life was developed: a campaign for law reform spearheaded by Gypsies, Travellers, and academic and practising lawyers.[2] It has focused on winning support to change the statutory and regulatory regime that presently fails to provide support and helps fuel intolerance towards these communities. A major first step was the drafting of the Traveller Law Reform Bill, which provided a focus for the campaign and attracted support from politicians from all major parties. In shifting the focus from the courts to Parliament and the executive, the movement illustrates the importance of lawyers' contributions, both in and beyond the courtroom.

Legal challenges remain a vital 'tool in the toolkit' of lawyers keen to make a difference. But lawyers shouldn't confine themselves to the 'courts of law', when they have much to contribute to the 'court of public opinion', and in the corridors of power in Whitehall, Westminster and increasingly Brussels, where public policy is developed with significant consequences for their clients. There is much that lawyers can and do achieve 'beyond the courtroom': drafting amendments to soften the blow of a bad Bill; contributing ideas for policy and law reform; engaging with officials on the detail of a policy or dreaming up a new law from scratch; lending their legal expertise to campaigns groups and coalitions; working with other lawyers to expose bad practices; and engaging the public with the law and legal issues via the media.

What is this book about?

Beyond the courtroom is a practical guide for those whose advocacy does not stop at the courtroom door. It is different from other books about campaigning because it has been written specifically for lawyers, legal advisers, law students and others working in or with the law. It is relevant to lawyers looking to change direction to work in-house in a charity or campaigning organisation, as well as to commercial lawyers keen to influence law and policy for their clients' benefit. And it is also aimed at organisations who seek to build relations with lawyers and make more strategic use of the law as a tool for social change.

I have already mentioned that test cases, although significant in campaigning for social change, are only 'one tool in the toolkit' for

2   The Gypsy and Traveller Law Reform Coalition.

Acknowledgements

This was a collaborative project and there are many people to thank.

I am very grateful to the following for reading and commenting on specific chapters: Robin Allen QC, Declan O'Dempsey, Chandrika Deshpande, Andy Harrop, Steve Hynes, Edward Kirton-Darling, Mark Mclaren, Susanna Mordaunt, Bob Nightingale, Hannah Pearce, Greg Power, Nicola Rogers, Michael Smyth, Rachel Sylvester, Helen Turnock and Martin Westlake.

Thank you to the following for sharing their views and experiences: Karen Ashton, Richard Austin, Richard Baker, Tim Baster, James Bridge, Helen Carr, Luke Clements, Richard Corbett MEP, Sarah Cutler, Elizabeth Crossick, Gareth Crossman, Michelle Dyson, John Finlay, Elspeth Guild, Jonathan Goldsmith, Stephanie Harland, Margaret Harrop, Michelle Lee, Lord Lester, Martin Penrose, David Ruebain, Lucy Scott Moncrieff, Roger Smith, Tim Spencer-Lane, Diana Sutton, Pauline Thompson, Graham Watson MEP, Jenny Watson, Alan Wardle, Sally West, Sue Willman, Nick Wright and Stuart Wright.

Everyone at LAG was a pleasure to work with. Special thanks to Esther Pilger who I worked with from the outset, and also to Owen Durnin who worked on the book from summer 2005.

Many thanks to Vera Baird QC MP for writing the foreword.

I am very grateful to my colleagues Michelle Mitchell, Neil Churchill and Gordon Lishman for enabling me to take a sabbatical to start the book whilst I was at Age Concern.

Thank you to my sister Nandita Ghose for making me put pen to paper in the first place and also for coming up with the title.

Most of all I would like to thank Andy Harrop for his unwavering encouragement and support. He helped me with all aspects of the book every step of the way.

campaigners and that they are often most effective when they are an integral part of a wider campaign. For these reasons, I do not devote a particular chapter to them; rather I have sought to refer to them throughout the book. In particular, I try to show the importance of working in partnership when choosing and working on legal cases with the aim of progressing or stimulating a campaign.

From my time in practice, I know that lawyers and advisers are extremely busy. Occupied with today's clients or tomorrow's cases, they do not have time for yet more reading. For this reason I have not sought to provide a detailed history or guide to campaigns and lobbying. There are many comprehensive books about these subjects already. I have tried instead to provide a handbook that will make it easier for you to bridge the gap between your cases and wider society and inspire you to take action, making best use of your existing expertise and resources.

As a lawyer you will be familiar with the legal system. This book focuses on the other two 'powerhouses': the executive (government) and Parliament – as well as the increasingly important European sphere of decision-making. The book takes you through the policy-making and political processes by which an idea becomes a practice, policy or law affecting thousands or millions of people. It demonstrates how and when you can have your say and influence the outcome. All lawyers know that cases can only be won or settled satisfactorily with knowledge of their opponents and of the judge: where they are coming from, their 'bottom lines' and their personal style. The same applies to campaigns and influencing, and this book looks at how to persuade a broad range of decision-makers to listen to your views and engage with your cause.

I have only included information about Whitehall, lobbying in the UK Parliament and on the main EU institutions. My experience does not extend either to influencing and lobbying in the Scottish Parliament or the Welsh Assembly or to local or regional government, and I would not have been able to do justice to the different ways in which lawyers can engage with the important activities of these bodies.

Where do I find the information I need?

Chapter 1 is an introduction to campaigning and the law. It includes a campaigns checklist for you to keep in mind as you read the book. Chapter 2 focuses on the workings of Whitehall: how to engage with ministers, civil servants and special advisers. Chapters 3 (legislation) and 4 (tools and techniques aside from legislation) focus on Parliament – its role in law-making and scrutinising government. Chapter 5 is about how to use the media as a channel to impact on all your key targets. Chapter 6 highlights the opportunities for influencing decisions made at European level. Finally, Chapter 7 looks at the power of partnership: how lawyers and campaigning organisations working together can achieve tangible changes to society. At the end of this chapter is a campaigns 'audit' and further checklists to help you and your colleagues put your ideas into action.

Katie Ghose
August 2005

Contents

CHAPTER 1

Campaigns: an introduction

continued

- Lawyers and their value as campaigners
- From the 1970s to the present day: key features of campaigning and the law
- Putting ideas into action: campaigns checklists

Upstream or downstream – what is campaigning about?

1.1 Many people are motivated in their daily lives by the idea of trying to create a more just and fair society. They want to reach out beyond their own personal circumstances to make a difference to a wider group. People contribute in a variety of ways – sometimes in their day job, as a nurse or social worker tackling problems at the 'coalface', or as volunteers assisting older neighbours or children in a local school. This type of work is located 'downstream', helping each and every individual with whatever problems they bring through the door. Essentially these people are on the receiving end of policies and practices, whether imposed by national or local government or other decision-making bodies and the everyday grind often doesn't allow the time to challenge what is happening 'upstream'.

1.2 Many lawyers will identify with this description, feeling that they spend their working lives 'downstream', dealing with a string of individual cases. But sometimes their frustrations with what they see make them want to go 'upriver' and discover what it is that's causing the problems and how it might be changed. When I was practising immigration law in the mid-1990s, I often despaired of the grotesque way in which my asylum-seeking clients were treated. They were victims I felt of a system and culture in which poor decision-making and a lack of respect for the individual were the norm. Ultimately it failed to protect many who had suffered persecution and torture in their country of origin. And through my individual case-load it was hard to see how the system as a whole might be made better.

1.3 For me campaigning is really about going 'upriver' and seeing what might be done to stem the tide, clean the water or do whatever it is that would have a positive impact on those further down. Mr Smith organising protests about plans for a new airport runway; trade union leaders calling on the government to withdraw its voucher scheme for asylum-seekers; millions of people the world over calling on rich nations to 'drop the debt' – all these are campaigns. What do they have in common? They involve a deliberate course of action with a clear goal in mind (and some smaller steps along the way) and a desire to achieve change that would impact on the wider community. They are an attempt to oppose, amend or improve a priority or a policy being drawn up by individuals or bodies in whom power is vested. They are motivated by a sense that something has gone wrong and that those in established bodies have either created the problem or cannot be relied on to put it right. Sometimes they set the agenda, raising the profile of an issue; sometimes they are reactive.

1.4   Campaigning has a strong public element – indeed individuals and organisations often resort to a campaign when behind the scenes influencing has failed to get the desired result. However, campaigns and influencing overlap. There are few successful campaigns that do not achieve their goals without some kind of 'backstage' activities – an MP having a private word with a minister for example, or discussions with officials about a compromise that might be reached.

Why should lawyers be interested in campaigns?

1.5   Lawyers have first-hand experience of an individual's particular circumstances that have brought them into the judicial system, but they are also faced head on with the wider consequences of existing law and policy. They are in a good position to look upstream and spot emerging trends and the wider impacts of a policy, law or practice (or the need for a new initiative). And when legal routes have tried and failed this puts them in a good position to influence policies and laws via other channels. An increasing number of lawyers wish to be more actively involved in shaping change – both of the legal system itself and of the laws that flow through it. Frustrated by draconian measures or ill thought through proposals, they want to make a difference early on – before they see their clients and before their clients get to court. Their position gives them a vital role to play in campaigns – especially but not only when the goals include law reform.

1.6   In a society in which the rule of law stands firm, campaigning for law reform can be a powerful way to effect change. For this reason many campaigns are aimed at legislative change – either pushing to reform existing laws (eg anti-abortion campaigners) or pressing the government to introduce new ones (eg lesbians', gay men's and bisexual's calls for equal treatment with heterosexuals). Laws that are under consideration are often subject to attempts both to amend them behind the scenes but also to more public campaigning (eg age organisations' attempts to persuade the government to scrap mandatory retirement ages as part of new anti-ageism laws in the workplace).

But lawyers also have an important role to play in seeking non-legislative change, in helping to change public opinion, educate decision-makers and in making the case for changes to policy or practice.

1.7 Lawyers have choices in the ways in which they seek to achieve social change. They can use the legal route by winning a test case that is not subsequently reversed (or which though reversed nonetheless has an impact). They can work on 'public interest cases' (a broader category of cases which use 'tried and tested' legal tools rather than necessarily testing a point of law). They can work with parliamentarians to achieve the amendment of an existing law or influence a draft law as it passes through Parliament. Or they can help win public support for a new law which the government then effects.

1.8 Lawyers can also focus on changing policy and practice, at local and national levels. For example, they can collect examples of bad practice and use these to bring pressure to bear. Using examples from one locality (eg a local authority or a housing benefit office) can effectively show how a problem is widespread and needs a systematic solution. They can often demonstrate the difference between the stated intention of a public policy and its effects in reality.

1.9 Lawyers can also have an impact by sharing information, ideas and techniques, both with other lawyers and more broadly. Offering training to lawyers and advisers and helping in other ways to publicise a prospective new law is one of the best ways to ensure take-up of new rights and that important points are tested in the courts early on.

Campaigns and the law: what can lawyers contribute?

1.10 Lawyers have three core strengths when it comes to campaigning. They have legal action or the threat of it up their sleeve which makes decision-makers sit up and listen; they have valuable knowledge from the 'sharp end' (their clients) about the effects of laws and policies; and they are experts, about the legal system itself as well as in their specialist areas which can help them support campaigns for legal reforms and input into policy making. They are also accustomed to dealing with powerful people like judges and bodies including central and local government which equips them well for the 'corridors of power'.

Legal challenges

1.11 Lawyers' involvement in legal challenges today continues to be an important part of their contribution to campaigns. Advising a campaigns group about a potential challenge (or the value in threatening one) can help put pressure on the government or others. Also, encouraging other lawyers to take cases on a similar point can help build up a case-load that is untenable for the courts.

1.12   Tony Prosser, in his 1983 study of test cases, found that 'the indirect effects of test cases' (awareness raising; building a portfolio of cases which helps stimulate policy change; increasing legitimacy of the groups bringing the cases which in turn improves their ability to influence) are 'more important than the direct effect'.[1]

1.13   A test case can certainly be a very public way to raise awareness of an issue or keep it high on the political agenda. Handled effectively some cases can also amount to a detailed investigation into an issue, accompanied by an account of the facts that becomes the accepted record of what happened. Acceptance of a certain history (eg of prejudice within an institution like the police) can help move an issue on and win recognition by the government of the need for reforms.

Evidence

1.14   Lawyers sometimes forget the value of being at the 'coalface', that civil servants in particular are thirsty for information about how policies are being experienced on the ground and that when it comes to persuading people of the need for change there is nothing more powerful than the story of a real person – especially when their experience is shared by others. Lawyers' clients are a vast and often untapped resource in campaigns. Clients dissatisfied with the outcome of their own case are often keen to see a broader campaign emerge – to ensure that others do not have to endure what they have.

1.15   One story, or a group of them, can present the need for a campaign in the first place. They can be the fastest way to spell out why action is needed and then help to keep it in the public eye. First-hand accounts (anonymised if necessary) are often the best possible way to make a point – not least because they are much more likely to be remembered than a sea of facts and statistics. They give a cause credibility and someone to identify with and may also help attract and sustain media interest.

1.16   Politicians are interested in individuals' stories, recognising that one person's problem may be a warning sign of a wider issue. Indeed, MPs' policy priorities are often heavily influenced by the issues they come up against most often in their weekly surgeries. The trend towards

---

1   T Prosser, 'Test cases for the poor legal techniques in the politics of social welfare', *Child Poverty Action Group Poverty Pamphlet*, 1983, p86.

greater 'user involvement' in policy making, reinforces the importance of individuals' experiences in policy making and campaigns.

Knowledge and expertise

1.17   Lawyers can bring a clear and proper understanding of all aspects of the legal system and the law in general: its strengths and failings and how it really impacts on citizens every day. The value of this cannot be underestimated, especially given the low level of public awareness about the workings of the law and legal institutions. They also have expertise in their chosen areas, such as crime, family or immigration law. This makes them invaluable public commentators – explaining how a case might impact on wider groups than the individual concerned.

1.18   Their expertise also makes them valuable behind the scenes, helping organisations, officials and ministers to understand the potential for or implications of a legal challenge or how a proposed legal reform might be drafted to achieve their objectives. Their confidence in dealing with powerful or influential people and institutions is an additional strength.

Campaigning and the law – key developments

Highlights from the 1970s and beyond

1.19   There is nothing new about lawyers seeking to have an impact beyond their individual cases or indeed in campaigners making strategic use of the law to challenge social injustices. In their book, *Pressure through law,* Carol Harlow and Richard Rawlings find that 'the use of the law by pressure groups to achieve reform and to establish rights may be as old as pressure groups themselves. Long before the twentieth century, test cases and pressure group litigation can be identified in Britain'.[2] They highlight as an early example the legal cases in England and Scotland in the 1700s that challenged slavery, and formed an important part of a wider movement for its abolition. Interestingly, as with the suffragettes, judicial decisions and comment were only one 'piece in the jigsaw'. Legislation and other government action were required before slavery was completely outlawed in 1834.[3]

2   C Harlow and R Rawlings, *Pressure through law*, Routledge, 1992, p12.

3   The purchasing of enslaved Africans was finally outlawed in the British Empire by an Act of Parliament in 1807. The abolition of slavery as an institution was achieved by the Slavery Abolition Act 1833.

1.20   Harlow and Rawlings provide a fascinating history of the 'use of law and legal techniques as an instrument for obtaining wider collective justice'.[4] I do not attempt an historical account here, either of test cases or lawyers' wider involvement in campaigns. Instead, I select some particularly interesting features of 'legal campaigning' from the last three decades of the twentieth century and the first few years of the twenty-first. These help to show the rich tradition of lawyers' involvement in social reforms, the barriers they may face and to set the scene for showing how lawyers today can be a powerful force for change. (I return to some of these themes in chapter 7, which looks at the importance of lawyers working in partnership, within their profession as well as with other organisations.)

Lawyers' engagement with social injustice

1.21   Although, as we have seen, test cases were nothing new, the 1970s marked a new phase in campaigning through the law, with lawyers actively involving themselves in social issues and organisations making more strategic use of the law. New sets of chambers were set up by barristers keen to break the mould and to focus their attention on people who were deeply disadvantaged or unjustly treated within the legal system. They aimed specifically to tackle discrimination and injustice suffered by particular groups – young, black men in the criminal justice system for instance. There was a realisation that entrenched attitudes in the legal system itself was at the root of some of the injustices faced by certain groups, and had to be challenged head on.

1.22   A significant need for advice on welfare law and particularly welfare benefits fuelled the growth of the independent advice sector, staffed by non-legally qualified caseworkers. Interestingly, Citizens Advice (then the National Association of Citizens Advice Bureaux), from early on allowed experiences of the delivery of information and advice to inform campaigns and policy work. It developed social policy as a twin 'aim', alongside the provision of free, independent advice, a feature which endures in its work today. Evidence of CAB clients' problems is a powerful tool in campaigning for changes in policies and services. They use case studies gathered from local bureaux as the basis for reports and often succeed in having them cited in parliamentary debates and in the media. This concrete evidence is hard for policy-makers to ignore, as is evident from their successes over the years. (See p20 for details of a recent success, when evidence provided by

---

4   C Harlow and R Rawlings, *Pressure through law*, Routledge 1992.

CA led to the introduction of a tenancy deposit scheme in the 2004 Housing Act.)

1.23   The 1970s saw the development of law centres which also aimed to use evidence from their cases for wider benefit.[5] Steve Hynes, Director of the Law Centres Federation, describes their emergence in the UK as a direct result of the failure of the legal aid scheme 'to meet the legal needs of people living in poor neighbourhoods'.[6]

1.24   Hynes also highlights the influence of the North American 'neighbourhood law offices' as part of a War on Poverty programme. An agreement with the Law Society, initially hostile to the potential competition, saw law centres develop services mainly in the areas of welfare rights, immigration, employment, housing and public law, where private firms had not tended to operate. Law centres aimed to be a different model of legal services, embedded in the local community and with an emphasis on campaigning for people's rights more broadly, rather than only working on individual casework (as legally aided solicitors would tend to do). They sought to effect change at local as well as at national level, encouraging local lawyers to challenge the bad practices that they saw emerging.

Test case litigation

1.25   The 1970s saw an explosion in test case litigation, much influenced by the US where there was a long record of strategic use of law. There was a growth in national organisations doing test cases as part of their core work. The National Council for Civil Liberties (NCCL, now Liberty) for example had been in existence since 1935 but only really got going in terms of legal challenges in this decade. Child Poverty Action Group (CPAG) was also explicit in identifying significant cases to test welfare benefits law as it affected children. At different times since, many other national organisations (notably, MIND and more recently Shelter) have developed and maintained a commitment to the value of litigation as a tool for achieving organisational objectives. Established test case organisations have sought to further integrate their legal services and work into their overall objectives and campaigns. CPAG is

---

5 The first was opened in North Kensington, London on 17 July 1970.

6 'Law Centres – providing access to justice', a paper by Steve Hynes, Director of the Law Centres Federation, presented during a visit arranged by the British Embassies in Buenos Aires, Montevideo and Santiago in Buenos Aires, 2004. This gives an excellent account of the history and development of the UK legal aid system and of law centres. See www.lawcentres.org.uk.

seeking to be more strategic, for example by running a case as part of a broader campaign or using evidence from cases to influence parliamentary committees.

1.26   Organisations without a track record in this type of legal work are also seeing the power of interventions and other devices as additional tools in their armoury.

Administrative law – a new tool for challenging state power

1.27   Administrative law and in particular judicial review developed during the 1970s and became a powerful mechanism for challenging the state on a range of broad social issues. This often saw the joining up of lawyers and campaigns groups. Cases often reflected the wider social issues of the times, with homelessness, for example, featuring prominently in the overall number of judicial reviews.

1.28   Administrative law saw a breakthrough in the late 1980s when organisations were allowed to take on a representative role and sue in their own name. Since then a number of non-governmental organisations (NGOs) have been able to demonstrate 'sufficient interest' and mount public law challenges.[7] The courts have adopted a fairly liberal approach and acknowledged the benefit to the development of public law in allowing these challenges, particularly where individuals are unlikely to come forward. Organisations including the World Development Movement, Greenpeace and the Joint Council for the Welfare of Immigrants have all taken advantage of this to take major cases. In *R v Secretary of State for Social Services ex p Child Poverty Action Group*, Woolf LJ noted that CPAG and the National Association of Citizens Advice Bureaux had raised important social welfare issues that might not be raised by individual claimants.[8] It should be noted however, that when the government introduced the Human Rights Act 1988 it created a more restrictive test in relation to human rights cases. See para 1.50 for more information about this.

The political climate

1.29   The 1980s and the beginning of the Conservatives' 18 years in office, brought a very different and more polarised political climate from the previous decade. Unemployment increased, social security benefits were reduced and their availability lessened and lawyers found them-

7   Supreme Court Act 1981 s31(3).
8   [1990] 2 QB 540.

selves faced with numerous social problems (including homelessness). At national level access to justice was not seen as a priority. There were left-wing local authorities and networks (eg the Local Government Information Unit) that were completely opposed to the national government's policies in most areas but were limited in terms of their ability to effect change, especially when their finance powers were curtailed. However, at local level there was a growth in information and advice provision (both local authority and independent services) to deal with the fallout 'on the ground' of significant economic decline. Publicly-funded lawyers were largely unable to get anywhere through the law reform route, and much of their work was focused on getting people their minimum entitlements, in terms of benefits and accommodation, etc.

Politics and the law: where do the boundaries lie?

1.30   The debate about the boundaries between politics and law has been around for a long time. It continues to be played out in tussles over the balance of power between the executive (government as policy-maker), the judiciary and Parliament and in particular on whether judges are straying into the domain of making decisions about public policy, the miners' litigation being a good example. These are important debates as they provide the backdrop to and may influence how lawyers feel about becoming involved in wider social issues and campaigns.

1.31   Britons can be suspicious of politics, especially party politics, sometimes treating it as a topic not quite 'polite' to discuss. Perhaps in reflection of this many lawyers see a clear separation between their domain (the legal system and the courts) and the political institutions of government and Parliament and don't think of themselves as natural policy-makers (even though many lawyers go on to a political career). Harlow and Rawlings describe an 'apolitical tradition of law' in the UK in which they see lawyers as 'quick to divest their case law of its political and social significance, reducing it to a boxed set of sanitised legal precedents'. However, they point out that this view of the law is 'challenged by pressure-group activity around the courtroom'.[9]

1.32   The US provides an interesting contrast, where there is a much more explicit link between politicians and lawyers and an expectation that a decent Washington lawyer will have a good grasp of how the political system operates and be able to influence behind the scenes.

9 See p6.

This reflects the differences in the political system, with horse trading taking place along the lines of 'I'll vote for this law if you do x for me in x state'. Law and public policy is a recognised career path, reflected in the number of firms with an explicit legislative or public policy practice. Lawyers are afforded an explicit role in communicating with state agencies to advance their clients' interests. In contrast few firms, (Clifford Chance and DLA Piper Rudnick Gray Cary are notable examples) offer anything comparable in the UK.

Judges v politicians or eunuchs v the kings?

1.33   Disagreement about the boundaries between judicial and executive power tends to explode around fundamentally important social and political issues. In 2005, in the US, a 7-year battle brought judges and politicians into direct conflict over the fate of Terry Schiavo, a woman in a coma for 15 years whose feeding was withdrawn following a court ruling. President Bush cut short a holiday to fly back to Washington to sign an emergency bill to send the case back to the federal courts soon after the feeding tube was disconnected. But the US courts at every level supported her husband's case that feeding be withdrawn and she died shortly afterwards.

1.34   Closer to home ministers of all political colours have come to blows with judges. In 2003 judges were fiercely critical of the government's hasty decision to scrap the post of Lord Chancellor – of major significance for the entire constitution. Former Home Secretary David Blunkett MP was following in others' footsteps when he said he was 'fed up with having to deal with a situation where Parliament debates issues and judges then overturn them'.[10] Judges and politicians came into serious conflict when the Law Lords found against the government in relation to its detention of terror suspects for long periods without trial in the wake of the attacks on the US on 11 September 2001.[11]

1.35   In *The politics of the judiciary* John Griffith sets out two views of the judge's role. He describes the traditional view as one of 'judicial neutrality' with judges acting as neutral arbiters with no interest in the external world and no policies or positions of their own.

---

10 David Blunkett made this statement in response to the High Court finding on 20 February 2003 that government measures to deprive asylum-seekers of social security benefits were contrary to their obligations under the HRA, H Kennedy, *Just Law*, p121.

11 *A and others v Secretary of State for the Home Department; X and another v Secretary for the Home Department* 16 December 2004 [2004] UKHL 56.

'On this view the judge is not to take into account any consequences which might flow from his decision and which are wider than the direct interests of the parties. He must act like a political, economic, and social eunuch, and have no interest in the world outside his court when he comes to judgement.'

Griffith goes on to present a 'more sophisticated version' of this view which places the courts squarely at the heart of a functioning, healthy democracy. They are the chief mediator between the individual and the state and guard against excessive use of power by the executive. They often deal with issues that have already attracted controversy such as race and immigration or the police and individual citizens' rights.

1.36 Griffith argues that in this role judges inevitably make political decisions and that it would be preferable to acknowledge this publicly than to pretend that a line is drawn firmly between the law and politics.

'If it is accepted ... that a judge ... is frequently required to make decisions which involve an assessment of where the public interest lies and so to make a political decision, then he cannot be said to act neutrally, although he may still be the person best suited to make that particular decision.'[12]

1.37 During the late 1970s and 1980s the courts were a 'prominent arena' for the political conflict between the trade unions and the government.[13] There were new laws and litigation (including the miners' strike and the disputes which centred on newspaper workers based at Wapping) which significantly curtailed the unions' powers and in particular the right to conduct legal strikes. John Griffith gives a good account of these developments in *The politics of the judiciary*.[14] His analysis of the case-law leads him to conclude that in general the judges roamed far and wide in interpreting new laws such as the Employment Act 1980 which limited secondary action,[15] almost always with the effect of curtailing the collective power of employees and unions. More generally, Griffith charts the ever-changing relationship between the courts and the government, from this example, which shows the judges aiding the government in a political endeavour to weaken 'countervailing sources of power or influence', through to examples of the judiciary standing up to the government's adoption of 'harsh policies' and actions 'on the margins of legality'. It may not be possible to generalise or to predict how robust or supportive judges will

12 J Griffith, *The politics of the judiciary*, 5th edn, Fontana Press, 1997, p57.
13 Ibid at p98.
14 Ibid at p63.
15 Action taken by workers in support of a trade dispute by other workers against their employers.

be of the executive at any one time, but it is a vitally important tension for lawyers to be aware of.

1.38   Griffith also highlights the 'extra judicial activities' that judges engage in outside the courtroom as further evidence of the difficulty of imposing a strict line between the 'legal' and the 'political'. The most senior judges are members of the House of Lords, and in addition to their judicial role are free to take part in its legislative and other activities. They may also be consulted by government departments about matters of law reform and are often called on to head up high profile commissions or inquiries.

What does the future hold?

1.39   As one might expect, there are many different views about the extent to which contemporary lawyers are interested in or engaged with the 'bigger picture'. Some lawyers see the generations active in the 1970s and 1980s as the last to be socially and politically motivated in using the law as a tool for social change and complain that new lawyers coming through are more commercially minded. Others observe at least as much, if not more, commitment by new generations to work beyond their own case-load and furtherance of their career. Lord Lester, a lawyer and member of the House of Lords, sees today's lawyers as 'much more public spirited, and knowledgeable about the social and political aspects of the law'.[16]

Lawyers

1.40   There are some real barriers for lawyers who wish to do more than deal with their ever-increasing case-load. Many publicly-funded lawyers say they feel overburdened with casework, working in a contract culture that demands high outputs and leaves time for little else. The decline of legal aid has heaped on further pressures in many areas of law and in some specialisms (notably immigration and asylum) lawyers are leaving the profession and firms are closing down. Some people, in addition, have undoubtedly been demoralised by laws introduced by the Labour government that came to power in 1997 that are as draconian as anything dreamed up by Conservative administrations and perhaps feel that they do not want to engage in behind the scenes influencing on matters of detail when they disagree with the fundamental principles behind a proposal.

16 Interview with Lord Lester, 23 May 2005.

1.41   In spite of, or perhaps because of, these pressures there continue
to be lawyers who actively seek out wider causes, involving themselves
in influencing and lobbying and finding new ways to work together as
well as in partnership with relevant organisations. There is no shortage of practitioners' groups bringing together lawyers and others to
share information about individual cases from their own areas and to
take forward policy work and campaigns. Legal aid cuts have hindered
publicly-funded lawyers keen to work on policy matters but it has also
inspired them to join forces to campaign together as the Access to
Justice Alliance. There have been laws such as the Civil Partnership Act
2004, affording new rights to lesbians, gay men and bisexuals, new
equality laws to protect other groups from discrimination and legislation in family and housing that have been welcomed by many practitioners and provide opportunities for lawyers to be involved in
explaining and encouraging people to make use of their new rights.

Law centres

1.42   Casework and funding pressures may have prevented law centres from
developing fully into the integrated casework and campaigns model that
was their aspiration. In particular, the contracting system and the shift
in balance of funding towards the Legal Services Commission has
inevitably increased the pressure to deliver on casework and restricted
the opportunities for strategic litigation and other activities. However,
some law centres do manage to retain a focus on these kinds of activities and as a whole they continue to have an active campaigning voice
through their umbrella body, the Law Centres Federation (LCF). The
LCF is active in seeking to persuade the government to fund 'strategic
legal work' (ie legal education, community based campaigning, etc)
and also in identifying creative new partnerships (including with private law firms). Other campaigns activity includes work on equalities
legislation and legal aid. Pending the government's review of legal
aid, their future funding arrangements are uncertain. It is possible
that the development of a salaried legal service could provide law centres with the flexibility to develop a holistic rather than a casework-
centred approach that many initially hoped for.

Private practice

1.43   In private practice there is a cadre of lawyers at all levels who make the
taking of significant cases and/or pro bono work a significant part of
what they do. The driver for many City firms to commit to a certain
level of pro bono work is their acknowledgement that it helps to

motivate and retain staff as well as helping their public profile. There are some innovative examples which suggest that firms are open to far more than the tried and tested ways of achieving these objectives. International law firm Eversheds worked with the College of Law to create 'Streetlaw UK'. Students are trained to run legal workshops in disadvantaged areas. The City law firm Clifford Chance has helped a number of NGOs in their lobbying on Bills to secure their goals – a rather different form of assistance from providing trainees to do advice surgeries. In April 2005 Allen & Overy announced that it would pioneer a new way to contribute money to London's voluntary legal agencies. Through pooling the interest from monies held in client accounts, the firm will be able to contribute to the funds needed to urge the government to boost civil legal aid funding.[17]

Judges

1.44   As far as judges go, in 1997, John Griffith wrote that they 'are refreshingly freer in their written and spoken thoughts about social as well as legal problems'.[18] Several years on there is every sign of this developing, with many judges taking on more of a public role, for example by making speeches or writing articles on topical issues. Baroness Hale of Richmond, for example, delivered a lecture for the British Institute of Human Rights on mental health, in which she wondered 'whether we can recognise a real human rights abuse when we see one'.[19] Lawyers should respond to this by 'tuning' into judges' interests and also seeking to engage them in wider debates.

Individuals

1.45   There continue to be inspiring examples of individuals making use of the courts in their own campaigns. The 'McLibel two', campaigners Helen Steel and David Morris, handed out leaflets criticising Mcdonald's, the multi-national company's practices. The two citizens took on a company and won at least a partial victory (followed by a European Court of Human Rights ruling that the lack of legal aid had denied the pair the right to a fair trial). It made a vital point about the

---

17   Allen & Overy will be donating the funds to the London Legal Support Trust. It is urging other firms to follow its example by signing up to this voluntary arrangement.

18   J Griffith, *The politics of the judiciary*, 5th edn, Fontana Press, 1997, pxi.

19   Baroness Hale of Richmond, 'What can the Human Rights Act do for my mental health', Paul Sieghart Memorial Lecture 2004, www.bihr.org.

inadequacy of the current legal aid scheme to offer real opportunities to individuals to safeguard their human rights.[20]

Campaign tools – public interest litigation

1.46 There have been useful developments in support of public interest litigation but much for lawyers to do to strengthen this category of legal challenge. In 1998 the government acknowledged that support should be provided for cases with a wider public interest. A funding code was introduced in 2000 which sets lower hurdles of the merits and cost-benefits tests for cases with a 'significant wider public interest'. A Public Interest Advisory Panel advises the Legal Services Commission on the significance of the public interest issues put forward by the applicant's solicitor. However, there remain real barriers in the overall approach towards public interest cases. Support is only available if an individual is poor enough to meet the strict eligibility criteria and remains poor enough throughout the case. Also, where cases settle, as they often do, the chance to resolve the broader point is lost. Ultimately the approach is still to rely on individual cases and their resolution to tackle problems that affect larger groups. Many lawyers have argued for years that a different approach, backed by a public interest fund that gave explicit support to organisations to litigate in the public interest would be a major step forward. Organisations would be able not only to identify the public interest elements of individual cases but to initiate 'pure public interest litigation'. Public lawyer Karen Ashton argues that this would mean that 'Public interest litigation would perhaps, at last, find its proper role in campaign strategies'.[21]

Working with organisations

1.47 As a whole the NGO sector continues to grow and to professionalise, although admittedly in some areas (including parts of the advice sector) funding cuts have severely compromised its ability to deliver. The growth in 'evidence-based policy' has put service providing organisations in a strong position to develop policy, research and campaign calls that are taken seriously by decision-makers. There is clearly a role here for lawyers to lend their expertise and share evidence gathered from their cases. An increasing number of barristers and solicitors have come from NGOs or the advice sector and therefore understand

20 *Legal Action* April 2005, article by Keir Starmer, p9.
21 K Ashton, 'Public interest litigation realising the potential', *Legal Action* July 2001, p4 supplement.

the benefits of partnership working. Likewise NGOs continue to develop a variety of legal services, often employing in-house lawyers as well as working with lawyers externally, all of which give many opportunities for joint working.

The Human Rights Act 1998

1.48   The Human Rights Act 1998 (HRA), which came into force on 2 October 2000, enables individuals to challenge breaches of their human rights by public bodies in the domestic courts, rather than having to go to the European Court of Human Rights in Strasbourg. Its potential value and impact has yet to be realised. There has certainly not been the take-up by individuals that some (the government) feared or others hoped for, nor the change in culture that it should have stimulated. However, provided that the HRA can be maintained on the statute book in the face of opposition from some quarters, it should continue to provide a real boost to campaigners for two reasons.

1.49   First, it is a different kind of law. Its capacity to 'trump dominant legislation' gives it an advantage over one of the old problems of test cases – parliamentary sovereignty or the ability of a minister to introduce legislation to override the court's decision. This is of course tempered by the fact that the courts can only point out an incompatibility of a law with Convention rights, and then leave it to the government to rectify this (via Parliament with new legislation). However, when the Act was passed the government made it clear that in the 'last resort' of a court making a declaration of incompatibility it would then act to remedy the situation.[22]

1.50   Second, cases involving human rights put a range of social and controversial decisions (including the right to life) squarely in the courtroom – and via the mass media with the public. At the very least it is a useful publicity tool to raise pressing social issues. Only a 'victim' or potential victim can bring a case under the Human Rights Act 1998; no provision was granted to interest groups along the lines of the 'standing test' outlined above. The government, clearly fearful of a stream of cases being brought by interest groups, has been much criticised for this approach. However, the courts' relaxed approach to third party interventions has enabled organisations to inform the courts about the wider social context of a case and persuade judges to take on board expert evidence about social trends that would otherwise be missing. Nathalie Lieven and Charlotte Kilroy provide useful

---

22   Then Lord Chancellor Lord Irvine of Lairg, Hansard HL Debates cols 1294–1295, 19 January 1997.

analysis of the impact of this approach in *Delivering rights: how the Human Rights Act is working and for whom.*[23]

1.51 Lawyers should take encouragement from the way in which the HRA obliges judges, in balancing between the individual's rights and major societal considerations to take a broader view than they might think was judicial in a traditional sense, listening to evidence from a wider social context and taking this into account in their decisions. There are lessons to be learned here for linking individuals' cases with wider social causes to campaigns.

1.52 What will the next three decades bring? Stuffy courtrooms are certain to continue to be a mirror of – or sometimes a battleground over – events occurring outside. Wherever we choose to place the boundaries between law and politics, or judges and politicians, the truth is that cases are inextricably linked with wider social change – the law sometimes reacting to developments and at other times blazing a new trail. Medical advances will stimulate further challenges involving the 'right to life' (or to death); workers' changing expectations will see business practices being challenged in court; and there will be fresh civil liberties cases, as politicians push more 'anti-terror' legislation, identity cards and other controversial measures onto the statute book. Many hope that the environment will at last take centre stage and that lawyers will play their part in challenges around pollution and climate changes. As, in spite of the likely demise of its draft constitution, the European Union will be an increasingly important source of policy and new laws for UK citizens.

From ideas to action: campaigns checklists

Effective influencing and campaigning start with three key questions

1.53 • What is the problem you want to solve?
• What is the solution that you seek?
• Who has the power to solve it in your favour (and who will influence this person or group)?

1.54 Although you may not realise it, you probably apply these same questions to your work every day as a lawyer. Your client has a problem – they are facing removal from the country after their asylum appeal

23 J Jowell and J Cooper, Hart Publishing, 2003, p115.

has been rejected; they are about to be made homeless or they are seeking to maintain contact with their child. You will be seeking legal solutions in court or a settlement outside that will give the client a fresh decision or compensation in recognition of what they have suffered. Good lawyers will deploy a range of tactics to get the best possible outcome; seeking advice from outside the profession where appropriate and questioning whether the law is the best route. Your targets will most often be judges but may often be other decision-makers for whom the threat of legal action may persuade them to reconsider. Before going into court representatives are often mindful of the particular judges – their interests and tendencies (eg by reading their entry in *Who's Who*)[24] – and may seek to adapt their arguments accordingly. Legal arguments will be deployed but judges may also be persuaded by broader considerations (particularly in Human Rights Act cases where they are explicitly called upon to balance the individual's rights against considerations about the impact on wider society).

1.55   Campaigns and influencing involve similar considerations. This checklist is a guide that you can apply to any issue, cause or campaign. It should be useful if you are working with an organisation on a specific issue or campaign or are at the early stages of identifying, with other lawyers, an emerging issue.

Case example: tenancy deposits

What was the problem?
Citizens Advice (CA)[25] had identified that some landlords were withholding deposits from tenants when they left the rental property.

Evidence gathering
Citizens Advice collected evidence of the problems faced by many tenants in getting their deposits back from landlords, and in 1998 published a hard-hitting report which generated publicity.[26]

---

24 Published annually, by A & C Black.
25 Formerly The National Association of Citizens Advice Bureaux.
26 'Unsafe Deposit', Citizens Advice, 1998.

What was the solution?
Citizens Advice took the view that regulation was needed in order to make a difference. From 1996 onwards, they called for a custodial deposit scheme, along the lines of models used in other countries, that would hold tenants' deposits during their tenancy and return them at the end.

Who had the power to solve the situation?
Landlords were obviously at fault but changing their behaviour seemed difficult without an incentive or sanction. Central government was the obvious target in terms of introducing legislation. However, in 1998, the Housing Minister, whilst acknowledging the problem, said that initially the government wanted to try a voluntary approach.

In 2003, CA joined forces with Shelter. They launched a new campaign to press the government to include a tenancy deposit scheme in the Housing Bill 2003 that was making its passage through Parliament.

Continued lobbying of MPs at local and national level, work in Parliament (including giving evidence at a select committee) and media work proved to be vital in building up support for change. Tactics included CAB clients sending postcards to their MPs highlighting the problem.

The result
The government announced that new provisions would be included in the Housing Bill 2003 (now the Housing Act 2004) to ensure that tenants' deposits would be safeguarded.[27]

What is the problem you want to solve?

Key questions

1.56 • Have you seen a policy or practice emerging from your cases that indicates a broader problem?
• Do you know enough about the problem – for example how many and what kind of people does it affect?
• What impact is it having on their lives and how serious is this?

---

27 Housing Minister Keith Hill MP made the announcement on 19 May 2004. See www.citizensadvice.org.uk for further information.

- Is the problem caused by central or local government policy or practice or by the drafting of the original statute?
- Is further discussion or research needed, perhaps involving a wider group of lawyers, academics or other experts in the field?

1.57   Many campaigns falter or fail to get off the ground at all because they did not start off with the necessary research. Veteran campaigner Des Wilson is passionate about the need for detailed research before kicking off a campaign. He sets out four clear reasons: first, if your instinct is wrong, you will save time and money in finding this out early on; second, you will reveal additional information that will bolster your cause; third, it will help you refine your objectives and messages; and finally, it will give you ammunition (and defences) when the opposition tries to attack you.[28] It is interesting to note the increasing emphasis the government places on research before conducting its own campaigns, first to establish public opinion through polling but often then to test out its own messages before going public.

What is the solution?

Key questions

1.58
- Do you have a solution in mind – eg legislative change or new guidance?
- Is a policy right in principle but being wrongly interpreted, for example, by local authorities or social security tribunals (perhaps due to inadequate guidance)?
- If legislation is needed, could a Bill be usefully drafted, to help focus minds and use as a campaigns tool? As a lawyer you should be able to help identify what is legally 'do-able'.

What will your solution cost?

1.59   This is a vital question and often ignored by campaigners. It is one that parliamentarians and others are certain to ask. You need to think about whether it would cost in the region of £1.5 million, £5 million and so on into billions of pounds and whether there are short-run initial costs followed by reduced annual costs. The progress of a campaign is often aided by having a package of low, medium and

28   D Wilson, *Campaigning: The A – Z of public advocacy*, Hawksmere plc, 1993, p70.

higher cost reforms. You should also do a cost-benefit analysis, eg would your legal reforms cut re-offending and thus cut costs to the public purse? Can you make an economic case for allowing asylum-seekers to work? Is more money needed or could existing resources be re-allocated in a different way? If you find a civil servant sympathetic to your case, you may even be able to encourage the government to do the costings itself.

Having thought through these issues you should be closer to narrowing down your objectives, which are vital for a successful campaign.

1.60   Your research may have indicated that most judges are so opposed to change in a certain area that wholesale law reform is the only way forward. You therefore decide to build up public support for a change in the law. Or in looking for solutions you may have found that achieving clear national guidance for local authorities could be a first step and other campaign objectives pursued only if this fails. You need to have clearly agreed objectives, particularly if you are working with a large group of lawyers and organisations in which people may hold different views.

Who has the power to resolve the problem and enact your solution?

Key questions

1.61   • Does power lie within central government – with a particular minister or ministers or at regional or local level?
   • If at central government, what level will the decision be made at – by a middle-ranking civil servant making a recommendation to a minister or is it so sensitive that the Prime Minister would become directly involved?
   • If judges were to start to make decisions in your favour what are the chances of the government then seeking to change the law?
   • Do businesses or business organisations (eg the CBI), trade unions or other organisations have any relevant decision-making power?
   • Is this a policy matter or a 'systems failure'? How does this affect who has the power to make a difference?
   • What part do the media have to play? Who are your likely supporters and detractors in different sections of the media?

What is the route to this target or targets?

Key questions

1.62   Sometimes there is a direct route to your target. Organisations including the Law Society and the Bar Council will have meetings with ministers on key legal issues. However, there is often no direct route to the person with power and influence or direct contact alone will not be enough to convince them. Instead you have to think about people who have influence over them who you may be able to get to.

1.63   What are the subjects they are passionate about? What are their values? Who are their closest colleagues, friends and advisers (formal and informal)? Who they are likely to listen to?

1.64   Politicians are certain to be influenced to some degree by grassroots views, eg letters from their own constituents or local businesses. Are there respected local organisations who support your cause, such as CAB who could add their voice at a local level? It is often necessary to build awareness of an issue before seeking to convince a politician that anything needs to be done about it. From 2002 onwards, Age Concern and Fawcett worked to raise awareness of the plight of older women in poverty. This helped to engage other organisations and make ministers aware of the particular failings of the pensions system for women. Sometimes politicians want to effect change, but need public support to do so. They want to be seen to be delivering popular changes that the public have called for. Chancellor Gordon Brown MP called on the children's lobby to be more vocal in their campaign's demands on child poverty, to help him prioritise resources in this area. Think creatively about how to influence people. Gordon Brown's staff are known to prepare a pile of reading for him to take on his summer holiday! You could think about a report or dossier of information that might appeal to your target.

1.65   Who are the people or bodies who may not be close to your target but who nonetheless could help you create a 'climate for change' – eg regional media in a minister's constituency who might support your campaign; a professional body such as the British Medical Association or a trade union; an influential think-tank whose interest will make your target think that they should listen too? Some of the campaigns' 'wins' secured by lawyers in recent years have been greatly assisted by the support of judges sitting in the House of Lords (eg Lord Woolf) that it is hard for the government to ignore.

1.66   Ultimately you need to think about building relationships with the key people – bearing in mind that most ministers are in a post for an average of 2 years. Don't forget to thank people when they help you achieve your goals – or a step along the way. People with influence are often forgotten when it comes to praise or acknowledgement – they appreciate it and are more likely to assist you again.

An influencing tree

1.67   A useful exercise is to draw an 'influencing tree'. This lists your key target(s) and around them all the people or institutions that you think will influence them (eg regional media, a close friend/fellow politician, a particular think-tank) – and in turn who influences these people. Seeing a map of targets and influencers helps to clarify and prioritise your actions.

Influencing tree: Asylum and immigration; action to persuade the government to stop detaining migrants and asylum-seekers whilst their applications are pending[29]

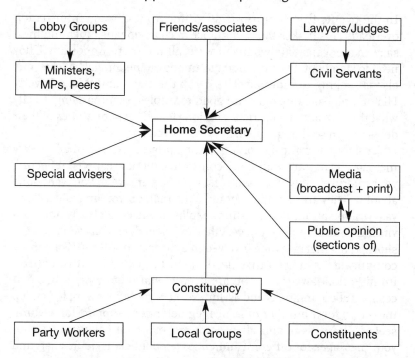

29 People can be detained at any stage of their application for asylum or their claim to remain in the UK. The use of detention is not restricted to those shortly to be removed. Length of detention varies, 6 months is not uncommon and the worst known case was 3 years.

1.68   This example assumes that the Home Secretary would be the key target and highlights key figures that might influence him or her. It is not exhaustive; campaigners in this area will have other targets, and much depends on the political climate at the time. Some organisations, like Bail for Immigration Detainees (BID) have been campaigning on discrete areas, eg trying to prevent the detention of children or the use of prisons for immigration detention as well as on immigration detention more broadly. The first question it raises is what the Home Secretary's views are on this issue. Do his private opinions differ from his public stance? Establishing your target's opinions is crucial in any campaign but can be a challenge!

1.69   Once these boxes are ticked and you are crystal clear about your objectives, there is a further question: how are you going to communicate your key messages and calls to action?

What are your key messages?

1.70   In the twenty-first century we all suffer from chronic information overload. This makes the importance of clear slogans, titles and message that encapsulate what you want all the more important. They need to stand out, to be memorable among all the things that everyone else is seeking to promote. The 'Drop the Debt' and 'Make Poverty History' global campaigns are good examples: summarising exactly what they are about – for richer nations to relieve poorer ones of their debts and in so doing to help alleviate poverty.

1.71   Vital for any campaign or influencing project, large or small, are key messages. They are your chief communications weapons, reflecting your interpretation of an issue or a situation and what you want done about it. They are as important for a one man or woman band as for a vast organisation; if you cannot explain your case clearly and convincingly you are unlikely to get others on side. Essentially you need 3–5 short points that everyone involved in a campaign will use. For a more complicated issue you may need more. For example, if you are an immigration lawyer and you are keen to start changing public perceptions about migrants and asylum-seekers you might want to develop messages for a number of issues (eg detention, support for asylum-seekers, fairness of appeals procedures, etc). You will want to tailor your messages for different audiences (eg politicians, journalists and members of the public).

1.72   Lawyers are sometimes accused of being self-serving in the issues they choose to engage with, especially when they relate to the legal profession and system. Thinking about the messages you want to get across can help guard against this. For example, when the government was seeking to scrap trial by jury for some cases the Bar Council and others managed to get across a consistent message about the threat this posed to the presumption of innocence, which they argued is core to our legal system. This helped to safeguard against allegations of barristers seeking to preserve their own livelihoods.

1.73 To communicate messages effectively, you need to find different ways to get them across. Service delivery organisations have a huge asset in the practical stories that explain a problem and sometimes point to a solution. Lawyers have a similar resource in the form of their clients and more generally the practices they see being played out in the judicial system. A story about an individual can be a powerful way to get your message across, as can new research (eg opinion polling showing overwhelming support for your reforms or bang up-to-date facts and figures demonstrating the true extent of the problem). Chapter 6 highlights the importance of choosing the right medium to get your points across and influence your targets.

- Problem
- Solution (including costs)
- Key targets (including who influences them and how to reach them)
- Objectives
- Messages

Keep this checklist in mind as you're reading the book. It should help you analyse the case studies in the book – as well as any campaigns or influencing work, past and present, that you have been involved in or seen others be part of. Did they tick all the boxes?

Further information

History and analysis

1.74
- Carol Harlow & Richard Rawlings, *Pressure through law*, Routledge, 1992.
- Test cases for the poor legal techniques in the politics of social welfare, Child Poverty Action Group Poverty pamphlet, September 1983.
- Roger Smith, 'Test case strategies and the Human Rights Act', *Justice Journal*, 2004, Vol 1, No 1, p65.

continued

> - How ideas turn into policies and laws
> - How to identify and influence your key targets: ministers, officials and special advisers
> - Navigating your way through the corridors of power
> - How to have your say in the policy-making process

Introduction

2.1 When we talk about lobbying we often focus on Parliament – perhaps because early uses of the term 'lobby' referred to the anteroom of a legislative assembly where interest groups gathered to 'ply their trade'. But to be effective, lobbying, or the act of influencing governmental actions, must involve engagement with policies and laws at the earliest possible stage. By the time a law reaches Parliament, ministers' views will have firmed up and they will be seeking to push a Bill through its stages quickly – mindful of the scarcity of parliamentary time. There are in addition proposals that are never subjected to Parliament's scrutiny. This isn't to say that influence cannot be brought to bear later on in the process, but involvement at the earlier, less public stages when ideas are still fresh and policies being formulated is a key time to have an impact. This means getting to know how to penetrate the Whitehall machine, through which ideas are transformed into policies or laws and impact on people's everyday lives.

2.2 As a lawyer you will often be motivated by the bad or even disastrous effects you fear a new law will have on your clients or on the field of law in which you practise. In this situation any lobbying you do will be focused on opposing new proposals outright, or on seeking to have their worst effects ameliorated. As a specialist you will have a valuable part to play in explaining why proposals will not work, often because you will have access to evidence from 'the ground' that will not be available to the government. You will be well placed to comment on the detail and point out obvious flaws, but your skills and interests also equip you to have influence in a more positive, or proactive way, by contributing new ideas for reform. Most lawyers are less accustomed to thinking of themselves as influencers in this sense – but much can be achieved with a small amount of knowledge about how the system works. If you are able to offer fresh ideas and positive solutions your 'hand' may be strengthened on those occasions when you want to be extremely critical.

2.3   Whatever your motivations you should not under-estimate how much you have to offer. After all much of Whitehall's work is about the law – its creation, shaping and development through to implementation and enforcement. Lawyers should be natural influencers in this area!

What is this chapter about?

2.4   This chapter looks first at the various sources of new ideas and policies; second at government and Whitehall, the institutions, structures and processes; third at your key targets, the people (primarily ministers, civil servants and special advisers) you will wish to influence and finally at how policy is made – the translation of an idea into a policy or law. At the end I highlight some key developments that help understand how government and Whitehall operate today (including freedom of information).

2.5   Throughout are tips on how to have influence, whether you have a brand new idea to share, wish to prevent something from happening or to modify a draft law before it passes to Parliament for scrutiny.

Turning ideas into actions

2.6   Where do ideas for policies come from? Who first dreamed up the words 'anti-social behaviour' and is it a new phenomenon or just a clever re-branding? Who thought that the notion of giving a one-day old baby a cash contribution to his or her piggy bank would catch on? Did Thatcher take the credit for her vote-winning policy allowing tenants to buy their council homes – or was it a crafty adviser? Which ideas respond to a real problem that is capable of solution by government and which are cosmetic – more important for how they sound than what they do? What do we mean when we speak of an idea 'whose time has come'? How could the taxi driver who suggested to me a Bank Holiday Monday every month (provided by everyone working an extra 15 minutes a day) find support for his idea?

2.7   The answer is that ideas for new policies, laws and practices can emerge from a number of sources: political parties, MPs' postbags and from within Whitehall itself.

The political parties

2.8 It is vital to know about the parties' policy-making processes. After all it is a major task of Whitehall officials to put into action the governing party's manifesto commitments. You need to be influencing the opposition parties too – not only because their turn in government could be just around the corner, but because their ideas may put the governing party under pressure to act, or to come up with alternative solutions.

2.9 Knowing about the ebb and flow of the parties' policy-making cycles can help you pinpoint the times when parties and individuals are more or less open to new ideas. As a general rule, during the last 2 years of a government's life (often 4 years in total), both government and opposition will be thinking ahead to the next term and the package of policies that will persuade the electorate to vote for them. This period is therefore crucial, especially as the manifestos may be finalised as late as a few weeks before election day.

2.10 There are significant differences between the ways in which the various political parties make policy – as well as differences between the processes when in government or in opposition. Within each of the major political parties, central teams of researchers and policy-makers will be responsible for developing new ideas and policies.

2.11 In government, however, the influence of the central party policy-makers will be less so than when in opposition. For example, it has been political appointees working from within Whitehall (eg in the Number Ten Policy Directorate) rather than at party headquarters who from 1997 have been primarily responsible for researching and developing ideas under the Labour government.

See chapter 4 for details of how each of the main political parties make policy.

Parliament

2.12 Closer to Whitehall, but still outside government, Parliament can be a source of new initiatives. Its select committees have increasing clout and their reports and recommendations are sometimes adopted. Occasionally a backbench MP will find interest being taken in their proposal for a Private Member's Bill.[1]

---

1 See para 3.166 for details of Hywel Williams, a backbencher who saw his Private Member's Bill for carers become law.

Pressures from elsewhere

Organisations

2.13   Pressure for change and calls for new initiatives may build up from outside government and Parliament – from interest groups and campaigners, think-tanks, trade unions, businesses and business organisations or local authorities. Think-tanks in particular have gained ground in recent years as sources of ideas and policy-developers. Techniques vary, from evidence-gathering and public campaigns to direct action. The actions of 'Fathers for Justice' (including flour-bombing MPs from the Commons visitors' gallery), have been widely criticised, but they have succeeded in getting the issue of separated fathers' contact with their children on the 'radar screen'.

2.14   The issue of pensions shows how external pressures can build up, pushing an issue high up the political agenda. A range of bodies from the financial services industry through to unions and charities have all called for substantial reform. It has gone from being a guaranteed conversation stopper to a regular topic raised by taxi-drivers! As it often does for complex problems with no obvious solution (or where the options are unpalatable) the government chose to create an independent inquiry. In 2002 a Commission chaired by Adair Turner, was set up to examine whether the voluntary approach to pensions saving was working. No doubt the government hoped that it would be easier to make tough choices on pensions if it was seen to be responding to an independent inquiry rather than simply acting off its own bat.

Public opinion

2.15   Politicians are often accused of being out of touch with 'real people'. However, ministers take seriously the issues that their own and other MPs' constituents report to them. Indeed they are arguably 'over-influenced' by these, sometimes wrongly believing that the concerns voiced in their constituency are mirrored across the country. In addition there has been considerable reliance in recent years on focus groups, although these are often used to test likely reaction to new ideas rather than to generate proposals.

Other countries

2.16   Other countries are an important source of ideas which are then adapted to the UK's needs and circumstances. Examples include the US Earned Income Tax Credit, an American federal tax credit for people on low incomes which influenced Chancellor Gordon Brown's

development of Child Tax Credit and Working Tax Credit, both introduced in 2003. The pensions debate has included discussion about
other countries' experiences, including the Australian system of
compelling people to save for their retirement.

Whitehall

2.17   As well as shaping ideas from the manifesto or other sources, officials in each department are an important source of new policies. Permanent secretaries and other senior officials will certainly have room
to make their own recommendations, often able to take fresh thinking
from one department to another. Their success rate will very much
depend on how open ministers are to their ideas. Officials in the
Department of Transport were said to have been determined for many
years to see compulsory seat belt legislation introduced and were
finally successful when a minister agreed with them. In general, in
areas in which a minister has less interest or knowledge, influence
may be easier to bring to bear.

Case study: Child Trust Funds – from idea to high profile policy
The experiences of asset-based welfare in the US kick-started
thinking in the UK about the provision of state grants ('baby
bonds') to children or young people that would be added to and
rise in value over time.[2]

The Institute for Public Policy Research (ippr) developed the
idea further. It carried out timely research and published a book
in 2000, promoting the policy.[3] To engage key targets in the idea,
ippr organised a seminar at Number Ten entitled: 'Opportunity
and Assets: the role of the Child Trust Fund'. The idea chimed with
the government's broader thinking about asset-based welfare and
instilling savings habits early on in life. This helped to attract
the support of senior politicians which can often make the difference in terms of a policy progressing. David Blunkett MP took
a keen interest, commissioning work when he was Education
Secretary to help progress the idea. It also fitted in well with the
Chancellor's focus on intervening in children's lives (and especially those facing disadvantage) from the earliest opportunity.

---

2   See for example, D Nissan and J le Grand, 'A capital idea: start up grants for
young people', Fabian Society, 2000.
3   Gavin Kelly and Rachel Lissauer, 'Ownership for all', January 2000, ippr.

> The government first announced its adoption of Child Trust Funds (CTFs) in April 2001 and it was formally launched in the 2003 Budget. The Chancellor's commitment was to provide every child born after autumn 2002 with a minimum of £250 (twice that for poorer families) to be invested, ippr continued to influence its development and to use it as a hook for other related ideas. Tactics included organising a seminar in 2004 with Ruth Kelly MP, then Financial Secretary to the Treasury, on the next steps for CTFs. In January 2005 they called for local authorities to make contributions to the CTFs of children in their care and looked at other issues around CTFs and local authorities. They began to work in partnership with the University of Oxford to ask how CTFs could be expanded into 'citizens' stakes'.

2.18   Whatever the origin of an idea, it is officials who will face the task of shaping it into a workable policy. The next sections look at how government and Whitehall are organised, how policy is developed and how to make your input.

The government and Whitehall

Where does power lie?

2.19   The 'powerhouses' of central government are: the Prime Minister (supported by Number Ten); the Cabinet (and the Cabinet Office); the ministers not in the Cabinet; and the network of government departments and agencies staffed by civil servants and led by ministers.

2.20   'Whitehall' was originally a royal palace, created by Henry VIII from the home of Cardinal Thomas Wolsey, his 'cleric-cum-bureaucrat' until he 'fell from grace'.⁴ It has grown to mean the relatively small number of senior, policy-making officials (sometimes dubbed 'mandarins') with a headquarters function.⁵ Many still work close to the site of the original palace in the government buildings up and down Whitehall but there is a trend for more staff to be located outside London.

---

4 P. Hennessy, *Whitehall*, 3rd edn, Pimlico, 2001, p17.
5 Sometimes it is used more generally to mean the entire network of government departments and agencies, and not only those engaged in policy-making.

The Prime Minister

2.21 At the top of the tree, as head of the government, is the Prime Minister who has virtually unlimited powers, able to select the people he or she wishes to work under them and to reorganise the structures within which they operate. There is no 'Prime Minister's Department'; instead the Prime Minister is supported by 'Number Ten' staff and by the Cabinet Office. Kavanagh and Seldon point out that the idea of a Prime Minister's Department that brings together units covering policy, party, media, diary, speechwriting and relations with government departments has been canvassed by many people over the years, from across the parties, but has never been adopted. Given that the Prime Minister does have access to support for all these matters, there never seems to have been quite the wish or drive to consolidate them into one major department, as is found in some other countries.[6]

Number Ten

2.22 The structure and personnel of Number Ten change fairly frequently. The basic structure is currently four units, dealing with policy and political issues, delivery and strategy. Like other ministers the Prime Minister also has a Private Office, in his capacity as head of government. The influence of Number Ten is felt throughout Whitehall with the Prime Minister communicating his or her views on key policies and Number Ten staff involving themselves with other departments on selected issues.

The Prime Minister's Private Office

2.23 The Prime Minister is assisted both by officials and by political appointees. The latter are responsible for the Prime Minister in his or her partisan role, including as party leader. The roles and titles of key Number Ten personnel seem to be ever changing. Under Tony Blair have been the following (but not necessarily all at the same time): a Chief of Staff (under Blair a political appointee), responsible overall for leading and co-ordinating operations across Number Ten; a Deputy Chief of Staff (created in 2005); a Director of Communications (formerly the Chief Press Secretary), a Director of Government Relations (whose role includes managing a range of relationships including with interest groups; voluntary organisations and businesses); a Director

6 Kavanagh and Seldon, *The powers behind the Prime Minister*, Harper Collins, 2000.

of Political Operations/Political Secretary (paid for by the Labour Party); a Chief Policy Adviser or Head of the Number Ten Policy Directorate; a Director of Events and Scheduling; and a Chief Adviser on Strategy.

2.24   Officials in Number Ten are led by the Prime Minister's Principal Private Secretary, who is often seconded from the Treasury. A senior civil servant, he or she liaises closely with the Cabinet Secretary and the Queen's Private Secretary. Under the current structure, this post-holder also heads the Policy Directorate. They have a major co-ordinating role, and work alongside a team of Private Secretaries, with responsibility for different areas (eg Economic and Home Affairs). Collectively the officials are responsible to the Prime Minister as head of the government.

2.25   A senior civil servant now acts as the Prime Minister's official spokesperson whereas in the recent past this was a political appointee.

2.26   Like other Cabinet Ministers, the Prime Minister has a Parliamentary Private Secretary (PPS – not to be confused with the Principal Private Secretary, a civil servant), an MP who acts as his or her 'eyes and ears' in Parliament.

2.27   Key support staff include the Diary Secretary and the Duty Clerk.

2.28   Most Number Ten staff are inwardly focused, although those working on policy will take responsibility for engaging the relevant outside groups.

2.29   As some of the following examples show, here is a lot of overlap between Number Ten and the Cabinet Office, with some units located within the Cabinet Office but reporting directly to the Prime Minister.

2.30   **The Policy Directorate** is the result of a merger between the Prime Minister's Private Office and the Policy Unit and is staffed by both civil servants and special advisers. Each is assigned to a specific government department and works very closely with them (in pairs). To some extent the civil servant will deal more with the management of Number Ten's current policy involvement and issues whilst the special adviser will be more focused on future ideas and policies. In terms of formulation of future policies, the Policy Unit will often agree statements and proposals together with the relevant department. In 2005 there was speculation that in the future officials and special advisers might be separated.

Tip:

2.31   • It is always worth checking who in Number Ten has responsibility for the policy area/s in which you take an interest and seeking to brief them at an appropriate point.

2.32 **The Political Office/Unit** focuses on relations with key political players, but its role can vary widely. It liaises with the party machine; government departments and the whips. Often it co-ordinates the manifesto process; and when the Labour Party is in power liaises with the National Policy Forum and the trade unions. It can play an important role in gaining support among the party at large for key policies and communicating concerns back to the government.

Tip:

2.33 • Its operation can vary widely according to which party is in power.

2.34 Both the Delivery Unit and the Strategy Unit often report directly to the Prime Minister but are part of the Cabinet Office so are dealt with in that section.

The Cabinet

2.35 In theory the Cabinet remains the chief decision-making body, composed of the Prime Minister and the most senior ministers (most heading a government department; some with another role, eg Leader of the House of Commons). In practice Prime Ministers decide on the extent to which they wish to govern by consensus, with the Cabinet as a key forum for discussion, or via a Cabinet with more of a 'rubber stamping' role. The Prime Minister controls the size and make-up of the Cabinet (usually around 16–24 members) and will have in mind a range of considerations in appointing or dismissing ministers. In addition to rewarding loyalists they may also choose to bring in ministers with differing views, on the basis that it is safer to have them on board than operating from the outside.

2.36 The Cabinet meets once a week (on Thursdays) and will focus on major issues where senior level decisions are required and/or where individual ministers have been unable to reconcile their differences. Tony Blair is said to have limited Cabinet meetings as a discussion forum, keeping meetings brief and preferring 'one-to-ones' with colleagues or set up informal ad hoc groups.[7] The doctrine of collective responsibility binds ministers, who are supposed to give public support to all Cabinet decisions, regardless of their personal views. Opinions vary widely as to how this operates but there have certainly been high profile resignations in recent times by people who felt strongly that

7 *The powers behind the Prime Minister*, p278.

they could no longer give public support to a major policy (eg Cabinet Minister the late Robin Cook over the Iraq war).

Non-Cabinet ministers

2.37   Every government contains around 100 ministers. Around 80 of these will not be in the Cabinet. In each department, underneath the Secretary of State will be Ministers of State, and beneath them, Parliamentary Under-Secretaries of State. There are also MPs who are unpaid ministerial aides – Parliamentary Private Secretaries (PPSs).

2.38   **Cabinet Committees:** Most decisions are made by committee, via a series of ministerial-level Cabinet Committees and sub-committees that bring together ministers from a range of departments. After the 2005 General Election Tony Blair announced that the committee system would be restructured to 'assume a more central role in the operation of the Government' and that he would chair a number of the major committees. A reduction was announced from 61 to 44 committees.[8] Officials also operate a series of 'shadow' committees to assist the work of the Cabinet Committees.

2.39   It is worth checking the committees that operate in your area of interest and the seniority and combination of ministers involved, which can give a clue as to how seriously the issues are taken. The officials who service the Cabinet Committees also play an important role. The Treasury has a representative on every Cabinet Committee whose job it is to ask: 'how are these policies going to be paid for?'. For a complete list of Cabinet Committees and their membership, etc go to: www.cabinetoffice.gov.uk.

Government departments

2.40   A stable feature of the UK government is its strict organisation into separate departments, each very much its own beast – with distinct cultures, policies and budgets – tempered of course by ministers coming and going every year or so with their own opinions and ways of working. Less stable are the changes that each administration makes to remit and structure, sometimes little more than rebranding, but sometimes involving major departmental mergers or abolitions. The descriptions that follow may go quickly out of date!

---

8   This was announced on 24 May 2005. See www.number-10.gov.uk for more details.

The Cabinet Office

2.41 The Cabinet Office was set up to be the machinery to make the Cabinet work and continues today to be a crucial bridge between the Cabinet and government departments. Headed by the Cabinet Secretary, the highest-ranking domestic civil servant (Head of the Home Civil Service), who works extremely closely with the Prime Minister, it is a department of several hundred staff. Its stated aim is 'to make government more effective by providing a strong centre' and its objectives are:

> 'support the Prime Minister in leading the government; to achieve coordination of policy and operations across government; to improve delivery by building capacity in departments and the public services and to promote standards that ensure good governance, including adherence to the Ministerial and Civil Service Codes'.

Its role includes ensuring that Cabinet decisions are communicated to non-Cabinet ministers and that they are implemented by each government department.

2.42 There have been various changes to the roles of Cabinet Office Ministers. Following the post-election reshuffle in 2005, there are now three ministers, all with a role in linking Number Ten and other parts of government. The Chancellor of the Duchy of Lancaster (Minister for the Cabinet Office) is a Cabinet Minister with overall responsibility for the Cabinet Office, a focus on better regulation and the public service reform agenda. The other two ministers are currently: Minister without Portfolio who under Tony Blair has also been the Labour Party Chair and whose responsibilities include links between the government and the Labour party; and a Parliamentary Secretary who supports the Chancellor of the Duchy of Lancaster. See www.cabinetoffice.gov.uk for further information.

2.43 There are two units it is particularly important to be aware of. **The Prime Minister's Delivery Unit** is a fairly new creation. It works closely with government departments, monitoring progress departments are making in the delivery of public services, including any barriers to success. With the Treasury, it works to ensure that each department is set up to deliver on its Public Service Agreements (PSAs) (see para 2.115 for more on these). It is based in the Cabinet Office and often reports directly to the Prime Minister or to the Chancellor (eg through presentations or draft speeches). The Chancellor of the Duchy of Lancaster has a watching brief over its work.

Tip:

2.44 • The Delivery Unit will be interested in evidence of a department's failure to deliver on a policy and suggested solutions. Lawyers may have evidence of the operation of a policy failing to work – for example the Child Support Agency failing to get much needed cash to single mothers – that they could feed into the Unit through an appropriate group, eg a voluntary organisation working in the field. For more details see www.cabinetoffice.gov.uk/pmdu for more information.

2.45 **The Prime Minister's Strategy Unit** sits within the Cabinet Office but again, often reports directly to the Prime Minister. The Chancellor of the Duchy of Lancaster has a watching brief. It is tasked with the longer-term strategic thinking that can easily be pushed aside amidst pressures for short-term solutions to pressing problems. It conducts reviews around very broad themes or policy areas, with a particular emphasis on areas cutting across a number of departments' responsibilities or 'knotty problems'. The Unit also compares the UK's performance with other nations and seeks to improve strategy and policy development across Whitehall. It has been a significant way for Tony Blair to promote his agenda and bring in radical ideas from outside government (in addition to civil servants, the Unit is staffed by secondees from business, the not for profit sector, think-tanks, etc) that he can see converted into concrete proposals. In addition to major reviews, it also carries out shorter projects, literature reviews and seminars, as well as in-house management consultancy on some problems. Much of its work is published as government policy, although some is published as recommendations to the government (rather than agreed policy).

2.46 The Unit's work operates across a range of policy areas and many of its projects are of direct relevance to lawyers. In 2000, for example, it carried out a review for the Prime Minister into adoption which was instrumental in the introduction of the Adoption and Children Act 2002. Another recent project was a joint research study with the Home Office into migration, which led to new policies in relation to migrants with certain skills – and in 2005 it published its strategy for transforming the life chances of disabled people.[9]

---

9 'Improving the life chances of disabled people', Strategy Unit, a joint report with DWP, DH, DfES and ODPM, January 2005.

Tip:

2.47 • Frequently the Unit works with other departments, either supporting them (eg it is supporting the DCA on the 'Fundamental Legal Aid Review') or instituting a project which a department then takes responsibility for implementing. The Unit will often consult and take evidence from external organisations, and in addition to looking for ideas to feed into ongoing reviews, the Strategy Unit may also be open to suggestions for new reviews. For more details see www.strategy.gov.uk.

HM Treasury

2.48 The Treasury is the UK's economics and finance ministry which exerts a firm hold over the rest of Whitehall, due to its control over public expenditure. It is responsible for formulating and implementing the government's financial and economic policy.

2.49 The ministerial responsibilities give a rough idea of the breakdown of the Treasury's work. The Chief Secretary is responsible for public expenditure and public/private partnerships; the Paymaster-General for the tax system; the Financial Secretary for banking, financial services and insurance and the Economic Secretary for enterprise and productivity.

2.50 As holder of the purse strings, the Treasury's power across government cannot be overestimated. This is something that campaigners sometimes forget. Your proposals may gain favour with the relevant department but they will have to get approval from the Treasury for the money. A first step in any campaign should be thinking through how much money your proposals will cost (and will there be any savings to government as a result). You may not have exact estimates (sometimes these are difficult to gauge) but you should at least be able to say whether reforms are in the bracket of less than £5 million, £5–10 million, £10 million upwards or whether it is in fact billions of pounds that are required. Governments are always looking out for relatively cheap reforms that will be popular (particularly around Budget time) so it is always worth thinking through a range of reforms you would like to see, some low-cost some more expensive.

2.51 The relations between Number Ten and the Treasury were subjected to continual and intense scrutiny throughout the Labour governments of 1997–2001 and 2001–2004 which showed no signs of abating after the General Election of 2005 as speculation mounted about when Tony Blair might stand down. This is nothing new. Asquith and Lloyd-George's battles of nearly a century ago are well documented and since then many other Chancellors and Prime Ministers have been at odds with one another, both on policy matters and on the question of succession! But whatever the reality of relations between the men or women at the respective helms, an understanding of how each set of offices works is crucial. They are the two powerhouses of government and therefore it is unsurprising that they vie with each other.

2.52   It is important to remember that in addition to the core work that falls to any Chancellor, the person in the job will also have their own interests and agenda. As Chancellor, Gordon Brown has been notable for his ongoing close interest in and commitment to the welfare of children, prioritising early on in office the battle against child poverty. Another continuing interest has been the debt of the poorest nations, in relation to which he has created a role for himself on the world stage.

2.53   Like the Prime Minister, the Chancellor will typically have a number of close advisers. Gordon Brown in particular has been notable for a very small and close number including Ed Balls, his former Chief Economics Adviser, who stayed with him until he moved on to become MP for Normanton in May 2005.

For more details see www.hm-treasury.gov.uk.

Other domestic departments

2.54   All lawyers will have an interest in the Department of Constitutional Affairs which was created in 2003 and brings together the former Lord Chancellor's Department, and (for administrative purposes only) the staff of the Scotland Office and the Wales Office. Its main areas of activity are: the criminal justice system (jointly with the Home Office and the Crown Prosecution Service); the asylum system (working with the Home Office); constitutional reform (in particular establishing a Supreme Court and a Judicial Appointments Commission); managing the courts and tribunals including appointment and training of the judiciary until the Commission is in place; provision of legal services including legal aid and overseeing the legal services market; the reform and revision of English civil law in a number of areas including freedom of information and human rights. It is responsible for a number of related bodies such as the Law Commission, the Judicial Studies Board and the Public Guardianship Office and is the sponsor department for the Legal Services Commission. The department's strategy for 2004–09 ('Delivering justice, rights and democracy') is published on its website as is more detailed information about its work (www.dca.gov.uk).

2.55   The Home Office is a major department dealing with all internal affairs in England and Wales not covered by other departments. Its basic remit comprises crime and criminal justice including terrorism and other threats of national communities; race equality and community cohesion, although many lawyers would argue that many of its own policies in these areas contradict each other! It also leads on immigration, nationality and citizenship. In a number of areas its work overlaps with that of the DCA. For more details see www.homeoffice.gov.uk.

2.56   The other domestic departments are: Work and Pensions (www.dwp.gov.uk); Health (www.dh.gov.uk); Education and Skills (www.dfes.gov.uk); Environment, Food and Rural Affairs (www.defra.gov.uk); Trade and Industry (www.dti.gov.uk); Transport (www.dft.gov.uk); and Culture, Media and Sport (www.culture.gov.uk). The Office of the Deputy Prime Minister is a major department rather than a Minister's Private Office. It encompasses local and regional government, housing and planning and regeneration (www.odpm.gov.uk). The Law Officers' Departments contains the Attorney-General (the government's chief legal adviser) and the Solicitor-General (their deputy) who have responsibility for the Crown Prosecution Service, the Serious Fraud Office and the Treasury Solicitor's Department.

Joined-up government: fiction or reality?

2.57   The separation between departments is reinforced by the competition between them, for money from the Chancellor and for parliamentary time for Bills. In addition personal differences or disagreements on policy matters between ministers in addition to 'territorialism' can affect the level of joined-up working.

2.58   However, there are a great many policy initiatives that do involve cross-departmental working. Public health is so wide-ranging that it must involve departments engaged in housing, health, work and education. Skills and workforce development are critical issues for the DfES, the DTI and the DWP. Childcare strategies are led by the DfES, but involve the DTI, the DWP and the Treasury. Setting up the Commission for Equality and Human Rights, although DTI-led, brings in a number of other departments including the Home Office (responsible for race relations); the DWP (responsible for disability issues); and the DCA (responsible for human rights).

2.59   There appears to be a movement towards greater cross-departmental working and increasingly the machinery to support this. Peter Hennessey credits Tony Blair with having made genuine attempts to improve 'cross-cutting policy development and implementation' since

1997,[10] citing the Social Exclusion Unit as an example which deals with policies that concern a number of departments. There is also more informal contact than there used to be between officials and special advisers based in different departments on specific issues or policies.

Who's who in Whitehall: identifying and influencing the key figures

2.60   In chapter 1 we looked at the importance of identifying your key targets – the people with the power to bring about the reform you are seeking (or to reconsider an ill-judged proposal of their own). The next section is about ministers, civil servants and special advisers. All are key targets and in most influencing activity and campaigns all will have to be engaged with in one way or another. Lawyers working in government are another obvious group for lawyers working outside government to make contact with. The following guidance applies, whoever your target is.

2.61   • You need to be acutely aware of your targets' preoccupations and their overall political agenda. Public services, for example, (their delivery, cost and potential reform) has been and is likely to continue to be a predominant political issue. Is there a way of linking your concerns, for example, about serious cuts to legal aid with this agenda? Acknowledging your targets' concerns does not mean compromising or changing your goal – but it does make it more likely that you will be listened to and therefore have an opportunity to make a difference.

2.62   • To achieve your goal you will need to work on different targets at different times. Building up relations with officials and special advisers can help you access a minister. Alternatively, if a minister becomes engaged in your idea, officials may be more responsive to your concerns. In addition to a particular department you should also consider targeting the relevant parts of Number Ten such as the Policy Directorate. You can also try the relevant person in the political party's own policy teams (based at the party's headquarters). However, it is worth remembering that these people are far more influential when in opposition than when their party is in government.

10   P Hennessey, *Whitehall*, 3rd edn, Pimlico, 2001, p748.

Ministers

2.63   **Role:** Being a government minister is a strange profession. Most are expected to run large departments, yet the majority have little or no experience of management – and to be successful, they have to be generalists, as do their civil servants. Subject to frequent reshuffles, ministers have to pick up a departmental brief quickly. They may have some knowledge of or interest in their allocated department or portfolio but they are just as likely not to. They have a mixed role – part managerial; part ambassadorial (for their department and the government more broadly) and part policy-making. They will also fulfil duties for their party as well as retaining their responsibilities to their constituency. Their activities will obviously vary according to their seniority – ie whether they are a secretary of state or a more junior minister.

2.64   **Activities:** The first lesson a new minister learns is that time is precious. There is very little of it left once their diary has been filled with engagements and meetings, bearing in mind that they still retain their constituency duties as an MP. The busiest days might start with an interview for breakfast media and go right through to a dinner or other evening engagement. Then they have to deal with the day's 'red box', papers and correspondence. Duties in Parliament will include departmental Question Time, being called to speak at meetings or give evidence to various committees or piloting a Bill through its various stages. The responsibility of managing the department falls in particular to the secretary of state but junior ministers will also play their part. Invariably ministers will vary in terms of how much they want to give strategic direction to the department and how much they want to be involved in operational matters.

2.65   In terms of policy matters, the level of a minister's involvement will vary, often depending on how important, controversial or political a proposal is. In relation to an important and/or controversial measure that could attract bad publicity a minister will be closely involved in all policy decisions. With more technical matters ministers may be less attracted to the detail of the policy formulation and happier to leave it to civil servants. For example, ministers were aware of the controversy that the Sexual Offences Act 2003 would attract and that opposition was likely, particularly in the House of Lords. As a result, the level of ministerial involvement was high in relation to all the major policy decisions. Consultation was extensive and ministers engaged with a range of outside groups – for example the Criminal Bar Association and other legal stakeholders, giving significant opportunities for influence.

2.66   One of the best accounts of the relationship between ministers and civil servants is contained in former Labour Minister Gerald Kaufman's biography – *How to be a minister* – although dated it gives a great feel for the challenges that ministers face.[11]

2.67   **Private Office:** Every minister has a Private Office to support them, generally comprising a Private Secretary who is in charge, Assistant Private Secretaries and a Diary Secretary. Secretaries of State will have a similar set-up but a more senior civil servant (a Principal Private Secretary) running the show and a number of Private Secretaries reporting to them. Private Office staff are the link between minister and department. They filter everything that comes in, deciding which letters and documents a minister should see and ensuring that the minister receives written briefings and advice as appropriate. A member of the Private Office accompanies the minister to every meeting or visit.

Influencing ministers

2.68   • It is very difficult to secure direct influence over a minister. You therefore need to think about a number of routes to influencing them, over a period of time. Officials and special advisers are your chief 'ways in'. They act as the ministers' gatekeepers and may even need your help to progress an issue.

2.69   • The minister's PPS (an MP who acts as their unpaid assistant) is another useful avenue, although their knowledge of the detailed policy that their minister is working on may be variable. If you meet with them they should at least be able to indicate their minister's areas of interest.

2.70   • Don't forget that other MPs are important for gaining access to a minister. They can flag issues with him or her, in writing or in person and if they have taken up an issue for you, may facilitate a meeting.

2.71   • Think about why a minister would choose to see you; what do you have to say that all the people in their diary won't already have briefed him or her about?

2.72   • Organisations will often write to new ministers welcoming their appointment, setting out key issues they hope to engage them on and sometimes requesting a meeting.

2.73   • Remember that ministers will often be looking for platforms across the country to give them the opportunity to publicise their government's policies but also for informal ways to meet with groups of citizens. Organising such an event can be a good opportunity to get some key points across (either directly or through others).

11   Faber & Faber, 1997.

Securing a meeting with a minister

2.74   Well-established, large organisations are far more likely to be able to secure a meeting with a minister than individuals or smaller, less known organisations. And you are more likely to gain access when an issue is already featuring on their radar and when they feel you have something useful to say or offer them.

2.75   • You will probably be asked by the Private Office a few days before the meeting for an indication of the issues or points you wish to raise. It is well worth putting your 'cards on the table' as you are more likely to get a considered response at the meeting. It is helpful to make direct contact with the policy 'lead' who may attend the meeting. Or, you can brief the Private Office staff. With enough notice, they will talk to the relevant policy official/s in advance and advise the minister accordingly.

2.76   • If you do secure a meeting with a minister you may only have a short space of time (30 minutes or less) to get your points across – they may well want to do lots of the talking – and about issues other than those you are keen to engage them with!

Civil servants

2.77   **Role:** Civil servants or 'officials' as they are often called perform a variety of roles. They are there to help the government of the day formulate policies; carry out decisions and administer public services. They have to cover a lot of ground, engaging in short term crisis management, medium term implementation of the governing party's manifesto pledges (over the lifetime of a Parliament) and longer term strategic thinking (sometimes sacrificed to the first two). Their first duty is to the minister in charge of the department in which they are working. The senior civil servants who engage in and lead on areas of policy are the ones of interest from an influencing perspective.

2.78   **Activities:** Day-to-day civil servants with a policy role are likely to combine the overseeing of current policies and developing new ideas. Increasingly they are also expected to engage with external stakeholders – an activity that parts of Whitehall are quite unused to! Linked with this, there are now more opportunities for secondments in other departments or out of Whitehall and signs of more openness to employing outsiders in the civil service. It is now common for civil servants to change roles and departments fairly frequently. They might work on a Bill, serve in a minister's Private Office or take up a policy lead on a specific issue.

Influencing civil servants

2.79 • You need to identify the civil servants specialising in your areas of interest – eg the team working on proposed new legislation. It can be difficult – particularly given the lack of uniformity across departments – to work out who does what and where interest, power, or influence lies. Lobbyists find that the easiest way to find out is to ask a civil servant they have contact with (eg by serving on an advisory group or meeting them at a conference), to explain how their department works – and how they interact with officials in other departments working on their policy areas. Over time this helps build up your knowledge.

2.80 • You need to work out who has sufficient status and/or interest to be worth engaging with. At one time the civil service was based on a series of grades[12] and you will often hear references to civil servants as 'the Grade 5' or 'the Grade 7'. Most departments have changed their structures, with 'Grades' no longer the official terminology, but in practice you will still often hear them used, and they remain a useful indicator of the level at which a person is operating.

2.81 • Grades 5–7 are the key policy officials; below that and people will generally be too junior to make policy and above that their responsibilities will be increasingly managerial. A Grade 7 would be a middle manager, perhaps heading up a section and would be given responsibility to manage a Bill team. Grades 1–5 are the senior ranks (1 is Permanent Secretary level and 5 is entry level to the senior civil service) and employed on a common basis across Whitehall. Altogether there are only a few hundred people who are working at Grades 1–5 level.

2.82 • If you have information that you think will be of interest you can call the relevant official and then follow this up with a short email and any relevant briefing.

2.83 • Outside organisations can occasionally play a useful role in bringing together officials and advisers from different departments (eg for an informal seminar) when they might find it difficult to organise this themselves (eg because of differences in levels of interest or of opinion between departments on an issue). This can be useful when you want to test out your proposals; to encourage officials to conduct further research; or come up with costings; or if one

---

12 Grades 1–7; below Grade 7 posts are called officers – Higher Executive Officer, Senior Executive Officer, etc.

department is particularly keen but needs the support of others to progress their ideas.

2.84 • Collective activities are generally more effective than as individuals and on relevant measures the government will consult organisations like the Law Society and the Bar Council as a matter of course. However, although ministers will be most interested in the views of major organisations, the civil servants should be willing to engage with an individual lawyer with a significant degree of expertise in an area who could provide useful information to influence a policy proposal.

Special advisers

2.85 **Role**: In contrast with civil servants, special advisers (or 'spads') are personal appointments made by a secretary of state; temporary positions and politically partisan. The minister can choose who they like although the appointment must be approved by Number Ten. Appointed by a particular secretary of state, when they move on the special adviser may move with them, the new minister may invite them to stay on (or they may be able to move into Number Ten if they have a relevant policy specialism). Special advisers fulfil three main functions: policy expertise; media relations; and a political role – providing a link with the party in power. These roles may be covered by one adviser or split between more than one person. They are a major source of support for their Cabinet Minister, acting as a 'sounding board' and helping keep them abreast of issues, ideas and advising on what to say and when to say it. They can offer alternative opinions from those coming from the civil servants. They offer support to other ministers in the department as well – for example giving junior ministers help with questions and speeches.

2.86 The official code which governs their work states that they:

> 'are employed to help Ministers on matters where the work of Government and the work of the Government party overlap and it would be inappropriate for permanent civil servants to become involved. They are an additional resource for the Minister providing advice from a standpoint that is more politically committed and politically aware than would be available to a Minister from the Civil Service.'[13]

2.87 **Activities**: A special adviser's workload would typically include some of the following: advising on departmental business, eg on party political

13 'Cabinet Office Code of Conduct for Special Advisers'.

activities or the party political implications of documents going to the minister; acting as a link between government and their political party, eg by briefing MPs and officials on issues relating to government policy and ensuring that the department's policy reviews and analysis incorporate ideas coming from the party; preparing policy papers that generate longer term thinking in the department including those which reflect the political viewpoint of the minister's party; ensuring that the minister's views are reflected in the party's policy reviews; liaising with external organisations; speechwriting and research, eg adding political content to briefings prepared by civil servants. Some will be tasked especially to spend time liaising with external organisations, exchanging ideas and views and their likely response to specific proposals.

2.88   They work with special advisers from other departments including from Number Ten. As a group they meet fortnightly to exchange information and views about common themes. There has been an increase in special advisers since 1997, from 38 to around 81 (at the end of 2004). However, the rise has mainly been in Numbers Ten and Eleven. Most other departments continue to have two special advisers. Reforms, including a cap on the number of special advisers, have been floated and it is possible that legislation (eg a Civil Service Act) will be passed in the near future introducing more regulation of these posts.

Influencing special advisers

2.89   • One of special advisers' functions is to provide a 'reality check' for their minister and one way to achieve this is to have links with external organisations who can let them know how policies are taking effect in people's lives. Building up a relationship with a special adviser over time is an effective way to get across your messages and policies.

2.90   • Special advisers will appreciate concise briefings with clear messages. They can advise on areas of particular interest to the minister which can help you shape any requests you might make, eg for a meeting or visit to your organisation.

Lawyers working within government

The Government Legal Service

2.91   The Government Legal Service (GLS) is the 'umbrella' or 'virtual' organisation that recruits lawyers to practise within government. There are around 1,900 lawyers and trainees employed in 40 government organisations. Each of the major government departments has a team of GLS lawyers (with the exception of the Foreign Office, the Crown Prosecution Service and the Office of the Parliamentary Counsel, who have separate arrangements). Essentially each department decides how they wish to run their legal work (eg the balance between in-house and external contracting). Teams vary – from one GLS lawyer in a fairly small, regulatory body through to more than 300 in the Treasury Solicitor's Department.

2.92 **Role**: In their day-to-day working lives GLS lawyers will be managed by fellow civil servants in their department. However, the GLS retains responsibility for their professional development, providing training and networking opportunities.[14] The GLS broadly divides jobs into 'advisory and parliamentary' and 'litigation/prosecution'. With just one client – the government – to serve, there is a vast range of advice sought and litigation to be managed.

2.93 **Activities**: Many lawyers will now work in many different departments or bodies and in varied roles over the course of their career. In addition to advising on current laws, they also advise on whether new laws are needed to implement new policies. In a large department like the Home Office several teams of lawyers will work on different areas (eg prison issues). For more about their role in the preparation of legislation see para 2.123. Some will operate in a specifically European context, advising on the implications of community law for domestic policy, for example, or preparing cases for the European Court of Justice. Others will spend time on a specific aspect of public service – working in the Official Solicitor's Office or at the Office of Fair Trading. Some will focus on changes to the judicial system itself. For more details see www.gls.gov.uk.

> Home Office lawyer David Seymour gave an interesting perspective on the demands on a modern government lawyer when he addressed a legal conference in 2004.[15] He pointed to the need for a clear understanding of the pre-existing statutory framework; of EU law and policies, including the Justice and Home Affairs 'pillar'; the rise in cross-cutting issues that mean engagement with a number of government departments and the 'major undertaking' of ensuring compliance of any new law with the

---

14 There are similar 'virtual' bodies operating across Whitehall, such as the Government Statistical Service, the UK's largest provider of statisticians.
15 The 16th Annual Judicial Review Conference 2004, organised by Thomson Sweet & Maxwell.

> Human Rights Act 1998[16] He also highlighted the growing trend for pre-legislative scrutiny – in effect meaning that at any one time government lawyers will be dealing with laws at three stages: consultation and preparation of new laws; pre-legislative scrutiny of another group; and intensive work on those before Parliament as Bills. To this can be added the challenges by way of judicial review of executive decisions made under existing law.

Treasury Solicitor's Department

2.94   The Treasury Solicitor's Department provides legal services (litigation and advisory work) to most of the major central government departments and other publicly funded bodies in England and Wales. It is an Executive Agency, responsible to the Attorney General and one of the largest legal organisations in the United Kingdom, with over 700 employees. Like any other agency it has a chief executive (whose official title is Her Majesty's Procurator General and Treasury Solicitor and Head of the Government Legal Service). It has to bid for work and over time has developed a diverse brief, covering anything from debt recovery to human rights to property advice and litigation.

2.95   It has a number of specialist groups (eg the Litigation Division and Employment and Commercial Contracts Group). It also provides a number of in-house advisory teams, 'co-locating' lawyers within a major department. For more details see www.treasury-solicitor.gov.uk.

How is policy made?

2.96   'What must be banished is any lingering idea that policy is some highly rational process in which expert technicians are firmly in control using highly tuned instruments to achieve easily predicted outcomes.'[17]

It helps to think of the government as being in many respects like any other big business or organisation. It has to develop, publicise and implement policy, to plan ahead and to work out how to tax and then allocate spending of the nation's cash.

---

16   Section 19 of the HRA obligates ministers to certify that a Bill is compliant with the HRA.

17   M Turner and D Hulme, *Governance, Administration and Development Making the State Work*, Kumarian Press, 1997.

2.97   It is useful to understanding the policy-making processes as they offer significant opportunities for engagement and influence. They provide useful information about a government's priorities and where it is minded to put its resources; public 'hooks' or 'levers' to push for a specific policy measure and lots of opportunities, including formal and informal consultations, to have influence.

2.98   There are five points to bear in mind when reading this section:

(1) Civil servants inherit the governing party's manifesto which will be full of proposals, some more developed than others. See para 4.131ff for more about how to influence the parties' manifestos. But not everything in the manifesto will 'see the light of day' (or at least not in its original form), and other policies will emerge over the course of a Parliament.

(2) Legislation and regulation are significant ways in which governments introduce new policies. But much is achieved via other routes, ranging from educating or persuading the public to change its behaviour through to spending programmes and from economic incentives to self-regulation.

(3) The government consults on all sorts of policy proposals and plans, large and small. You shouldn't only consider responding to a consultation on legislation; there may be elements of strategies, plans, reviews, etc that you may also have an interest in and which the government will consult on.

(4) You need to think about the financial cycle. Taxing and spending are key ways in which the government seeks to change behaviour (tax credits for working parents is an example of this). But you also need to know where money to fund a proposal will come from. There is little point securing a commitment unless there is cash allocated to make it happen.

(5) Remember that policy officials at any one time will be working on proposals at a very early stage of formulation right through to working on a Bill as it nears the end of its passage through Parliament.

2.99   A final point: check if something is a genuinely new policy or proposal as opposed to a re-announcement!

> **The policy process: a summary**
>
> **Key stages:**
> - Identification of the problem or issue;
> - research;
> - consultation, partly to gain additional knowledge;
> - framing of options;
> - further consultation;
> - narrowing of the options;
> - political will: securing the relevant minister/s agreement to a recommendation.
>
> There is bound to be overlap between these stages. Once agreed (which may involve other ministers) the policy will need to be effectively presented and clear information provided. If legislation is needed there are a number of additional 'hoops' to jump through (see para 2.122 for more information). Above all, a policy may be presented by ministers as having emerged from a seamless process when this is far from the case!

From 'the big picture' to the detail

2.100   As the manifesto is very 'broadbrush', departments then need to find a manageable way to develop the policies and detailed proposals to achieve the government's objectives. There is no 'template' for achieving this, but strategies, plans and reviews are all part of the process. These can range from major 10-year programmes for a department through to much more detailed policy proposals. As indicated above, these may take the form of a consultation or have a consultative element to them or be a firmer statement of intent or activity. Some of them fit into the spending and financial cycles (see below), others less so. As a result their value in terms of how influential, long-lived or likely to be fully implemented is variable.

2.101   The traditional method of consultation and policy development has been through a green paper (consultation) followed by a white paper (a statement of intent). However, the process is now more complex and the terminology is changing all the time.

Long term plans and strategies

2.102   There is a well-developed trend of publishing longer-term plans, eg ten-year plans in relation to health or transport. Recently published longer-term strategies include 'Opportunity Age', a strategy for an ageing society launched by the Department for Work and Pensions in 2005 but presented as a cross-government strategy. As with many plans, this combines statements of government policy and planned activity together with an element of consultation.

2.103   A more recent development has been the publication (starting in summer 2004) of the first five-year plans for health, education, crime and transport. For example, the Department for Education and Skills published a five-year strategy for 'children and learners'. A further series followed – including a five-Year Plan on Immigration and Asylum which included tighter restrictions on permanent settlement in the UK (eg granting refugees permanent status only after 5 years, if the situation in their home country has not improved).

2.104   This series of plans are being drawn up mainly by domestic departments in collaboration with Number Ten. They are widely seen as an attempt by Number Ten to wrest back some control over planning and spending from the Treasury – and as a tool to generate new ideas and longer-term thinking. The first plans tied into spending reviews that had already been decided, whereas subsequent ones are likely to be linked in with future spending reviews. The plans give indications of the key priorities for the government and as such they can help organisations focus their influencing efforts accordingly. They are consultative in nature, offering ideas for development, rather than being a fixed 'business plan'.

2.105   Plans can sometimes take the form of a 'white paper'. In early 2005 the government published two skills white papers within a month of each other.[18] Both reviewed previous plans but also looked at least 5 years ahead, mapping out proposals and anticipated outcomes.

Reviews

2.106   The government may also signal its particular interest and commitment to an issue through announcing a review, sometimes but not always involving more than one department. This opens an issue up for debate, with opportunities for discussion or consultation and new policies and legislation likely to follow. The Treasury will always be involved if there are financial implications.

2.107   Reviews may be internal or external. For example, in 2005, the government announced two equality reviews, an independent, external review to be headed by Trevor Phillips, Chair of the Commission for Racial Equality, tasked with examining the deep-seated

18   *Skills: getting on in business, getting on at work*, 22 March 2005; 14–19 *Education and skills white paper*, 23 February 2005, Department for Education and Skills.

causes of inequality in society and an internal government review to be run in parallel, looking at discrimination legislation with a view to creating a Single Equality Act, to be led by the DTI.[19]

Case examples: policy-making in action

Flexible working for families

The DTI and the Treasury conducted a major review into parents and work, consulting on a number of options around leave and flexible working. A green paper entitled 'Work and parents, competitiveness and choice' was followed in 2002 with a Work and Parents Taskforce which made recommendations in relation to flexible working. One of the outcomes was the legislation to introduce a right to request flexible working for parents with children (and a duty on employers to consider such requests) (the Employment Act 2002). This agenda was further developed through a consultation ('Work and families: choice and flexibility') which sought views on proposals including the extension of maternity pay, maternity allowance, etc and the extension of the right to request flexible working to new groups of people (eg parents of older children and carers of sick and disabled adults). Some of these were floated in the 2004 Pre-Budget Report.

Childcare

Childcare is an interesting policy area where Labour signalled a clear interest from early on in government and followed through with a number of different strategies, reviews and plans. A National Childcare Strategy was launched in 1998, with a particular emphasis on expanding childcare provision in disadvantaged areas. In 2002 the inter-departmental childcare review, 'Delivering for children and families', was published by the Strategy Unit. This set out a broad vision for a strategy up to 2010 and also linked with the spending reviews, highlighting for example how new money committed in the 2002 spending review was helping to further this agenda. A further step was the announcement in December 2004 by the Treasury of a 10-year childcare strategy: 'Choice for parents, the best start for children'. The consultation process was set to include a number of countrywide events to gather views from parents of different backgrounds and income levels.

19 For more details see www.theequalitiesreview.org.uk and www.womenandequalityunit.gov.uk.

The financial and budgetary cycles

2.108 HM Treasury has to keep track of how much money the government has, and how it is going to be spent.

2.109 There are three cycles: the Budget cycle (which takes a broad overview of the economy and sets taxes); the estimates cycle (which is about how much public spending to authorise); and the reporting cycle (whose focus is how and on what money has been spent). In effect these different cycles separate taxation from spending. For just 3 years (1993–96) the Conservative government issued a unified Budget in November which set out both taxation (for one year) and spending plans (for 3 years). Aside from this, tax and spending have been kept separate.

Pre-Budget Report and Budget

2.110 There is now a Pre-Budget Report (PBR) in late November/early December and a Budget in March (or early April). The PBR is important from an influencing perspective as it is partly consultative. It is a progress report, which includes an assessment of the state of the economy and gives a sense of the government's policy or spending priorities. It may flag future plans, eg to alter taxes or for spending but does not alter taxes there and then.

2.111 The PBR may also provide a convenient and high profile point to announce a major review. As part of the 2001 PBR, the Chancellor issued a document on child poverty, giving the 'context for policy decisions to come in the Budget and Spending Review of 2002 and the years to follow'. The document indicated areas where the government was particularly open to outside views.

2.112 The PBR is often followed by various select committees examining the implications for their policy area. It is always worth including both the PBR and the Budget into plans for influencing and campaigns. Advice varies on how many of the numerous submissions from external groups that are submitted for the PBR and Budget are actually read. However, the exercise of putting together a submission (which should be very short – just a few pages long, preferably with a one-page summary) can be helpful in terms of distilling your wish list. Given the amount of publicity that both events attract they can be useful hooks for your campaign – particularly if you can join up with other organisations to issue a public call to the Chancellor.

2.113 From the government's point of view the Budget is an opportunity to announce new policies. It is a major test of their popularity with the public and they will feel under pressure to deliver across the board.

The 2005 pre-election Budget was a good example of this, with the Chancellor variously praised and criticised for a package of measures aimed a cross-section of society: families, older people, children and business.

Case example: 'penalised for being ill'

If you can think of a simple new policy that does not cost too much but is guaranteed to be well received and to make a real difference to a key group the Budget can be a good opportunity to have it realised. Many organisations campaigned for years to see an end to an archaic rule dating back to the creation of the NHS: the cuts to the pensions and benefits of older people in hospital for long stays. The first victory came when Age Concern used the passage of the Pension Credit Bill through Parliament in 2001–02 to put pressure on the government to amend the rules. The government announced that the rule would not kick in until 13 weeks, giving relief to the 20,000 pensioners previously affected (at any one time). In the 2003 Budget the Chancellor announced a further relaxation – only people in hospital for more than a year would see any deductions – and unexpectedly included in the 2005 Budget was the announcement that the rule would be scrapped altogether. This would be of minimal cost (only affecting the small number of people unlucky enough to be in hospital for more than a year) but created a warm reception among older people and groups working on their behalf and some good publicity as a result.

Spending reviews

2.114   Although taxation continues to be handled on an annual basis, since 1997 the Labour government has attempted to introduce a more long-term approach to spending, aimed in part at enabling departments to plan their work more effectively. The model for the 1997 and 2001 Parliaments was to make a major announcement (the spending review) every 2 years (in July) that set out plans for the next 3 years (from the April following the announcement) for spending for each government department. An overlap year between spending reviews gave the opportunity for upward revisions in previously announced plans. For example, the 3-year 2004 spending review (announced in July 2004) started in April 2005 and will run until April 2008. In July 2005 Chancellor Gordon Brown announced that the next spending review would take place in 2007 (a one-year delay). This positions him well, should he take over as Prime Minister from Tony Blair in 2008 or 2009, as he would have set his own spending plans for the period from 2008/09 – 2010/11, rather than leave them to his replacement in Number Eleven.

Annual reports and Public Service Agreements

2.115 In between spending plans, each department publishes an annual report (usually between March and May), which includes more detailed information about its future spending plans. The report must include an assessment of progress towards achieving its objectives. A key Treasury tool for measuring this are the Public Service Agreements (PSAs): undertakings by each department to deliver (in the form of measurable targets) in the period covered by the spending plans. Select committees are becoming increasingly adept at using PSAs to hold government to account during their inquiries.

Spending reviews 'in a nutshell'
Spending Reviews are a fundamental tool for the review of departments' policies. They are based on a 3-year forward look and are updated every 2–3 years. Under the Spending Review, HM Treasury negotiate with a department to set fixed 3-year administration budgets (Departmental Expenditure Limits). In return for this funding, performance targets are set through a Public Service Agreement. These define the key priority areas/improvements that the public can expect.'[20]

Consultations

2.116 In theory the government can do whatever it likes. In practice, consultation, within and outside Whitehall has become an integral part of the policy process. One way or another, new policies involve people being exhorted, encouraged and required to change their behaviour. If done properly, consultation can develop policies that are more likely to be accepted, operated and sustained 'in the real world'.

2.117 Lawyers often respond to consultations on proposed new legislation. However, government plans, strategies, reviews or other proposals can also be consultative or contain a consultative element within them, even if this is not obvious from their presentation. The Chancellor's 10-year childcare strategy, for example, invited views.

---

20 'Opportunity Age: Meeting the challenges of ageing in the 21st century', 24 March 2005, p103.

2.118   There are no fixed rules for consulting prior to introducing legislation and as a result the process varies. However, the Cabinet Office good practice guidelines are nearly always followed.[21] Governments issue frequent consultation documents (in recent years becoming more open to outside influence) and indeed outside organisations often complain of being 'overconsulted' or 'consultation fatigue' – or at least not having the time to respond adequately to all the consultations they would like to in the time available (3 months is the standard time allowed under the Cabinet Office Code on Consultation and is generally adhered to). However, in spite of complaints about 'consultation fatigue', the government will feel the heat if it fails to consult at all. An excellent example of this is the hot water the government got into when it announced a major constitutional reform as part of a standard summer reshuffle. It hurriedly announced plans to abolish the post of Lord Chancellor and to create a new department (of constitutional affairs) without any prior consultation or indication of what was planned, and came in for a great deal of criticism for its 'hastily concocted compromise'.

2.119   A typical method of consultation on legislation is through a document (traditionally a 'green paper'), which sets out fairly general proposals and invites comment on the broad principles behind an idea – whether reform is necessary or desirable and what it might achieve. Internally, other departments will need to be consulted (in particular the Treasury but also other departments affected and, if relevant, the devolved administrations). This is often followed by a more concrete policy statement (a 'white paper'), setting out the government's vision for the project, the direction in which they want to take it and giving more detail about how they see it working in practice. The government may invite comment again but at this stage the room for influencing the shape and outcomes of the legislation will be at a more detailed level. The government may progress straight to a white paper or to a Bill without prior consultation, but this is not usual practice. As with any other consultation, departments usually publish a summary of the responses that they receive to green and white papers. Whilst these public processes are going on, there will also be less formal discussions with external groups. Of course not all consultations relate to legislation and it's vital that lawyers engage with these too, as their clients may be just as affected by a policy change that does not require a new law as by one that does.

21   Code of Practice on Consultation, Cabinet Office, Regulatory Impact Unit, January 2004.

Responding to consultations

2.120 Whatever the nature of the document, official, public consultation responses are one way in which lawyers can make their views heard. Practitioners groups and bodies like the Bar Council and the Law Society often respond to government consultations. Many government lawyers speak of the added value that practising lawyers bring from their field. Their knowledge of what will work in practice – ie when new laws start to impact on people's lives and cases start to filter through the courts – is invaluable, as is their ability to point out the unintended consequences of proposals.

2.121 • There is no standard form of consultation or criteria to follow. Typically it will be in questionnaire style, with some questions allowing for a Yes/No answer and others allowing for comment.

• Departments prefer people to respond using the 'pro forma' supplied. However the problem with this is that it may not allow you to make all the points you wish in the order or way you would like to. In addition, the government may simply count up the number of Yes/No responses to certain questions rather than read the detail. (The government is sometimes accused of 'weighing' the quantity of responses rather than looking at the merits of the arguments.)

• Consultation responses will be dealt with in different ways and accorded different weight. Sometimes an unofficial 'A' and 'B' list is in operation, eg 'A' list responses being read by a senior official and 'B' list by a junior official or consultant. You need to get yourself on the 'A' list!

• It is vital to be selective about which consultations to respond to and the 'added value' that as a lawyer you can bring to the particular consultation. Consultation responses do not have to be long or to respond to all the parts of a document; they can be very brief and selective as to the issues they cover.

• Ideally your first contact with officials should not be when you submit the response. Try to make contact with the relevant official beforehand. A QC or other senior lawyer could usefully make contact, explaining that they will be responding and their particular areas of concern.

• Try to get your submission in at least a week before the deadline – it is more likely to be read and you will be popular with officials!

• Decide on the tone you wish to adopt. You may feel very strongly about the proposals but decide that in order to build relations with officials you will adopt a more moderate approach at this stage – and be more strident at other stages of the process. You may decide that you are going to take a 'hard line' throughout. Remember that responses will be published unless confidentiality is requested.

- The civil servants responsible will have boxes full of consultations and will be reading much of the same material in each response. Finding a different way to get your views across will be welcome and make your response stand out. For example, you could highlight one or two points where your expertise as practitioners is particularly valuable (perhaps with some recent case examples or evidence).
- Most departments have a consultation unit or team which receives comments or complaints about any consultation processes.
- In addition to inviting written submissions, there may be other avenues like road shows, or a series of regional seminars (with support sometimes sought from organisations to co-host or input into these).

Case study: Commission for Equality and Human Rights

In developing its ideas for an integrated equality and human rights body (a Commission for Equality and Human Rights), the government conducted a particularly wide-ranging external consultation process. First, it issued a consultation document in October 2002 entitled 'Equality and diversity: "making it happen" which was followed by a number of regional events, seminars and meetings including an all-day conference. This was followed by a period of consideration of the issues over several months by a taskforce (bringing together representatives from equality organisations, unions and business, etc) and the subsequent publication of a white paper, 'Fairness for all', in May 2004. This was a more detailed document setting out more concrete proposals and including the government's response to a number of points made in the initial consultation. This was followed by a further period of consultation (in particular with black and minority ethnic groups many of whom had opposed moves towards a single body). Alongside the public consultations there were behind the scenes negotiations with organisations including the existing equality Commissions. Work on the Bill began in 2004, and once disagreements among stakeholders had been resolved, a slot was secured in the December 2004 Queen's Speech. However, the Bill was debated for the first time just days before Parliament dissolved for the 2005 General Election. It was quickly reintroduced and began its passage through Parliament after the election.

Whitehall's role in legislation

2.122   Once an idea has been formulated and become agreed policy, it will sometimes, although not always, require legislation to take effect. A core function of Whitehall therefore remains the preparation of new legislation although this features more highly in some departments than in others (eg the Home Office which always has a large number of Bills). Chapter 3 deals in detail with legislation once it has gone to Parliament to be scrutinised. This section looks at what happens before it gets to that stage.

Drafting legislation

2.123   Although a lawyer's role may be thought of as legal or technical, in practice many government lawyers play an important role in policy formulation, often working with policy advisers to work up policies and then instructing the parliamentary counsel (drafting specialists), to draft laws accordingly. Many will have a 'bridging role' and be involved in seeking the views of outside groups. Primary legislation is drafted by parliamentary counsel whereas lawyers based in the relevant department draft secondary legislation.

2.124   Parliamentary counsel provide a service to all departments and will move from Bill to Bill as needed. They tend to be highly skilled academic lawyers. Their job is to draft laws that will achieve the desired policy objectives. However, the result may not always be plain English!

Securing agreement within Whitehall

2.125   There is a two-stage process to secure approval for legislation. First, the sponsoring department will need to secure approval of the policy from the Domestic Affairs Cabinet Committee. Second, when the objectives are clearer, approval is sought from the Cabinet Committee on the Legislative Programme (LP – whose members include the Leaders and Chief Whips in both Houses) which recommends to the Cabinet the proposals that should be included in the next Queen's Speech. As well as approving Bills, they discuss which House they should start in, how much time they are likely to need and the level of any likely dissent.

2.126   Parliamentary time is precious and there is fierce competition for a slot in the Queen's Speech, with some departments invariably getting more Bills than others. The government often commits to introducing legislation 'when parliamentary time allows', in effect giving no more than an in principle commitment to legislating at some future point.

2.127   Throughout the process of securing approval, a Bill may be drafted and re-drafted several times, often taking account of points made by outside groups. However, there will inevitably be matters, some technical some substantive which will still need attention when the Bill is under consideration in Parliament.

Influencing the process

2.128   • If you are keen to see a measure in place but concerned about a lack of political will to deliver it, you may need to lobby MPs and ministers to include a specific Bill in the Queen's Speech.

• If this is unsuccessful it is worth identifying another Bill that the measures could be slotted into. If the government is broadly supportive of a measure it may be more persuaded to commit to it if it is not going to take up extra parliamentary time.

• Often you will be opposing a Bill or parts of it. Ministers want the Bill to go through Parliament as smoothly as possible. Even if a large majority means that they can be pretty much guaranteed enough votes, they do not want to attract bad publicity, annoyance and frustration from their own side and opportunities for the opposition to score points. As a result ministers will be keen to hear from groups or organisations who they know have the reputation and strength to attract support from parliamentarians and others.

• Generally speaking, sharing your views at this stage will benefit your cause. By the time a Bill reaches Parliament, ministers will be much more reluctant to publicly concede significant changes. Earlier on in the process, before a draft Bill or Bill is published, taking on additional points or suggested changes will be much easier. In addition, if the government understands the points you are making, although they may not agree with them, the debates in Parliament may be more useful and constructive. You will be better able to brief friendly MPs about where the government is coming from. It will also help you establish areas in which the civil servants may wish to be constructive and see some changes being made – useful when the Bill is going through Parliament.

Implementation

2.129   The introduction of new laws requires effective publicity, including guidance about their meaning and how they will be enforced. Lawyers have an important role here, in advising on how to communicate new policies (eg employment rights for a new group or new initiatives on domestic violence) as well as on the detail of Codes of Practice and other guidance that can make a real difference in how new laws are put into practice.

Key features and recent developments

2.130 Five key features are useful in understanding how Whitehall operates today and give an indication as to how its machinery may develop in the future:

- the division between party politics and the duty to govern;
- different styles of government;
- the emphasis on improving and changing the delivery of public services;
- an increased focus on evidence-based policy making;
- greater openness and engagement with outside groups.

Party politics versus the duty to govern

2.131 A key feature of any administration is the separation of party politics from the government's obligation, through non-partisan civil servants, to deliver a range of public services. One Permanent Secretary called it 'the thin golden line that must not be crossed'.[22]

This separation is sometimes called into question. Some of Tony Blair's reforms, it is argued, have blurred the traditional divide between government and party – the growth in the number and influence of special advisers; the introduction in 1999 of civil servants into the Number Ten Policy Unit to play a policy role; or his early securing of extra powers for political appointees to give instructions to civil servants.[23]

2.132 There is however nothing new about governments bringing into office their own like-minded political appointments, as a counter-balance to non-partisan civil servants or about the more general issue of where party politics end and running the country begins. There was more-or-less continual disagreement about the role of Marcia Williams, Prime Minister Harold Wilson's 'Personal and Political Secretary' during the late 1960s and more broadly about where the lines should be drawn between the official and political functions of Number Ten.

---

22 P Hennessy *Whitehall*, 3rd edn, Pimlico, 2001, pp748 and 845.

23 Within days of Tony Blair becoming Prime Minister in 1997, an Order in Council had been made allowing both Alistair Campbell, then Chief Press Secretary and Jonathan Powell, Chief of Staff, to play a political role and issue instructions to civil servants.

Initiatives under the Heath and Thatcher governments were also criticised for blurring the line between the civil service and party political
appointments – and it was under Heath that the network of special
advisers began to develop, explicitly to supplement civil service advice.

2.133   More than 30 years later, the numbers and the conduct of some of
the advisers under the 'New Labour' administration appeared to bring
matters to a head. A few months before the 2005 General Election,
Lord Butler of Brockwell, Cabinet Secretary under Thatcher, Major,
and for the first year of Blair's first term, launched a blistering attack
on the growing influence of political appointees, which, he argued
were listened to all too often to the exclusion of the 'fuddy-duddy civil
servants who may produce boringly inconvenient arguments'.[24] (Iron-
ically it was Lord Butler who approved the 1997 Order in Council that
authorised certain political appointees to give instructions to civil servants.) However, many civil servants are positive about the role of special advisers who they feel add value to policy making and help protect
the independence of civil servants.

2.134   Following various inquiries and under pressure from a number
of sources Tony Blair made some changes. The government acted on
several of the recommendations made by Bob Phillis' Independent
Review of Government Communications.[25] It replaced the Government Information and Communication Service (GICS) with a new
unit (Government Relations) led by a Permanent Secretary based in the
Cabinet Office and reporting to the Cabinet Secretary and assisted by
a civil service deputy secretary who would be the Prime Minister's
official spokesperson. The government also removed executive powers
from the Director of Communications and Strategy. It has agreed to
look at other areas, with a view to redefining the overall role of government communications and to opening up the lobby briefing system.

2.135   There are likely to be further reforms in this area, with calls from
some quarters for a Civil Service Act to regulate the Civil Service and
special advisers. Indeed a draft Civil Service Bill and consultation was
published in November 2004; however it failed to re-emerge in the
2005 Queen's Speech immediately after the General Election.[26]

24 *Spectator* interview, December 2004.
25 The Independent Review of Government Communications, chaired by Bob
Phillis was launched on 11 February 2003 and published its final report on 19
January 2004.
26 This was one of the recommendations of the Committee on Standards in
Public Life. Its Ninth Report 'Defining the boundaries within the executive:
ministers, special advisers and the permanent civil service' was published in
April 2003.

Styles of government: controllers versus consensus-builders

2.136 Each government (and Prime Minister) has a distinct style of government. It also structures its machinery and deploys its resources in different ways – often reacting directly against the patterns of the outgoing government. Blair's 'most commanding of command-premiership models' was doubtless stimulated by having observed John Major's consensual style lead him to struggle and ultimately fail to keep a grip on his Cabinet.[27] John Major's style in itself was a reaction to Thatcher's disregard for Cabinet-style government. Certainly the Blair governments of 1997–2001 and 2001–05 were characterised by a centralisation of power at Number Ten. It will be interesting to see whether the government's reduced majority (to 67), following the 2005 General Election will lead to a change in leadership style or indeed if a new leader would be different (for example, reverting to more of a consensual, Cabinet-style government). A Gordon Brown Prime Ministership would not necessarily herald this type of approach, given his preference as Chancellor for working closely with a small team of advisers.

Public services: delivery and reform

2.137 All Prime Ministers in the last three decades or more have engaged directly in the fundamental question of how to deliver quality public services and there have been some strands of continuity amongst the deep political differences. The trend towards executive agencies was started by Thatcher, embraced by John Major and continued by a Labour government. John Major focused in particular on the citizen as consumer rather than mute receiver of services, and further developed the practice of procurement (ie of government contracting from other sources rather than always being the direct provider of services).

2.138 Since 1997 the Labour government's drive to reform public services has increased still further pressure on civil servants not only to be 'thinkers' but to engage in delivery – in making things happen. With the major increases in spending for many departments, the pressure has inevitably increased to show results and that policies are taking effect 'on the ground'. Tony Blair went so far as to call the shift in

27 P Hennessey, p747.

focus 'from policy advice to delivery ... a change of operation and of culture that goes to the core of the civil service'.[28]

Evidence-based policy making

2.139   An interesting feature of modern policy-making is the increasing demand for evidence rather than an ideological base. This has affected political parties, government and organisations alike, who strive to base their policies on evidence rather than on an ideal or series of ideas they intuitively feel is the right thing to do. 'Evidence-based' policy-making is seen as the norm and the accepted way to make your case. Even in opposition, with limited research facilities, parties are expected to research and develop detailed and costed proposals. Being a policy maker has become a profession in its own right with plenty of opportunities inside and outside government to be a policy researcher or specialist. As a result, all the political parties rely on other organisations for research and information. You will always strengthen your position if you can point to some new facts, figures and interpretation in aid of your case.

2.140   It is interesting just how many well-researched policies are rejected when they are first presented only to re-emerge years later, when the climate is judged to be right. Council tax is a good example. In the late 1990s, people within local government, trade unions and think-tanks, such as the New Policy Institute (NPI), were calling for radical reform of the council tax. Ministers rejected the need for change, but several years later, with growing public anger about the system, the government began to announce its own review and is considering the ideas originally put forward by NPI and others.

Open government

2.141   John Major can take credit for a major programme of opening government up to public scrutiny, taking a number of initiatives including being the first Prime Minister to publish the full list of Cabinet Committees. Tony Blair continued this trend, in his first term bringing in the Freedom of Information Act 2000, which came into force in January 2005. It creates a general right of access to information held by public authorities and as such provides an additional tool for campaigners. When an individual demands information from a public body like a

---

28 M Stanley, *How to be a civil servant*, Politico's, 2000 p3.

central government department or health trust, the authority is under a duty to confirm or deny its existence, unless a specific exemption applies. Guy Vassall-Adams, a barrister at Doughty Street chambers explains its impact:

> 'In addition to providing members of the public, campaigning organisations and journalists with a new means of accessing information on issues of public interest, the Act will be a powerful tool for lawyers seeking information of relevance to their cases.'[29]

2.142   Vassall-Adams points out that in addition to 'making creative use of the right to know in their own cases', lawyers will have an important role to play in explaining to individuals and organisations how it works, how to draft an initial request for information and in assisting applicants with appeals where disclosure is refused.[30] However, it is worth noting that the usefulness of the Act for campaigners and lawyers is certain to be restricted, among other reasons, by the way in which the public interest test operates and how in practice exemptions are applied.[31]

2.143   More generally, many NGOs have commented on a change of culture. They point to the increased openness of Whitehall to the 'third sector', with officials actively seeking views and advice on the development of new policies, NGO/government partnerships to deliver services and secondments of officials to the voluntary sector (and vice versa) helping to promote mutual understanding.

Further information

Historical

2.144   •   The *Yes Minister* (and *Yes Prime Minister*) television series are worth watching; they are acknowledged for containing much realism amongst the satire! Former Cabinet Secretary Robin Butler revealed how he and William Waldegrave, then a foreign office minister, found themselves watching an episode of the programme together, as the minister waited to see if the Scott inquiry into selling arms to Iraq would result in his resignation. They remarked on the programme's similarities with the minister's predicament![32]

---

29 *Legal Action*, January 2005, p15, article by Guy Vassall-Adams which explains the FIA including its exemptions.

30 *Legal Action*, January 2005, p19.

31 See also the DCA's website at www.dca.gov.uk/foi/foiact.htm and the Campaign for Freedom of Information's website at www.cfoi.org.uk.

32 *Yes Minister: the view from Whitehall*, Radio 4 programme celebrating the series' twenty-fifth anniversary, producer Anthony Worrall.

- Peter Hennessey is acknowledged as the expert on Whitehall. The most recent edition of his book *Whitehall* was published in 2001 and although it had been updated in parts (including a 1990s epilogue) the author points out that it is essentially a late 1980s book.
- For historical detail about how different governments have organised their power bases, see Kavanagh and Seldon, *The powers behind the Prime Minister,* Harper Collins, 2000.

Current

2.145 • The website www.civilservant.org.uk accompanies the useful book *How to be a civil servant,* written by former senior civil servant Martin Stanley and is updated from time to time.
- The website www.direct.gov.uk has a wide range of information about government services, how government works and useful links to other sites.
- See www.knowledgenetwork.gov.uk/elmr/minister.nsf for a list of ministerial responsibilities (including agencies).
- There are various guides that are frequently updated that list detailed information about government, Whitehall and Parliament (including details of departments, committees and MPs/peers). Good examples are the (PMS) Parliamentary Companion, published by PMS Publications and Vachers Parliamentary Companion, published by Vacher Dod Publishing Ltd (both updated quarterly).
- Departmental websites vary in their usefulness. Some have organisational charts that can throw light on the basic directorates, teams, etc.
- *The civil service handbook* is the most comprehensive source of information, but bear in mind that it is only published annually so may be out of date.
- *The greenbook* ('Greenbook', *Appraisal and evaluation in central government*) is a Treasury document that gives guidance to civil servants when they are working out the impact of a major new policy (eg carrying out a regulatory impact assessment). Officials will appreciate input from lawyers (eg advising on the number likely to be affected or the cost of savings of a new law or policy). See www.greenbook.treasury.gov.uk for more details.

CHAPTER 3

From Bill to Act: making your mark

Continued

- Why lawyers should get involved *before* laws are passed
- How a Bill becomes an Act: key stages of the parliamentary process
- Scrutinising primary and secondary legislation
- Engaging parliamentarians with your key issues
- Tips for drafting amendments and briefings

'There are two things that should not be observed in the making; laws and sausages' [1]

Introduction

3.1   For lawyers, the law is the means to a certain outcome for a client and on occasion the opportunity to bring about changes that will impact on a wider group. In our common law system, lawyers and judges have a crucial role in shaping the law case by case, as they pass through the courts.

3.2   For governments, new laws are the principal way in which they hope to mould society and leave a lasting legacy. As well as being necessary to enforce social and economic reforms, the law is one of the most effective ways for a government to advertise its programme to the public and to signal a change of direction for society. It is politicians, with ears and eyes attuned to the electorate who decide on the new laws that will be introduced or amendments made through Parliament to existing laws. It is therefore this group – their motivations and the processes that they follow – that we need to examine to understand how to influence this part of the law-making process.

What is this chapter about?

3.3   Chapter 2 focused on how to influence laws at an early stage. This chapter is about how lawyers can use their skills to influence laws once they are being scrutinised by Parliament, either in draft form or as 'fully-fledged' Bills. It takes you through each stage of primary legislation (Bills), explaining how and when you can monitor a Bill's progress, influence its content and secure information that will assist you once a Bill becomes an Act. It will focus on public Bills (government Bills and Private Members' Bills) and then look at secondary

1   MP being summoned by pager to a vote on fox-hunting legislation in 2004.

or 'delegated' legislation and the more limited opportunities for scrutiny that accompany this type of law.

Legislation, legislation, legislation ...

3.4   No government ever seized power and then thought that a period of quiet reflection and consolidation without any new legislation would be the ticket needed to impress the electorate. Instead, every government eagerly proceeds to mark their term in office with a raft of primary and secondary legislation, some amending existing laws, others that are brand new. Included in these will be an increasing number of laws emanating from Europe that have to be enacted, whether or not the government of the day agrees with them.

3.5   In 2004, Commons Leader Peter Hain acknowledged that he and his fellow ministers were often accused of being 'legislative junkies',[2] but all governments seek to make their mark through a heavy legislative 'load'. In both 2002–03 and 2003–04 (the last full session before election year), the Labour government succeeded in getting 33 government Bills onto the statute book. This looks slim when compared with 1995–96 (the last full parliamentary session of John Major's Conservative administration), when 59 'public and general' Bills became law.

3.6   Many laws serve more of a symbolic than a practical purpose. Take the controversial Bill that paved the way for 'foundation hospitals'.[3] This was one of the most publicised and fought over Bills in the 2002–03 parliamentary session and widely seen as emblematic of Blair's wish to be seen both as reforming the health service and taking a different approach to the use of private companies for the delivery of public services. Yet commentators have said that there was no need for new law, as the hospitals' new powers were so limited that they could have been exercised under existing provision.[4]

3.7   This approach to new laws is especially visible in the last session before a General Election, when the Queen becomes a convenient medium for the government to convey its election messages. The

2 House magazine conference, 9 December 2004.
3 Health and Social Care (Community Health and Standards) Act 2003.
4 'I am told, for example, that there was no need for a new law to establish foundation hospitals. The powers of the new hospitals were so limited that they could have been applied under existing legislation. Even so, such a fuss had been made about the boldness of the measure that a huge amount of parliamentary time was wasted.' Steve Richards, *The Independent* 23 November 2004.

government's emphasis on crime and security in the 2004 Queen's Speech is a case in point, with no fewer than five Home Office Bills (and an additional three in draft form) promising action on a variety of 'security threats', at home and abroad. At the time it seemed increasingly likely that a General Election would cut short the parliamentary session by several months. It was therefore widely recognised that only a handful of these measures would become law. But in the meantime, they would have served a useful purpose, in the government's eyes, of conveying a certain message to voters about law and order.[5]

3.8   Particularly when it has a hefty majority it can seem as though a government can railroad its legislative programme through regardless of any opposition. But sometimes the government gets the temperature wrong – underestimating the strength of feeling about an issue. The Gambling Bill 2004 is a good example when at a very late stage Labour backbenchers and others raised serious concerns about its impact (eg on lower income groups), attracting embarrassing headlines for the government. Even pre-legislative scrutiny and extensive consultation are no guarantees of a Bill's smooth passage. At times the Mental Capacity Bill 2004 had a rocky ride, especially when Labour MP Clare Curtis-Thomas revealed how her mother, having completed an advance directive, had subsequently communicated a change of mind. The flurry of media coverage that ensued was a fillip to the 'pro-life' lobby who were arguing that the Bill would bring in euthanasia via the 'backdoor' and led the government to make some concessions. (See paras 7.85–7.93 for the full case study.)

3.9   The reduction of Labour's majority from 167 to 66 in the May 2005 General Election is certain to alter the government's approach (eg making it more sensitive to backbenchers' views) and strengthen the hand of backbench MPs from the government side who do not agree with key policies or their party's approach on all issues. Although 66 is still a decent majority by which a government would expect to get much of its programme through unscathed, it gives far more room for meaningful opposition, either from its own side or from other parties in Parliament whose voting strength will have increased. There is the additional factor of some government backbenchers who are approaching a third term of their party being in office but have not been promoted and may therefore feel more willing to speak out on key issues.

---

5   Many of the Home Office's proposals including identity cards fell when the election was called but were subsequently reintroduced.

Why should lawyers take an interest in laws before they are enacted?

3.10   For lawyers working at the 'sharp end' it can be frustrating and demoralising when they see badly drafted laws being introduced that they don't agree with and have been subjected to inadequate scrutiny. Some are turned off by the political processes, seeing only injustices that ensue and procedures they feel are pointless to engage with. But as the people who have to help individuals deal with the consequences of new laws, lawyers must engage with the key procedures, both to be able to explain to clients and colleagues how new laws have come to be and their likely effects but also to understand how to have an influence on the final form they take.

3.11   An example from the 2003–04 session makes a powerful case for lawyers' involvement. Who would have predicted that the Asylum and Immigration (Treatment of Claimants, etc) Bill 2003 would be amended so as to alter the government's plan to place Home Office decisions beyond the scrutiny of the higher courts? It was only through the involvement of lawyers that this issue was identified in the first place, and they and others successfully lobbied parliamentarians, with the result that the 'ouster clause' was removed. Although the government's concession still left the Bill in a deeply flawed state, nonetheless to secure any change at all to a draconian law that had widespread Conservative party support in addition to a large Labour majority is an impressive example of how lawyers working together can make a difference to draft laws. See p130 for details.

3.12   The 2004–05 legislative programme was dominated by the Home Office, which had 8 out of the total of 37 Bills that were announced (including three in draft). The Department for Constitutional Affairs also had a full load – introducing the Criminal Defence Service Bill; the Inquiries Bill and the Judicial Pensions Bill. It carried over the Constitutional Reform Bill and the Mental Capacity Bill from the previous session. There were numerous other Bills of interest to lawyers (eg the Disability Discrimination Bill which extended existing laws to cover transport and extended the definition of disability). However, in an election year it was obvious that few would make it onto the statute book.

3.13   The 2005 post-election Queen's Speech was typically packed, with no fewer than 45 Bills mentioned and a handful more likely to be introduced in the course of the session. The programme included a number of draft Bills and a few reintroduced from the previous session. The Home Office as usual was set to dominate with the following

Bills: legislation to introduce identity cards; another Immigration and Asylum Bill (including provisions to remove the right of refugees to remain permanently and a new points system for migrant workers); a Violent Crime Bill (with a particular focus on the under-18s); Counter-Terrorism Laws (first to go through pre-legislative scrutiny); Management of Offenders Bill (to impose an obligation on judges to take into consideration the numbers in prison before imposing a sentence); a Fraud Bill; a Charities Bill; the outlawing of Incitement to Religious Hatred; and the long-awaited Corporate Manslaughter Bill.

3.14   Following consultation (via a green paper) a Bill to reform incapacity benefit will be introduced, as well as legislation to cut housing benefit fraud. Education legislation is to give parents and inspectors more control over schools and 'foundation status' extended to primary schools. A Childcare Bill is to impose a duty on local authorities to secure sufficient childcare provision in their area. Legislation will give the courts more flexible powers to facilitate contact and enforce contact orders made under the Children Act 1989 and seek to tackle child trafficking from abroad (The Child Contact and Inter-Country Adoption Bill).

3.15   Employment lawyers will be interested in the detail of the Parental Rights Bill whose provisions include the extension of maternity leave and the opportunity for mothers to transfer some leave to fathers. A Health Bill brings together new measures to tackle the 'super-bug' MRSA and to further the ban on smoking in certain public spaces. An NHS Redress Bill introduces compensation for patients who have suffered mistreatment without having to go to court.

3.16   Pensions, an issue which has risen to the top of the political agenda, is to be the subject of a draft Bill, with measures to include action to plug the 'savings gap'. Other finance measures include consumer credit legislation to modernise the law and increase protection for vulnerable consumers.

3.17   The Mental Health Bill which has been widely criticised, has been reintroduced. It establishes a new legal framework for treating people with a mental disorder without their consent.

3.18   There are a number of proposals aimed at reforming parts of the legal system. The Legal Services Bill (in draft form) will overhaul the regulation of the legal profession (setting up a Legal Services Board) and pave the way for barristers and solicitors to operate in partnership or be owned by outside investors and companies. A Compensation Bill aims to limit the growth of what the government terms 'compensation culture', clarifying the law of negligence to make clear the boundaries of 'legitimate' challenges. The Coroners and Death Certification Bill will reform the antiquated system of coroners' inquests and tighten up the death certification system (in response to the inquiry into the murders carried out by the doctor Harold Shipman). Less progressively a Judicial Pensions Bill will allow judges to protect their pensions from a new tax regime to be introduced.

3.19   The legal aid reforms in the Criminal Defence Bill should be noted by civil as well as criminal lawyers as a signal of the government's determination to cut spending on legal aid as a whole. This Bill will introduce means testing for legal aid in magistrates' court cases.

3.20   Discrimination lawyers from all areas should be engaged in the Equality Bill which provides for the creation of an integrated equality and human rights Commission, with a remit on gender, race, disability, age, sexual orientation and religion and belief.

Engaging with the passage of a Bill: your motivations and objectives

3.21   The most successful campaigners and influencers are those who are crystal clear about their aims and objectives. They know exactly why they are spending time trying to influence a process or decision. The same goes for Bill work which can be time-consuming and if done in the wrong way ineffectual. So the first rule is that you need to be clear about why you are doing it.

There are three main reasons for seeking to engage with the passage of legislation through Parliament:

3.22   (1) Gain clarity including specific assurances in debates about the intentions behind the Bill – and the effects the government intends it should have.

(2) Improve the law – secure changes to the wording of the legislation that make a good Bill better or (more commonly) lessen the blow of a bad Bill.

(3) Use the Bill as a campaigning tool to register protest about a particular issue – or as part of a wider campaign – to help build up pressure on government for change.

Gaining information and clarification

3.23   Involvement in a Bill will give you familiarity with the detail of the law. This will be invaluable both in advising people ahead of time and once it is in force and affecting your clients. The process also lends itself to opportunities to clarify the intentions underlying specific clauses and to push for further details to be supplied. As much of the important detail is left out of primary legislation it is even more important to use parliamentary debates to ask for clarification of the government's intentions. Ministerial statements can be useful at a later date – both to aid with campaigns and in certain very specific circumstances to aid interpretation of an Act during legal proceedings.

Improving the law (or ameliorating its worst effects)

3.24 Securing amendments can be very difficult given the government's control over the process (and in particular if there is a large government majority). The system is largely geared towards propelling a Bill through with only limited alterations. However it is not impossible to have a Bill amended. Sometimes an issue builds up a 'head of steam', attracting broad support and the government will give way, rather than be defeated.

Legislation as a campaigns tool

3.25 Used as part of a campaigns toolkit, draft legislation can be an excellent way to draw attention to an issue. As well as highlighting issues concerning the content of the Bill itself, a Bill can also be used to highlight related issues that are not strictly speaking within its subject matter. For example, Age Concern used the passage of the Pensions Bill[6] to raise its campaign calls to action around the plight of women pensioners. Labour MP Vera Baird tabled a new clause which drew attention to the 64 per cent of pensioners who are women and yet the high proportion among them who are in poverty. The outcome was a commitment by the then pensions minister Malcolm Wicks MP that the Department of Work and Pensions would produce a specific report about women and pensions. This was a very useful concession which ensured that ministers, officials and others continued to pay attention to the issue and provided a hook for further campaigning.

3.26 Before you decide on your reason/s for engaging with a draft law you need to think about the government's motivations and to understand these you need to reflect on public opinion (or the government's perception of public opinion) – inevitably a major driver of policy. To what extent is a new law in keeping with, ahead of or behind public opinion? Is it a direct response to a demand from the public – an issue that is being widely spoken about on the doorstep? Or is it about the government seeking to trail blaze – to lead the public in a certain

6 The Bill gained royal assent on 18 November 2004.

direction without any indication that this is where people wish to go?
And which section of public opinion is it aimed at? Is it part of a
broader agenda – to enhance the rights of a certain group – over a
longer period? Is it a law that the government sees as central or tan-
gential to its overall agenda – or one that it has committed to as a
direct result of external pressure?

3.27   All these questions are worth asking as you think about the part you
can play in influencing legislation. They will give you clues about the
motivations behind a new law and where it fits into the government's
overall programme. This information will help you assess how to influence the process; how much effort (and what kind) to put in – and to
identify where wins, large or small, are most likely. They should also
help you clarify why it is you care about the proposals and the impact
you think they will have on people's lives.

Which Bills make it to Parliament?

3.28   Even when consultations have been carried out and a Bill is already in
draft form, there are no guarantees that it will be in the Queen's
Speech. The Prime Minister will be looking for the programme that as
a whole will help win over the public and effect change across a number
of areas of life. As we have seen, in a pre-election year the desire to
impress certain messages on the electorate will be even more acute.
Which proposals will be in or out is therefore essentially a political
decision, something that lobby groups sometimes forget – being totally
convinced of the need for legislation in their area. More laws will be prepared by hopeful ministers and officials than there will be room for and
the Prime Minister and colleagues will be especially nervous of legislation that could be a political liability. The final decision will be made
only a few days before the Queen's Speech, which (election years aside)
is typically in late November or early December.

3.29   Even once ministers and officials have carried out work to prepare
a Bill, organisations need to keep up the pressure, demonstrating
public support (eg by letters from constituents or positive media
coverage). Otherwise it could well be left out of the Queen's Speech.

The passage of a Bill through Parliament

3.30   Although we are told that Parliament is being modernised, the passage of a Bill still contains some puzzles from past centuries. Why does nothing happen at first reading? Where does whipping come in? And can the guillotine still be used? This section takes you through each part of the process.

3.31   **Summary:** At the end of chapter 2 we left the process at the point when a Bill had been drafted and could begin its passage through Parliament. A final hurdle is for the Bill text to be submitted to the relevant authorities in the House in which it is to start. The Clerk of Legislation (Commons) and the Public Bill Office (Lords) checks that it is in technical order (eg that everything in it is covered by the long title).

3.32   Every Bill has a short title and a long title. The short title is simply an easy way to refer to a Bill (eg 'This Act may be cited as the Constitutional Reform Act 2005'). It is found towards the end of a Bill (just before the schedules). The long title must encapsulate all the purposes of the Bill and appears near the beginning.

3.33   Most Bills start their passage in the Commons but some start in the Lords. They complete their stages in one House before passing to the other House for scrutiny. The process is literally made up of three 'readings': first, second and third, all opportunities for each House to consider or debate the Bill in general terms. These are almost always interspersed with a committee stage (after second reading) which allows for detailed consideration of the Bill by a small number of MPs, followed by report stage (also called 'consideration'), when the committee reports to the whole House. Usually Bills takes several weeks or months to pass through Parliament but it is possible for a government to rush a Bill through all its stages in one day. The Human Rights Act 1998 took a year almost to the day from its first debate in the Lords to its last debate in the Commons. In contrast, the Anti-Terrorism, Crime and Security Act 2001, which followed the attacks on New York on 11 September 2001, was rushed through Parliament in a month. Sometimes a Bill gets batted between the Commons and Lords until agreement is reached. The House of Lords sat for one of the longest periods in recent years (from 11 am on Thursday 10 March 2005 until 7.31 pm the following day) as the Prevention of Terrorism Bill 2005 passed from House to House with little prospect of compromise. When both Houses have agreed on the text (or the Commons has decided to enforce its will by using the Parliament Acts), royal assent is given.

3.34   **Preparation:** Having done your initial preparation – thinking about the government's motivations – you need to establish your own aims and objectives. Why is it worth trying to influence this particular Bill – not forgetting to take into account how far 'down the line' it is in the process of becoming law. You can use the campaigns checklist from chapter 1 to help your thinking.

3.35   The Law Society and the Bar Council, legal campaigns groups and practitioners' associations have a variety of mechanisms for seeking to influence legislation. Serving on key committees (eg the Bar Council's Law Reform Committee), building up good relationships with committee members or encouraging colleagues to get involved are important ways to ensure that they have a diverse membership and are actively engaged in influencing legislation. Some groups (eg the Immigration Law Practitioners' Association (ILPA)) have a legislation committee. This helps ensure that new proposals are tracked from an early stage, publicised among practitioners and that lawyers are proactively making proposals rather than simply reacting to government consultations, etc. A dedicated legislation committee or structure that covers primary and secondary legislation in a certain subject area should be an integral part of any legal campaigns group. Otherwise the chance to make a difference to new laws can be easily missed!

Key questions

3.36   • You need to identify what kind of Bill this is – is it a highly controversial measure or more of a technical Bill? Where will opposition to it come from? Are you wholeheartedly opposing it or are there parts that you welcome and others that you object to? If it is a Bill that you mainly support is your main interest in seeing it get onto the statute book quickly? If so you will want to limit the number of amendments you seek to have tabled.

   • You need to find out when the Bill is likely to start its passage so that you can have a plan of action. This could be immediately after the Queen's Speech or not for a while (or it may be scrutinised as a draft Bill).

   • As soon as the Bill is published (or before if you can get your hands on a draft) you need to dissect it, identifying key clauses that you are seeking information about or to amend and starting to look at how amendments or new clauses might be drafted or best used as hooks for raising wider issues. The explanatory notes published with the

Bill (or soon afterwards) can be useful for throwing light on its intentions.

- Organisations and groups will often get together a group of people to go through a Bill as soon as it is published, clarifying the effects it will have and the main objections they have, as well as any points of clarification they will be seeking. Some practitioners' associations do this exercise at the earliest possible opportunity. In a coalition or informal network it can be time efficient to divide up areas and clauses, sharing out responsibility for drafting amendments and briefings and for approaching parliamentarians.
- You need to identify your key targets. These should include the Bill manager (see below for more information about them) as well as other organisations who may plan to work on the Bill – and those who intend to oppose it. Partnership working can be very effective, with parliamentarians often appreciative of having one point of contact or joint briefings from a number of organisations.
- With a reduced although still substantial majority following the 2005 General Election (in August 2005, 66) the government is more vulnerable. It is worth checking MPs or peers' voting records on similar Bills or issues. For example, most of the 40 Labour MPs who opposed elements of the immigration and asylum legislation passed in the 2001–05 Parliament remain in Parliament. Combined with a number of Opposition MPs they could be a powerful force.
- Remember that MPs are generalists and even those who have signalled an interest in a Bill or have some previous knowledge will rely on expert outsiders for policy advice and specialist knowledge.

Key targets

3.37 **Parliamentarians:** Lawyers and organisations seeking to influence the passage of a Bill are likely to have some existing MPs or peers they have worked with and can rely on for support. Having one or two of these as champions for your cause can make a real difference. But you will also need to engage with new people who will take up your issues, as there are no guarantees for example, that any of your supporters will end up on the Bill committee. You need to be tactical about this and identify the people who are most likely to be able to help you achieve your goals. Westminster is built on fiercely partisan divides and these differences are played out during the passage of many Bills. In terms of winning concessions, there is little point under a Conservative government having a raft of keen Labour and Liberal Democrat MPs all heavily briefed in your support if you have not one government backbencher even willing to listen to your case. You need to think about the best way to get your issues raised and that means engaging with people from all the parties – (charities are obligated anyway to lobby on a cross-party basis). You also need to bear in mind that during committee stage, when a Bill receives its most detailed scrutiny, your targets will be a small number of MPs, many of whom will be totally loyal to the government.

3.38   Before a Bill begins its passage or when it is at an early stage interested outsiders will identify those parliamentarians most likely to have an interest, briefing or meeting with them individually or with the help of a keen member arranging a briefing meeting for several MPs (or peers) from the same party. Once the Bill reaches the other House it is a good idea to do the same exercise, again seeking an interested member to organise a meeting of MPs or peers.

3.39   A lot of Bill work takes place behind the scenes. An issue may appear lost, because a minister takes a tough stance during a debate. They may however be privately more sympathetic (but not wanting to appear so, especially to the Opposition). Or they may disagree strongly, but if effectively lobbied by MPs or peers in private (whilst also being put under pressure in public), may decide to concede rather than risk a humiliating defeat.

3.40   **Briefing MPs and peers:** It is far more productive to send briefings to a handful of MPs who are genuinely interested, who will attend the debate and with whom you have made contact, than to issue blanket mailings. However, you may wish to send your first briefing or letter to a larger audience in order to identify who will be most interested. If you are working with a particular MP or peer and hoping that they may speak in a debate it can be a good idea to give them some additional briefing, eg a paragraph on an issue they are especially interested in.

3.41   As well as your core group of parliamentarians it is generally worth sending any briefings you prepare to the minister's office; his or her special advisers and parliamentary Private Secretary (PPS); frontbench spokesperson for the Opposition parties and any relevant organisations. There are very few occasions when an 'ambush' approach really works (except perhaps when the government's majority is wafer-thin). Generally you will get a more considered response if the minister is aware of the issues that are to be raised by an MP or peer and it will help make them aware of opposition to (or support for) their proposals. If you are working with government backbenchers they will pass information on anyway. Tips on how to brief at each stage are included in the next section. See appendix 1 for suggested templates.

3.42   The House of Commons Library prepares a briefing document for MPs before a Bill starts its passage – so it's always worth sending them your briefings as they may include key points in this document. You can telephone the library (via the main number 020 7219 3000) to check when they are preparing the briefing and who you should send information to.

3.43   **Civil servants:** The Bill manager (or principal) is the lead civil servant who takes responsibility for the Bill throughout its passage. He or she will have a team of officials (including lawyers) who will be continually on hand for the minister, advising him or her at each stage and drafting notes on the key issues and any amendments. Sometimes the team members will have a co-ordinating role, relying on other officials for their policy expertise. At other times, officials with the detailed policy knowledge will be on the Bill team itself. They are easily spotted flanking the minister with bulky files in the committee corridor or on the floor of the House in the advisers' box! The minister's focus is getting the Bill through with as few amendments as possible – apart from relatively small changes which the government feels able to accept are an improvement and do not alter its fundamental purpose. An organisation that has been involved in influencing at an early stage may already have good relations with relevant civil servants. Securing a meeting between an organisation's representatives and the Bill principal is very useful. They will often be happy to have a brief meeting or a telephone conversation to hear about areas of concern. It benefits them to be forewarned of the stance that an organisation is going to take and amendments that are likely to be tabled. In return you may get some useful indication of areas where the government may be willing to compromise. Sometimes they will be receptive to suggested changes although they will not be able explicitly to acknowledge this. You should include the Bill principal on your list of people to send your general briefings to.

Pre-legislative scrutiny of draft Bills

3.44   This has become much more common since 2002 when agreement was reached on the proposal to publish more Bills in draft and subject these to pre-legislative scrutiny. Since then a handful of Bills have gone through this process each session. The 2004 Queen's Speech for example, included eight Bills in draft form. Essentially it involves scrutiny by the relevant departmental select committee (or joint committee of both Houses) of draft legislative proposals. The process is much the same as any other select committee enquiry. Evidence is taken from outside experts – both oral and by way of written submissions as well from relevant ministers and officials.

3.45   This process offers a real opportunity to influence measures at a stage in the political process when they are much less formed and therefore there is less face to lose by politicians if changes are made. The process has been generally well received, with participants feeling that it has led to better drafted and thought through legislation. There is an opportunity to submit oral and written evidence.

3.46-
3.52

Case example

The Mental Capacity Bill 2004

Summary: During 2003 the Mental Capacity Bill was scrutinised by a Joint Committee (chaired by a peer) before being introduced into Parliament in the summer of 2004. From the outset the committee emphasised that its role was confined to examining and reporting on the draft Bill.

Activities: The committee took evidence from over 100 witnesses including lawyers, legal bodies and campaign groups. Many of the concerns they raised were put to ministers when they attended a committee session. The Law Commission submitted a memorandum, highlighting its contribution (including several consultations and reports), and urging the committee to look again at sections which had been omitted from its own draft Bill.

During its deliberations the committee wrote to Lord Filkin, the minister responsible, seeking clarification about certain points (eg access to information and confidentiality). Some useful responses were received, with the government indicating that consequential amendments would be forthcoming.

At the end of 2003 the committee published its key findings and recommendations. Its reports included issues that members thought important, as well as those raised in evidence. In its response the government agreed with a significant number of the recommendations, which were reflected in the redrafted Bill. Overall the process was widely acknowledged as having led to a better Bill (although lobby groups argued for further improvements and indeed secured further changes when the Bill was going through its parliamentary stages). However, the committee strongly recommended that more time was needed for its work.

The Mental Health Bill

Summary: As the Mental Capacity Bill was going through the Commons 'for real', a second version of the Mental Health Bill began its pre-legislative scrutiny. The first version had been produced in 2002 and the overwhelming response from carers, professionals, campaigners, services users, charities, etc had been to oppose it, on the basis that the proposals were draconian and overly focused on the need for compulsory detention powers.

Activities: In response to the Joint Committee's recommendations on the mental capacity legislation, the Joint Committee charged with the Mental Health Bill was given an additional 3 months, increasing its scope for oral hearings especially. Various concerns were raised and many argued that although mental health law was in urgent need of updating and reform the Bill did nothing to achieve that, reflecting instead a lack of understanding about the reality of mental health service. The committee was critical of the draft Bill, saying that it still put too much emphasis on protecting the public from a small number of dangerously ill people and could be used to impose compulsory treatment on those who had done no wrong and would not benefit from it.

The Mental Health Bill was included in the 2005 Queen's Speech. The government's response to the committee signalled agreement in some areas but rejected criticism that the Bill placed too much emphasis on public safety and not enough on patients' rights. The government confirmed that the Bill would include measures to compel people to be treated in the community and to detain some with personality disorders before any crime had been committed.

Government Bills

House of Commons

Human rights 'audit'

3.53   The Human Rights Act 1998 introduced an obligation on ministers to ensure that any new Bill is compatible with the European Convention on Human Rights.[7] They have to publish a written statement to this effect. Officials therefore have to examine the proposals and lawyers will advise ministers about a Bill's compatibility with the ECHR. The Joint Committee on Human Rights (JCHR) plays an important role, scrutinising each Bill, and reporting its views. There is no automatic, 'stand-alone' debate on the issue of a Bill's compatibility with human rights. It is therefore well worth briefing parliamentarians if you have concerns about these aspects of a Bill (and referring them to any JCHR reports) as they can raise concerns during the Bill's passage through Parliament.

First reading

3.54   **Summary:** The introduction and first formal presentation of the Bill to Parliament. No debate takes place.

3.55   **The process:** The Bill will have been brought to MPs' attention by its inclusion in the daily Order Paper. The minister (or whip acting on his or her behalf) reads out its short title. A notional day is named for the Bill's second reading. The actual date for the second reading will be announced in the weekly Business Statement (on a Thursday).

3.56   **The outcome:** This stage forms the order to print the Bill (and post on the Internet: www.parliament.uk/bills/bills.cfm – a useful site which has details of all current bills and their stages).

Second reading

3.57   **Summary:** The first debate about the Bill: its 'spirit and purpose'. The major principles are discussed rather than the detail and no amendments can be proposed. Typically, but not always, two weekends are left between printing and the second reading.

3.58   **The process:** The minister responsible for the Bill's passage, often but not always the secretary of state, makes an opening and closing speech highlighting the main issues. Opposition frontbenchers also speak about the Bill and backbenchers from any party have an

---

7   Section 19(1)(a) of the Human Rights Act 1998.

opportunity to speak. Those MPs wishing to be selected to be on the committee for the next stage must attend second reading and if possible speak in order to indicate their interest. An opposed Bill will be voted on at the end of debate – either simply for or against it receiving its second reading, or on a 'reasoned amendment' which states the exact reasons why it is being opposed. For key Bills MPs will be 'whipped' (ie ordered) to be present to vote by their respective party whips (but this is no guarantee that they will attend the debate itself). For free votes (eg on issues of conscience such as abortion) there is usually no whip.

3.59   **Example:** The first Commons debate on the Mental Capacity Bill 2004 was a fairly typical second reading, lasting several hours. Junior DCA minister David Lammy MP made an opening speech, allowing several interventions from colleagues from all sides. Both Opposition spokespersons (Tim Boswell MP for the Conservatives and Paul Burstow MP for the Liberal Democrats) made substantial speeches, largely welcoming but pointing out concerns. At the end, Health Minister Rosie Winterton MP summed up the debate – referring to points colleagues had made during the debate.

3.60   **Influencing MPs:** Lawyers and organisations should brief MPs for the second reading debate. Briefings should ideally be sent to MPs a few days before but in practice if they arrive the day before a debate (or even on the day) and the MP is interested there is a good chance that it will be read. A second reading briefing should be brief (2–4 pages is ideal with a cover page summarising the key issues), to the point, and highlight the most important issues that you want to see raised. It should welcome measures as well as raise criticisms. This is vital – backbench MPs on the government side in particular loathe it when outside groups fail to acknowledge any good (as they see it) to be achieved through a new law. Even if you can see nothing good at all in a draconian new law you should find something positive and welcome it in the first paragraph. Your briefing is much more likely to be read and your arguments appreciated when you do criticise the Bill's provisions if you have come across as someone with a sense of perspective. See appendix 1 for a sample briefing.

3.61   **Timings:** Second reading debates are part of the 'main business' of the parliamentary day. This means that they typically take place from around 4.45 pm onwards (on Mondays) or from 1.45 pm (Tuesdays–Thursdays).

3.62   Attending the second reading debate (or watching it on the parliamentary channel) can give you a good feel for the issues and for the approach that government, Opposition and backbenchers are going to take towards the Bill. You can simply turn up at the House of Commons and request to go in the public gallery. Or a parliamentarian may be able to arrange a ticket for the gallery for you beforehand.

3.63   **Outcome:** The government is rarely voted down at second reading and thus stalled at this early stage. In spite of fierce opposition including from their own MPs, which could, together with the official Opposition result in defeat, in practice MPs will allow the Bill to continue its passage but continue to oppose it. With a large majority defeat will in any event be impossible to secure, but in addition the Opposition will often be keen to make political capital as the Bill progresses. Significant opposition from the government's own side at this stage or where there are exceptionally strong feelings on all sides signal a stormy ride during the rest of the Bill's passage.

3.64   Usually, second reading is followed immediately by a 'programme motion' that sets out a timetable for the Bill (a 'programme order') as well as any 'money resolutions' that are needed.[8]

3.65   You must take note of the proposed timetable as this will allow you to plan your amendments and briefings. For example, if clauses 1–4 are to be dealt with in the first two sittings, as soon as you have the committee list, you can be approaching MPs about draft amendments for these. At the same time you could be asking colleagues to be working on draft amendments for later sections of the Bill, dividing up the work as appropriate.

See the box on p95 for more information about Programme Orders.

Standing committees have been around for some time. In 1882 the system was reformed and two standing committees created to consider bills: one on law, justice and legal procedure and the other on trade, manufactures and shipping. They were designed to prevent the Irish party from taking up too much of the time of the whole House with committee stages of Bills!

Committee stage

3.66   **Summary:** After second reading most Bills go to a small cross-party committee of MPs (called a standing committee) for detailed scrutiny

---

8   Money Resolutions are needed to authorise any part of a Bill which involves a 'significant' charge on funds belonging to central government. Ways and Means Resolutions are required where taxes or other charges are to be levied by any part of the Bill.

of their provisions. At any one time there are at least eight standing committees in operation, each considering a different Bill. When a committee discharges its duty of studying a Bill its membership changes and it proceeds to scrutinise another. They each have a letter (eg standing committee A) and in addition there are up to two specifically assigned to deal with Scottish Bills (known as 1st and 2nd Scottish standing committees).

3.67   **Membership:** The committee has between 16 and 30 MPs (in practice it is usually around 18). A committee of selection (which includes whips of the three main parties) chooses the committee's members. They will be in proportion to the numbers of MPs that each party has in the current Parliament – thus securing a majority for the governing party. It also has regard to the member's level of interest, eg as shown by their attendance at second reading and to representations from members, whips and the government department. Their names will be published on a Thursday morning and can be obtained from the House of Commons Information Office.[9] The government's side will comprise people chosen for loyalty whose role is to ensure that the Bill passes through committee with as few amendments as possible. This will include a number of Parliamentary Private Secretaries (PPSs) – ministers' assistants. However, the governing side will also include MPs with a keen interest in the subject of the Bill. This latter group are crucial to engage with as although they are unlikely to be overtly disloyal, they may well be pleased to raise issues and concerns about the Bill and press for some changes. Committee membership also includes a minister from the relevant government department and Opposition frontbench spokespersons and backbenchers – again, including a number with a keen interest in the Bill's content. A government and Opposition whip will also sit on the committee, their role being to ensure colleagues are there for votes and to negotiate with the other side about timings and progress rather than to play an active part in the debates. Each Bill committee is chaired by a senior backbencher (a member of the 'Speaker's Panel of Chairmen'). A Clerk (usually from the Public Bill Office) is allocated to each committee.

3.68   With such a small number of MPs compared with membership of the House as a whole, they are generally all needed at every sitting in order to maintain the party balance – and from the government's standpoint, to get the Bill through.

9   Tel: 020 7219 4272.

3.69   **Activities:** In theory, the purpose of the committee stage is to enable detailed scrutiny of and voting on the Bill, clause by clause and line by line. The practice is somewhat different with MPs themselves describing the process as one 'tended to be devoted to political partisan debate rather than constructive and systematic scrutiny'.[10] There is a fundamental tension between the government's mission, which is to get the Bill through quickly and unamended, and the Opposition's goals, which may be quite the opposite. Indeed the greater the policy differences – and therefore arguably the greater the need for measured examination – the more likely it is that government backbenchers will stay silent or make short, supportive comments only in order to get the Bill through. In practice most committees are a mixture of highly politicised debates and more thoughtful scrutiny of a Bill's provisions.

3.70   With a strong government majority and MPs from the governing party chosen partly for their tendency to support the government it can be very difficult to amend a Bill during committee. However, committee stage offers ample opportunities for issues and concerns to be raised and for useful clarifications or concessions to be secured. Some of the more useful discussion occurs when a 'probing amendment' is tabled, aimed at discovering more about the intentions underlying a particular clause rather than a confrontational debate leading to a vote. Furthermore, it is not impossible for amendments to be won, particularly with a slimmer majority. It is also vital at this stage to signal the aspects of a Bill about which there is disagreement. This puts the government on notice that they will not be left alone on certain issues and can help build up a 'head of steam' for parliamentarians to pick up later on in the process. For less contentious areas, raising concerns at this stage gives the government the opportunity to go away and reconsider its position, sometimes coming back at a later stage with a new position or amendment.

3.71   **Timings:** Committee usually starts 2 weeks after second reading. The length of this stage varies, depending on the size of the Bill; how much controversy it is attracting and other negotiations taking place between government and Opposition. It is agreed in advance through a Programme Order. Committee stage can take anything from one day (eg the Employee Share Schemes Bill[11]) to several weeks or months (eg the Proceeds of Crime Bill[12] which took over 3 months), with sittings

---

10   Select committee on the Modernisation of the House of Commons, First Report, 23 July 1997.

11   Now the Employee Share Schemes Act 2002.

12   Now the Proceeds of Crime Act 2002.

taking place twice-weekly, usually on Tuesday and Thursday mornings and afternoons from 8.55–11.25 am and then again from 2.00 or 2.30 pm. This allows MPs to take part in business going on in the chamber.

Timings and control

Much of parliamentary life is still governed by 'the usual channels' – discussions, negotiations and informal agreements between government and Opposition whips. These channels are used in part to thrash out issues around timetabling of legislation. In the past, when these channels failed and governments wanted to stop the Opposition from spinning a Bill's proceedings out (sometimes for so long that it was in danger of falling) they also had recourse to a powerful weapon to cut short debate: a guillotine (or a type of 'Allocation of Time' motion). The guillotine remains in place. However, a new way of agreeing – in advance – how much time should be spent on a Bill – has been introduced, significantly reducing its use.

'Programme Orders' are another type of Allocation of Time motion that are moved straight after second reading and set out the timetable for the rest of the Bill's stages in the Commons. They are intended to be a 'half way house' between informal agreement and the use of the guillotine. Sometimes they are based on agreement between the 'usual channels'; in other cases there is disagreement and the Opposition opposes the motion.

If a timetable concerns sessions that will be open to all MPs (ie committee on the floor of the House, report or third reading), a programming committee is appointed which divides up the Bill and allots each part time that it thinks appropriate. When the timetable concerns proceedings in standing committee, a programming sub-committee of the standing committee is convened and carries out a similar exercise. You need to know what is decided as it will tell you on what days certain clauses will be discussed.

Programme orders have given governments another weapon to use to exert control over proceedings. However, timetabling in advance does make it easier for those seeking to influence the process to plan when to approach MPs with a view to tabling amendments and when to brief them. Although initially successful in promoting a more consensual approach since 2000, they have been heavily criticised especially by Opposition members who argue that they have not been accompanied by more effective scrutiny (eg through special standing committees) as was hoped.

3.72   **The process:** At the first session of the committee, business is dealt with, including consideration of the programming sub-committee's recommendations about the timetable for committee. This allows a 'free for all' debate in which any issues relating to the Bill can be aired. After that the committee will proceed to go through the Bill, looking first at each clause in turn, then at the schedules. They must agree or disagree to a motion that each clause or schedule 'stand part' of the Bill (ie be left in or deleted) – whether or not there is a debate at this point is up to the Chair. Suggestions for new clauses and new schedules are debated at the very end, only when the clause-by-clause scrutiny has been concluded.

Amendments

3.73   Amendments will be tabled a few days before the committee first meets and will continue to be put down during the rest of committee stage – in the name of one or more government and Opposition members. In fact any MP is free to table an amendment but only committee members can move it and speak to it.

3.74   **Selection and grouping of amendments:** The Chair can select and group amendments – a powerful role which does not exist in the House of Lords. This means that not every amendment that is tabled will be discussed. This may be because they are 'out of order' (eg deemed to be irrelevant, outside the scope of the Bill or aimed at 'wrecking' the Bill altogether rather than amending one part of it). Or even if an amendment is in order, the Chair may decide to exercise his or her discretion not to select it. The Clerk assists the Chair in choosing amendments for debate. Selection at committee stage is fairly generous however, with preference given to the member in charge of the Bill. Deadlines are fairly tight (eg amendments will need to be tabled on Friday for a Tuesday session). A marshalled list will show all the amendments tabled so far.

3.75   **Order of amendments:** The Chair also has the power to decide the order in which amendments are debated and voted on. Although the committee will basically go through the Bill clause by clause, amendments are sometimes grouped by subject, meaning that MPs will in effect be examining a number of clauses at the same time. Most amendments are not put to the vote. After discussion, it is common to hear an MP agree to withdraw their amendment – perhaps because the minister has agreed to 'consider the matter again'; some clarification has been offered; or simply because its promoter can see that a vote will achieve little. MPs can check what has happened to amendments the following day from the 'Standing Committee Proceedings' part of the Vote Bundle, the daily working documents of the House of Commons.

3.76   **Sitting in on committee sessions:** Committees are always open to the public. To get a feel for how they work and how you can best get your issues raised, sit in on part or all of a session. You can arrive at any-time during a session, entering through the entrance marked 'Public' (committee members go through the door marked 'Members'), although if a committee is discussing a topic of particular interest to out-siders the room may fill up early on. There will be lists available of the amendments tabled so far and you will see the Opposition on the right and the government on the left. The minister and the Opposition frontbench spokesperson will be at the front of their respective benches, nearest the Chairman. You are likely to see the whips going in and out of the room negotiating on timing and other issues – as well as gov-ernment backbenchers taking advantage of the time to do their corre-spondence. As committee stages are now tightly programmed you can find out in advance which clauses are being debated at which sessions. Just as in the main chamber, each sitting's deliberations will be pub-lished in *Hansard*, put on the parliamentary website 2 or 3 days later and consolidated into one document once committee stage is over.

Influencing MPs during committee

3.77 • Once the committee list is published you need to establish any likely allies. You need to do this quickly as the first committee ses-sion is likely to be the Tuesday following the selection. It is useful to find out the background of the MPs on the committee (eg by referring to their websites) so that you can establish if they are likely to have an interest in any of your issues.

    • You should make contact (eg with a one-side letter, enclosing the second reading briefing) with any MPs you think may be inter-ested in your issues – raising any specific amendments or new clauses that they might be interested in and asking if they might table them. If they are interested, you can follow up with more detailed briefing.

- It is extremely useful if you can persuade one of the MPs from the government side to raise one of your issues. Bearing in mind that they are likely to be supportive of the government, they will be more likely to table amendments or speak to another member's amendment that are relatively uncontroversial or are aimed more at probing the government for more information than at challenging the principles behind the Bill itself.
- You will also want to work with Opposition MPs, who as well as tabling their own amendments will often be receptive to suggestions from outside groups for additional amendments and briefings.
- During committee stage you can sometimes catch members for a quick word in the committee corridor just before or after the session.

Drafting amendments and new clauses

3.78
- These do not need to be technically perfect – they need to be written simply, to make sense and to relate to an appropriate clause. When an MP tables an amendment, clerks in the Public Bill Office are always happy to advise on the wording and technicalities. If an amendment were to reach the stage of being accepted by the government then work would be put into making sure it was technically correct and operable.
- Amendments are first printed as 'Notices of Amendment in Standing Committee' and any outstanding ones then reprinted before each sitting. They are included in MPs' Vote Bundle; you can get information about them from the House of Commons information office and they are on the parliamentary website.

Briefings

3.79   You will need to provide a separate briefing for each amendment (or group of amendments if they are related). They need to set out clearly the purpose, intended effect of the amendment and the difference it would make to the Bill's overall purpose. Remember that in addition to supplying briefings for amendments or new clauses that you have suggested, you may also want to brief on other amendments that have been tabled. See appendices 1–3 for a sample amendment, new clause and accompanying briefings.

3.80   You could also think about the kind of ministerial statement that would be useful in response to an amendment. It can be difficult to elicit clear and precise statements by ministers about a specific provision. As the section at paras 3.182–3.192 on *Pepper v Hart* reveals, ministers are increasingly reluctant to make statements during debates that may later be used in court under this doctrine. But it is still worth thinking about the kind of statement that might be useful and briefing parliamentarians accordingly. For example, a minister might make a broad statement acknowledging that future change along the lines of an amendment should be considered. Or the minister might make a general statement about the intention underlying a Bill (whilst disagreeing that anything more explicit needed to be on the face of the Bill to illuminate this intention). These kind of statements can help give ammunition to campaigners, eg if the government later signals a different interpretation of the policy and could help stimulate legal challenges.

3.81   It can also be useful to ask parliamentarians to make specific requests for information – eg to ask when relevant Codes of Practice or guidance will be published.

Other types of standing committee

3.82   Some non-controversial Bills and largely technical Bills giving effect to Law Commission recommendations will be referred straight to a **Second Reading Committee** rather than being discussed by the whole House. When this happens they are given a formal second reading by the whole House with no debate. There are also the following: **Welsh Grand Committee;** the **Scottish Grand Committee** and the **Northern Ireland Grand Committee;** various standing committees on **delegated legislation, European documents** and on **regional affairs.** The Welsh and Scottish committees have been retained post-devolution, in spite of representations from some quarters that they would not be needed, with any necessary debates taking place on the floor of the House or in Westminster Hall. See para 3.213 for more information about the standing committees on delegated legislation and paras 5.162–5.170 for more information about European standing committees.

3.83   Sometimes the procedure is different from that outlined above. A Bill may be debated by a **special standing committee** or by all MPs **(committee of the whole House).** Or, very rarely, a Bill may go to a **select committee** instead of a standing committee. This is usually confined to Hybrid Bills (part private, part public Bills – of general interest but affecting the interests of particular individuals or organisations, eg the Channel Tunnel Bills). For more information about select committees see chapter 4.

Special standing committees

3.84   **Summary:** Occasionally there is a different and longer opportunity for a standing committee to scrutinise a Bill. This happens when an MP's request for a Bill to go to a 'special standing committee' is granted.

3.85   **The process:** Any MP can request that a Bill goes to a special standing committee. They do this by moving a motion in the House following second reading.

3.86   **What does the committee do?:** The committee then has up to three 3-hour public evidence gathering sittings to help inform its discussion of the Bill's provisions (preceded by a private deliberative session). These must take place within 28 days. The Chair does not have to be from the usual panel used for standing committees and may instead be the Chair of the relevant departmental select committee. During this period it acts very much like a select committee. When these sessions are over the committee reverts to being a normal standing committee and proceeds to go through the Bill clause by clause. The modernisation committee recommended greater use of this procedure, which in theory offers a less partisan and confrontational approach with an emphasis on later discussion being informed by outside, expert opinion. However, in spite of this recommendation – and perhaps because it takes longer and offers less control to the governing side – in practice it has been little used (only once in the 1997 Parliament, for an asylum and immigration Bill and once in the 2001 Parliament, for the Adoption and Children Bill[13]).

3.87   **Influencing the process:** There are obvious opportunities here to influence consideration of the Bill by being called as a witness or submitting written evidence. Or if not formally called you can send briefings highlighting any concerns about the Bill to members of the committee.

Committee of the whole House

3.88   **Summary:** A committee of the whole House is when all MPs are able to consider a Bill at committee stage.

3.89   **Timings:** Takes place after second reading.

3.90   **When is this type of committee used?**

- When a Bill is of major constitutional importance
- When the government wants to secure very rapid passage of legislation (eg the Northern Ireland Assembly Elections Bill in the 2002–03 session)

---

13   Now the Adoption and Children Act 2002.

- When a Bill is uncontroversial
- For parts of the Finance Bill

3.91   **The process:** This is similar to a usual standing committee – the only difference being the potential for a larger number of MPs to be present. If a Bill is dealt with by a committee of the whole House and is not amended it goes straight onto third reading, missing out report stage. But if it is amended, there is a report stage as usual.

3.92   Discussion of a Bill in this way or in the more usual standing committee is subject to negotiation between the parties. Factors will include the government's wish to rush legislation through or the Opposition being keen for the higher profile that debate in the chamber offers. There are no set criteria so, for example, the Human Rights Bill was debated by the whole House.

3.93   **Influencing the process:** There may not be the level of detailed discussion, or for as long a period, as with the more usual committee stage. However, it does mean that instead of targeting a limited number of MPs, you have the opportunity to issue briefings to all MPs, as you would for a second reading debate. Having a debate on the floor of the House does give it a much higher profile which can help with publicity.

3.94   The next two stages: report and third reading are often collectively called the 'Remaining Stages'.

Report

3.95   **Summary:** A 'mini-version' of committee stage, open to all MPs. An opportunity for limited further discussion of the Bill.

3.96   **The process:** If the Bill has been amended in committee the Bill will have been reprinted. Any MP has the opportunity to table amendments or new clauses and to speak to them. These must not be identical to those already covered during committee stage. However, if there has been substantial discussion about a matter of importance, the speaker may select new amendments on this topic in order to give the whole House an opportunity to contribute. There are three differences from committee: (i) the debate takes place in a different order: first, new clauses, then amendments to clauses; new schedules and then amendments relating to schedules; (ii) there are no general 'stand part' debates on each clause as happens in committee – only debates on specific amendments as selected by the Speaker; and (iii) overall, a much smaller number of amendments will be selected than at committee.

3.97   **Timings:** Depending on the size and nature of the Bill – how controversial it is for example – report stage will last for a few hours or at most be spread out over 2 days. It is unusual for a Bill to go through committee stage without being amended at all. But if this happens there is no report stage and the Bill goes straight to third reading. Don't forget that the House can overturn amendments that have been made at committee.

3.98   **Engaging with MPs:** You will need to brief active committee members, who are likely to speak during report as well as a wider group of MPs who can join in at this stage. You may have an opportunity to ask a sympathetic MP to table an amendment or new clause at this stage, particularly those you have worked with during committee (bearing in mind that they cannot be identical 're-runs').

Third reading

3.99   **Summary:** Final stage of the Bill in each House and like second reading a debate on the principles. Usually takes place immediately after report stage at the same sitting. No amendments can be tabled – apart from a 'reasoned amendment' to register opposition to the entire Bill – but these are rare.

3.100   **The process:** It is this stage which allows the House to take an overview of the Bill – literally to 'read' or reconsider the Bill now that it has been through detailed scrutiny. It is often good-natured, with MPs congratulating each other on the contributions they have made. It has to receive a majority vote at this stage in order for it to proceed further. It then goes to the Lords (a paper copy is walked there by a Clerk, whilst electronic copies are also sent through) for consideration or, if it started in the Lords, to receive royal assent.

3.101   **Timings:** Often a very short debate, lasting for around an hour. Sometimes it can be taken formally with no debate, although this would only happen for uncontroversial or more minor Bills.

3.102   **Engaging with MPs:** If this is being taken straight after report you will want to do a general 'Remaining Stages' briefing with more tailored briefings for any amendments/new clauses you are interested in for report. It's a good idea to send any interested peers this briefing, as it will bring them up to speed with your concerns to date.

Case study

Stonewall has successful lobbied for a raft of legislation aimed at achieving equal treatment in the law for lesbians, gay men and bisexuals as well as removing certain legal provisions that are deeply offensive and harmful to these groups (eg section 28 of the Local Government Act 1988). When the Civil Partnership Bill came under threat as it was going through Parliament in 2004, the organisation found that a group of family lawyers were valuable allies. Some peers were attempting to 'wreck' the legislation by introducing amendments to extend its provisions to other co-habiting family members such as mother and daughter. The Solicitors Family Law Association wrote to peers urging them to support the Bill, which aimed to provide a legal framework for same sex couples in long term, committed relationships. They pointed out that these amendments would be an 'absurdity' and that far from improving the situation of co-habiting family members (which they acknowledged needed examination) might in some circumstances worsen it. The SFLA was able (through the expertise of its Cohabitation Committee) to lend considerable expertise, credibility (as a non-partisan group) and concrete examples of why the amendments were completely unworkable. This helped to keep the Bill 'on track' and on 18 November 2004 it received royal assent.

House of Lords

3.103   Seeking to influence the passage of a Bill through the Lords is similar to the Commons but with a few key differences:
- Committee stage is open to all peers.
- There is no selection of amendments – all will be debated.
- The extra opportunity for amendments to be tabled at third reading.
- Party strengths are different from the Commons. On 1 July 2005 there were slightly more Labour than Conservative peers (215 and 208 respectively); 74 Liberal Democrats and 187 cross-benchers. An influx of Labour peers after the 2005 General Election made Labour the largest party in the Lords for the first time, albeit not giving it an overall majority.

3.104   Above all, there is a much less partisan and co-operative approach which means that you are more likely to be working with peers prepared to work on a cross-party basis. In addition there is a core of cross-bench (independent of any of the political parties) peers to work with – many of whom command substantial respect from colleagues. However you need to remember that government Bills will still be whipped. In addition, the House of Lords is changing. Further reforms and the addition of more Labour peers may make it more partisan.

First reading

3.105   **Summary:** Formal as in the Commons. There will be a gap of at least 2 weeks but often longer, between first and second reading.

3.106   **Select committee on delegated powers and regulatory reform:** The Lords take a keen interest in the extent to which primary legislation gives delegated powers to ministers. Each Bill is at this stage considered by this Lords committee, which considers whether the Bill's provisions for ministers' powers to make secondary legislation are appropriate and whether any of these powers are to be subjected to an inadequate degree of parliamentary scrutiny. Almost always it reports before committee stage so that its findings can be considered during that stage. This process is all the more important as the Commons has no equivalent of this watchdog – despite calls for one to be introduced. Its recommendations are often accepted.

3.107   **Engaging with peers:** Between first and second reading (or just before the Bill's introduction) is a good time to be meeting with individuals or a group of peers to brief them about key issues. The Lords is much less partisan than the Commons and peers may therefore be willing to attend a cross-party meeting to discuss a Bill. Or, depending on the issue, a series of meetings with peers from different parties and the cross-benchers may be the best course of action. All peers thinking of taking part in debates on a Bill will appreciate information about what has been covered in the Commons and the government's responses to date. It is therefore invaluable to refer to the Commons debates in the Bill in any briefings for them, providing succinct summaries of any important points made. They will then be better armed when the government makes certain points or offers justifications for key provisions. Sending briefings to the government whips and Opposition whips' offices is a good way to get them to spokespersons. But to reach other party peers you will need to contact them directly. However, the 'cross-bench convenor' will make available briefings to all independent peers (by email or having copies available in their office but will not post them out to members).

Second reading

3.108   **Summary:** The debate takes the same format as in the Commons with a general discussion of the principles underlying the legislation.

3.109   **The process:** As in the Commons, the minister responsible for the Bill in the Lords will make an opening speech. With the Mental Capacity Bill 2004, Lord Falconer, Secretary of State for Constitutional Affairs, kicked off proceedings. Unlike in the Commons the minister was allowed to complete his opening remarks and 'commend the Bill to the House' without interruption. This was as usual followed by speeches by Opposition spokespersons and then backbenchers. The House was reminded at the outset that a 10.00 pm finish would be achieved if the list of 24 speakers (in the Lords, peers request to speak in advance of debate) limited themselves to 8 minutes per speech. Junior Constitutional Affairs Minister Baroness Ashton of Upholland made the closing remarks, acknowledging many of the speakers as well as the earlier scrutiny by a committee.

    By convention no vote is taken, on the basis that it would be improper for an unelected chamber to reject a Bill putting into effect a manifesto commitment.

3.110   Unlike in the Commons, peers put themselves on a 'speakers' list' if they want to speak in a debate. Maintained by the government whips office (www.lordswhips.org.uk) this is useful for deciding who to brief. The list closes on the day of the debate. Other peers can intervene before the winding up speeches, but there will be very limited time available once all the people on the list have had their turn. However, speakers' lists do *not* operate for the final stages of a Bill (report or third reading).

Committee

3.111   **Summary:** Detailed scrutiny of the Bill and less confrontational than in the Commons. It is now usually taken in 'Grand Committee' rather than on the floor of the House but still remains open to all peers – although in practice only ministers, frontbenchers and a few keenly interested backbench peers will attend. This practice has freed up time on the floor of the House for other business.

3.112   **Timings:** Government and Opposition whips will negotiate the number of days the Bill will be in committee. Depending on the Bill, committee stage will last anything from one short session through to several days (the Health and Social Care (Community Health and Standards) Bill 2003 spent 6 days in committee).

3.113   **The process:** Unlike in the House of Commons, there is no selection of amendments. This means that any amendment tabled by a peer, unless technically flawed, will be debated. However, amendments are grouped together, according to their general theme or topic and this can limit the extent to which a peer can ensure their amendments stand out. Grouping is carried out by the government whips, in consultation with those tabling amendments. It is supposed to avoid repetition when several similar amendments have been tabled, or amendments are linked by a common theme.

3.114   There are no procedures such as 'guillotines' or programming motions to govern the use of time, as in the Commons. In theory this could lead to peers opposing the Bill and obstructing proceedings by drawing debates out. In practice this does not tend to happen, in reflection of the more co-operative and less partisan spirit in which the Lords tends to conduct its business. No votes are taken during committee.

3.115   **Influencing the process:** You should check who spoke at second reading, as a guide to who may stay involved at committee stage. Some peers will be receptive to suggestions for amendments or to supporting amendments tabled by others. You may need to act quickly – eg if committee stage is to be completed in one or two days. Amendments and briefings should be drafted in similar way as for MPs. But for a thorough guide to how to set out amendments to Bills when they are in the Lords go to www.publications.parliament.uk/pa/ld/ldamend.pdf.

3.116   Deadlines for tabling amendments are posted on the government whips website: www.lordswhips.org.uk.

Report

3.117   **Summary:** Further consideration by the whole House of the Bill and, as in the Commons, an opportunity to table and debate a small number of amendments. Proceedings can hot up at this stage, with the government anxious to get its measures through and peers often keen to see significant concessions.

3.118   **The process:** If the Bill has been amended in committee it will have been reprinted. Any peer has the opportunity to table amendments or new clauses. However, these must not be identical to those already covered during committee stage. The debate will focus on new amendments, alterations to any amendments made during committee stage, and new clauses. As in the Commons, a much smaller number of amendments will be debated than at committee.

3.119   **Timings:** Depending on the size and nature of the Bill – and how many amendments are tabled – report stage will take up one sitting or last for a few days.

3.120   **Influencing the process:** Report offers another good opportunity to brief peers and encourage them to table amendments or new clauses.

You will need to identify the most important issue/s from committee that you would like to see prioritised and include in your briefings any points made (eg by the minister) that could usefully be pursued. Unlike committee, at this stage votes will be taken.

Third reading

3.121 **Summary:** Final stage of the Bill. The final opportunity for peers to suggest amendments to a Bill (unlike in the Commons where amendments cannot be tabled at third reading) and for this reason is crucial for those inside and outside Parliament seeking to make changes. Usually takes place at a separate sitting from report stage (unlike in the Commons).

3.122 **The process:** A small number of amendments or new clauses will be tabled and debated. A new angle must be found: they cannot be replicas of earlier amendments.

3.123 **Timings:** Third reading is completed within one sitting, often taking place a week or more after report stage.

3.124 **Influencing the process:** It is at third reading that the Bill may sometimes be amended, often with relatively low-cost and modest changes, but nonetheless ones that will make a difference to its impact. The opportunity for amendments at this stage is significant for those seeking to alter a Bill. Ideally, you will be able to persuade peers to raise again the one issue that you think is worth pursuing and may lead to a concession. The government may well come armed with something that will persuade peers to withdraw their amendments rather than push them to a vote.

The final stages: consideration of Lords' amendments

3.125 If the Bill has gone through the Lords without being amended, a message is sent to the Commons to this effect, and the Bill goes straight for royal assent. If, as is more common, it has been amended by the Lords, it returns to the Commons for consideration. The Commons will either agree to the amendments, agree to them but with their own amendments, or disagree entirely. If they agree, the Bill goes for royal assent. If they agree but with their own changes the Lords are asked to agree these. If the Commons disagrees with the Lords' amendments, the Bill will be returned to the Lords for them to consider the Commons' reasons. If the Lords decide to reject the Commons' reasons the Bill again goes back to the Commons for reconsideration.

Ping pong – ending in agreement

3.126   It's fairly common for a major bill to be batted to and from each House once or twice before agreement is reached. A Bill may be amended by the Lords, for example, returned to the Commons a week later and quickly sent back to the Lords again before receiving royal assent. During this process behind the scenes negotiations will be taking place to try to secure agreement on any remaining contentious issues.

Ping pong – with no agreement

3.127   The ping pong that results where there is severe disagreement will in the most extreme cases lead to the use of the Parliament Acts, a weapon deployed by the Commons to overrule the Lords. Where each House has stuck to its guns and offered no alternative the Commons can act to impose its will after one year without the consent of the House of Lords (but only by reintroducing the Bill in identical form). The most high profile case to attract this treatment in recent times is the Hunting Act 2004 – only the eighth time since 1911 that the Acts had been used to defeat the Lords.

Ping pong – with eventual compromise

3.128   When the government is up against the wire and does not wish to delay the introduction of legislation, it has to compromise. In March 2005, the government had just days to go before existing powers to detain foreign terror suspects without trial expired. It was seeking to push through a new law – in response to a law lords' ruling that the existing powers breached human rights laws.[14] Concessions were made at an early stage in the Lords to the Prevention of Terrorism Bill 2005, with government amendments aimed at transferring house arrest powers from politicians to judges. But this was not enough to avert outright opposition by many peers who wanted to defeat the Bill altogether. After a series of crushing defeats by peers to the core of the legislation, a 30-hour 'ping pong' session between the two Houses finally ended when the Prime Minister conceded that MPs should be able to review the law in a year's time.

---

14   The Prevention of Terrorism Act 2005 was the government's response to the damning ruling of the law lords on the detention without trial of foreign nationals under Part IV of the Anti-terrorism Crime and Security Act 2001 in *A, X & Ors v Secretary of State for the Home Department* [2004] HL.

Other scrutiny

3.129 Every Bill will also be considered by the Joint Committee on Human Rights and by the Lords Constitution Committee which both looks at the constitutional implications of any public Bill as well as carrying out more general policy inquiries. See para 4.111 for more information about the Joint Committee on Human Rights.

Consolidation Bills

3.130 These Bills, which seek to bring together existing laws in a consolidated and more coherent form, will often be of interest to lawyers – or indeed lobbied for by them. The Joint Committee on Consolidation, etc Bills is tasked with examining these Bills. However, as they are only involved once they have been introduced (they always start in the House of Lords) and deal only with the form not the merits, they are not the body to lobby to secure commitment to legislation in the first place. But if you have a specialist interest in the technicalities of a consolidation bill you may want to follow their deliberations.

3.131 The Tax Law Rewrite Committee is a joint committee with a similar function: to scrutinise draft laws aimed at consolidation and simplification.

From a Bill to an Act: receiving royal assent

3.132 Royal assent is the agreement of the monarch to the Bill becoming an Act. It is now a formality and happens quickly, sometimes on the same day as the Bill's remaining stages are concluded in Parliament, sometimes later. However it does not signify that the legislation has come into force.

Coming into force of an Act

3.133 When does an Act come into force? Each Act is different. Some take effect immediately; some at a date specified in the Act; and others by Commencement Order – a type of delegated power that gives the minister the power to specify at a later date when the Act should come into force. These are not mutually exclusive. In fact it is common for part of an Act to come into force immediately; for other parts at a date specified in the Act and other parts as provided for in a Commencement Order. The Disability Discrimination Act 1995 for example contained a number of Commencement Orders. The employment provisions came into effect on 2 December 1996, about a year after royal assent, whilst the introduction of certain other provisions was staggered. The duty to make reasonable adjustments to policies, etc did not come into force until October 1999 and certain transport duties took effect in 2000 and 2001. These allow governments to introduce change gradually – something they are particularly keen to do when they are introducing regulations that affect businesses.

3.134   'Sunset clauses', as their name suggests are the opposite of staged commencement. They are designed to allow elements of a Bill to fall after a stated period of time. They can also be used as a form of protest. Peers used a sunset clause as a device to show that they opposed the Prevention of Terrorism Bill 2005 in its entirety and wanted to kill it off.

3.135   Parliamentarians and lobbyists used a 'sunrise clause' to help put pressure on the government to delay a key element of the Community Care (Delayed Discharges) Act 2003. This gave local authorities more time to put structures in place to deal with the new requirements.

Putting the law into practice: Codes and guidance

3.136   Once a law has become an Act, the government turns its attention to awareness-raising and implementation. For example, the Disability Rights Commission was tasked with preparing a new Code of Practice in relation to new duties on transport providers contained in the Disability Discrimination Act 2005. The government will often consult on codes and guidance and those preparing them will be on the look out for examples to help bring it to life. Lawyers can input into the codes and guidance that are frequently prepared and are vital for showing individuals and organisations the meaning of a new law, how it will affect them and any actions they should take. In particular they can provide both hypothetical and real examples from their everyday practice that will help people understand and apply new laws. Do they have unreported cases that might be relevant for example, or have they been approached by clients they were unable to help due to the existing law?

3.137   **For further information:** The Public Bill Office can answer queries about a government Bill or standing committees more generally.[15] Progress can also be checked in the Weekly Bulletin. You can get information about when an Act or part of it will come into force from the government department responsible.

15   Tel: 020 7219 3251/8.

House of Commons

First Reading: The short title of the Bill is read out by the minister responsible or a whip; there is no debate but the Bill is then printed.

MPs and peers vote at all stages of the Bill.

Second reading: The first major debate on the principles of the Bill. Amendments cannot be tabled at this stage.

Committee: Typically lasts several days (over a number of weeks). A committee of MPs (weighted according to their number of representatives in the Commons) scrutinises the Bill clause by clause.

Report: A debate back on the floor of the House. A small number of amendments are debated.

Third reading: A short debate on the principles of the Bill. No amendments can be debated or made. Often follows straight after report stage on the same day.

House of Lords
Goes through the same stages as the Commons with three important differences:

- All members of the House of Lords can take part in the committee stage.
- All amendments tabled for committee stage will be debated; there is no selection.
- Amendments can be tabled at third reading.

First reading: The short title of the Bill is read out by the minister responsible or a whip; there is no debate but the Bill is then printed.

Second reading: The first major debate on the principles of the Bill. The issues will be revisited afresh, regardless of the debates that have already taken place in the Commons.

Committee: Open to all peers to take part, whether it takes place on the floor of the House or in Grand Committee.

Report: Further debate on the floor of the House. A smaller number of amendments are debated.

Third reading: Final consideration of the Bill before it returns to the Commons. The final opportunity for peers to debate and accept or reject amendments.

No Lords' amendments – Bill proceeds to receive royal assent.

Lords have amended the Bill – goes back to Commons for consideration of Lords' amendments.

The Commons considers any amendments made by the Lords and accepts them – the Bill proceeds to receive royal assent.

The Commons considers any amendments made by the Lords and rejects them (or amends them) and sends the Bill back to the Lords for re-consideration.

The Lords consider the Commons' rejection or suggested alterations to their amendments and decide not to continue their opposition – the Bill proceeds to receive royal assent.

The Lords decides to reject what the Commons has suggested and the Bill returns to the Commons.

Negotiations take place. The Commons exerts its will and uses the Parliament Acts to force the Bill through. Or, a compromise is reached and both Houses agree the final text.

The agreed text of the Bill is submitted for royal assent, now a formality.

The Bill becomes an Act and is printed.

Act comes into force although sometimes different parts come into force at different times.

Case study: government attempts to end trial by jury thwarted again

Illustrates: The importance of sustaining opposition over a long period.

Summary: The Criminal Justice Bill 2002 included proposals to severely limit the right to trial by jury: in serious fraud and other long and complex cases, where defendants chose trial by judge alone and where there was a perceived risk of jury intimidation. Thanks to the efforts of the legal profession, campaigners and parliamentarians the government was forced to make significant concessions.

Background: Since 1999, the government has brought forward numerous proposals aimed at limiting the number of jury trials. The Mode of Trial Bill 1999 was rejected outright by the House of Lords not once but twice. Plans for a third attempt were only dropped because of the forthcoming 2001 general election. Home Secretary David Blunkett who replaced Jack Straw was completely undeterred. He plucked various elements from a review of the criminal justice system published by Lord Justice Auld in October 2001 which the Home Office responded to by publishing a white paper on Criminal Justice, which trailed plans to limit jury trials. Interestingly the plans did not go as far as some of Lord Justice Auld's suggestions (eg to remove trial by jury for offences like theft and criminal damage), but via a 'flagship', Criminal Justice Bill, in the Queen's Speech that year, the government nonetheless proceeded with plans that would significantly reduce the right to trial by jury.

Working in partnership: A number of groups voiced fierce opposition to the proposals and sought to argue that removing the right to trial by jury did nothing to aid victims of crime and would only increase the chances of wrong verdicts (as well as criticising other aspects of the Bill). Matthias Kelly QC, who was Bar Council Chairman at the time, predicted that 'a powerful coalition' of parliamentarians from all parties, the legal profession and civil liberties groups would wage an intense battle. Joint work was in evidence from the outset, when the Criminal Bar Association, Liberty, the Legal Action Group and the Bar Council issued a joint statement in time for the first major Commons debate on the Bill. Peter Rook QC, then Chair of the Criminal Bar Association co-ordinated a working party on the Bill which helped to sustain pressure on Parliament.

The issues: In addition to the concern about jury trials, many also opposed controversial proposals to remove the 'double jeopardy law' (under which defendants cannot be subjected to a retrial when they have been found not guilty of certain serious offences) and to allow far greater admissibility of previous misconduct.

Strategy: In addition to opposing other aspects of the Bill, the sustained focus and activities of individuals and organisations helped to win support in Parliament. Crucially, the strong stance taken by campaigners in the run-up to and when the Bill commenced its passage, helped to form the ground for peers' defeats to be inflicted in the Lords.

Activities: Organisations' activities included sustained analysis, briefings, drafting amendments and seeking publicity for their views, and work publicly and behind the scenes with parliamentarians.

Parliamentary work: On the issue of trial by jury, campaigners' efforts were aided by cross-party opposition from the Liberal Democrats and Conservatives and importantly the staunch support of a number of Labour backbenchers, including lawyers who examined the proposals at a Labour backbench committee session.

Media coverage: The issue was already a media story, having received coverage when other attempts were made to limit jury trials. In January 2002 the Bar Council, the Law Society and the Criminal Bar Association had publicised their opposition to any weakening of the right to trial by jury through a survey showing overwhelming public trust in juries ('Jury trial support rock solid').[16] This helped to sustain media interest in the issues with each stage of the Bill's passage (and especially when the government was defeated) providing a new news 'hook'.

16   BBC on-line, 30 January 2002.

Turning points: The government was defeated at a late stage of the Bill in the Commons when 33 Labour MPs supported a Conservative and Liberal Democrat amendment to scupper the attempt to restrict trial by jury in complex fraud cases.[17]

The government was given a further taste of what was to come when criminal barrister and Labour peer Baroness Mallalieu voiced her opposition during second reading, saying that the government was attempting to 'chip away at the edges' rather than to have a proper debate about the wholesale removal of jury trials.[18]

The government suffered major defeats, with cross-benchers, Conservative and Liberal Democrat peers joining forces, voting down the section allowing judge-only trials in complex fraud cases. They also voted to restrict the extent to which the Bill would allow evidence of previous convictions to be heard in court and rejected provisions for defendants in any Crown Court case to opt for a judge-only trial.

Outcomes: As the Bill bounced to and from the Commons and Lords on the last day of the parliamentary session the government was forced to compromise, promising that the proposal for fraud trials without juries would not go ahead without cross-party agreement and a further parliamentary debate and vote in both Houses. The proposals for defendants to elect a non-jury trial were not pursued. However, in June 2005 the government announced that it would be seeking to put into effect the agreement, by having a vote in both Houses, with a view to securing an end to jury trials in complex fraud cases.

Principles of success
- The government's arguments kept changing, for example shifting from arguing that juries were not up to the complexities of complex fraud trials to concern that citizens could not spare months to sit on such juries. Campaigners had to respond to these shifting sands; it was important to main-

17   Hansard, HC Debates, 19 May 2003.
18   Hansard, HL Debates, col 607, 16 June 2003.

> tain a principled stance – for example, continuing to speak out
> about the importance of the presumption of innocence.
> • Campaigners kept up continual pressure. Liberty and others
>   engaged members of the public in their work and overall, a
>   powerful coalition built up, involving a range of interests,
>   which it became impossible for the government to ignore
>   whilst the Bill was going through Parliament. However it is an
>   example of the government ultimately being determined to
>   push a law through, in spite of being faced with considerable
>   opposition.

Carrying Bills over

3.152   In addition to making best use of Allocation of Time motions (see box on p95 above) another way in which the government can safeguard legislation from Opposition attack and ensure that more Bills are passed is the power to carry over Bills from one session to another. This was introduced in 1999, enabling the Financial Services and Markets Bill 1998–99, to be carried over into the 1999–2000 session when it was part way through its committee stage. Since then this procedure has been used on a number of occasions, including with the Mental Capacity Bill 2004 which was allowed to complete its Commons committee stage at the end of the 2003–04 session, and be reintroduced into the Commons the day after the Queen's Speech, at the beginning of the 2004–05 session. A total of three Bills were carried over into the 2004–05 programme.

3.153   However, this does not work in a General Election year, when any Bills that have not completed all their stages by the time Parliament has been dissolved will fall and have to start from scratch (all their stages in both Houses) in the next session.

Private Members' Bills

3.154   These are Bills that offer backbenchers the opportunity to make law. There are four types of Private Members' Bill:

(1) Ballot Bills (Commons)
(2) Private Peers' Bills (Lords)
(3) Ten Minute Rule Bills (Commons)
(4) Presentation Bills (Commons)

Private Members' Bills are another type of Public Bill. All offer a useful opportunity to raise an issue in Parliament and to gain some publicity – and a handful will actually become law! They are particularly useful for those seeking to engage in law reform as they offer the opportunity to draft the legislation; test the key issues it raises and to gather support. As it is rare for an individual to have the opportunity to take a Bill through, they may be as unfamiliar with the process as a non-parliamentarian!

3.155   A few MPs have had a real impact on policy through Private Members' Bills. Janet Anderson MP introduced two Bills which subsequently influenced government policy – one which sought to make stalking a criminal offence, the other to establish a national register of paedophiles. She has also piloted through Parliament a Private Members' Bill to make it an offence to use hand-held mobile telephones while driving a motor vehicle, which again the government responded positively to, by introducing a similar offence.[19]

Ballot Bills

3.156   **Summary:** These are Bills that are sponsored by the 20 lucky backbench MPs who enter the annual ballot and have their names picked out of the 'hat' (in this case a despatch box).

3.157   **The process:** On the Tuesday and Wednesday of the second week of the parliamentary session MPs can enter their names for the ballot. So, in 2005 the Queen's Speech took place on the 17 May; MPs entered the ballot the following week and 20 names were drawn out on Thursday 26 May at midday. These few will be given priority in introducing their Bills. In theory MPs can choose whether or not to enter – but in practice the whips will load on the pressure – not wanting MPs from other parties to end up with all the opportunities. Around 400 of the total number (646) will generally enter. The lucky few will then be inundated with requests from organisations to take up their idea for a Bill. Some MPs will already have decided which Bill to pilot – others will only decide after reflecting on the ideas they receive. Some may be willing to receive a ready-made 'handout' Bill from the government (particularly if they have an eye on the career ladder) – a small but important (in the government's eyes) measure that there will have been no room for in the Queen's Speech. For these Bills considerable support will be available from officials from the relevant department.

19 On 1 December 2003 a law was introduced which outlawed the use of a hand-held mobile phone whilst driving, SI No 2695, The Road Vehicles (Construction and Use) (Amendment) (No 4) Regulations 2003.

3.158   **Timings:** Private Members' Bills have to go through the same procedures as any other Public Bill in order to become law. However, the timings for their introduction and passage are different. Private Members' Bills are only debated on the floor of the House on Fridays – the day when most MPs have returned to their constituencies. And committee stage (if they get that far – the government takes up most of committees' time with its Bills) takes place on Wednesdays. Should a Bill get through its Commons stages, a peer will need to be identified to take it through the Lords.

3.159   The 20 MPs have just under 3 weeks from being picked to decide which Bill to present. Bills have to be introduced to Parliament on the fifth Wednesday of the session and the evening before the short and long titles and supporters' names must have been finalised. On that Wednesday all the MPs have to be present in the chamber, and when asked by the Speaker must name one of the allocated Fridays for the date for the Bill's second reading.

3.160   If you are working with an MP on a Bill they will then need your assistance to get it into a reasonable draft form.

Influencing the process: seeking to get your Bill introduced

3.161   Drafting a Bill is an excellent way to generate ideas and crystallise thinking about what you or other people really want. Private Members' or Private Peers' Bills have often helped to raise an issue and prompt governments to act: the first race relations legislation, new laws on civil partnerships and the Human Rights Act 1998 were all preceded by Bills introduced by backbenchers. Precursors to the Disability Discrimination Act 1995 were introduced as Private Members' Bills by numerous MPs and peers before the government was persuaded to introduce its own legislation.

3.162   Again, you need to establish your aims and objectives – what will the introduction of a Private Member's Bill achieve (if you get that far)? Is it the best way to gain interest in and publicity of your issue? You need to be clear about the aims and objectives – is it primarily to increase awareness which in the long run you think could lead a government to introduce the legislation or is there some chance that the government might not oppose it and of it becoming law? Or is it a measure that the government might actively want to see become law but which they won't put aside time for as a government Bill but would be happy to hand out to one of the MPs selected in the ballot? You need to bear in mind that supporting an MP or peer throughout the entire process is intensive and time-consuming.

3.163   If you decide that a draft Bill might help with your issue or campaign you need to be thinking about it and preparing your case well before the ballot takes place in November or December. Having a draft Bill ready may help persuade an MP to take it on – and your skills as a lawyer will be invaluable in helping an organisation or an MP translate an idea into draft legislation.

3.164   In an ideal world, a supportive MP keenly interested in your idea will be selected in the ballot. Unfortunately there are no guarantees of this so you will need to contact all your MPs with your idea. You could send a short letter to all MPs at the beginning of the summer recess (late July) giving them information and a copy of the Bill if it is already in draft form. This may give you a helpful indication of any who might be interested, who you can then contact immediately after the ballot. However, you may want to exclude from this mailing any MPs who you think will be utterly opposed and might delight in killing off a Private Member's Bill on your chosen topic!

3.165   Some MPs will have a clear candidate if they are picked. Others may know the issue but not have decided on the exact Bill and a few will be open to a variety of suggestions. Some may be attracted to a Bill which will give them some profile – so if you have already managed to gain some publicity for your proposals this may help. Do not worry about the exact wording of your Bill – it simply needs to be a draft and to convey roughly what it is about. If it gains favour with the government it will be completely redrafted by Parliamentary Counsel anyway.

Case study: carers' legislation

Dr Hywel Francis MP approached Carers UK when he came second in the ballot. Personal experience is often a factor in members' choice of legislation. In this case, the MP was motivated in part by his son Sam who had Down's Syndrome and who he and his wife cared for until he died at the age of 16. In a short space of time the Carers (Equal Opportunities) Bill or 'Sam's Bill' was pulled together. After passing through its initial stages in March 2004 the government pledged its support to an amended version of the Bill which aimed to provide greater support for carers (including access to information).[20] Solicitor Luke Clements was involved in drafting the Bill, although he recalls that the only words from his draft that survived the scrutiny of Parliamentary Counsel are the long title!

---

20 The Carers (Equal Opportunities) Act came into force on 1 April 2005.

Working on a Bill that has been introduced

3.167   Once a Private Members' Bill has been introduced, in theory it will proceed through the same stages as any other Public Bill. In practice most Bills of this type will not make it all the way. The MP will try to make a tactical decision to get the first slot of the day for second reading to minimise the possibility of it running out of time. They will need a minimum of 40 MPs to be present to vote at the end of this debate (and its other stages) – a tall order given that most will want to be out of London on a Friday. London MPs are crucial to cultivate here. Private Members' Bills are easily scuppered. An archaic rule allows a member to prevent a Bill from proceeding any further by raising a point of order. The MP can guard against this by briefing a friendly MP to get in there and raise the point of order first! This precludes the hostile MP from sabotaging the Bill.

3.168   Even if you are not working directly with an MP to promote a particular Bill, you may have an interest in another Bill. You need to assess what kind of Bill it is and why it is worth trying to influence – bearing in mind that even if a Bill is not destined to get beyond second reading or committee stage these debates can still offer an excellent opportunity to raise your concerns. Briefings need to follow a similar format as for government Bills although a useful additional point to make is why the Bill should be allowed to progress to the next stage.

Private Peers' Bills

3.169   **Summary:** Private Peers' Bills are the same as Private Members' Bills introduced by MPs. The key difference is the freedom peers have to introduce a Bill at any time rather than being picked in the ballot. However, the chances of successful passage are slim – of the 12 private peers' bills introduced in the 2003–04 session none became law.

3.170   **The process:** The process is more-or-less the same as with government Bills. If the Bill has government support and a serious prospect of being passed, it will need to start early in the session, so that there is time for it to complete its stages in the Lords and in the Commons as well.

3.171   **Timings:** Once the Public Bill Office has approved the text, a Bill can be introduced on any sitting day. Rather than a fixed timetable being set down, as is usual in the Commons, the member sponsoring the Bill takes responsibility for liaising with the government whips' office to fix a date for second reading and subsequent stages. If it gets through the Lords, an MP will need to be identified who is willing to take it through its Commons stages. However, even with this support it is virtually impossible to get the necessary time to go through its Commons stages, as peers' bills are at the end of the queue.

3.172 **Influencing the process:** Campaigners often forget about Peers' Bills. But peers will often be open to suggestions for Bills to introduce – and hopefully able to pilot them through at least all their Lords stages. For campaigners there is the great advantage that you can engage a peer with a draft idea and if they want to take it up there will not be the question mark posed by the ballot. It can be another good way to float an idea and get some publicity and to debate challenging ethical or moral issues which governments will be reluctant to touch. Many peers introduce similar Bills from session to session, in an attempt to keep plugging away at an issue. A good example is Lord Joffe's Patient (Assisted Dying) Bill from 2002–03 which resurfaced as the Assisted Dying for the Terminally Ill Bill in the next parliamentary session. Most unusually for a Private Members' Bill and greatly assisted by the work of the Voluntary Euthanasia Society it was scrutinised by a special Lords select committee which took evidence from over 100 witnesses.

Ten Minute Rule Bills

3.173 **Summary:** These are draft Bills used by backbenchers to raise a topic of their choice in Parliament. They are more of a parliamentary 'tool or technique' (see chapter 4 for more about these) than a realistic opportunity to get another law added to the statute books.

3.174 **Timings:** Ten Minute Rule Bills begin on the seventh week of a session. There are opportunities for two MPs per week (on Tuesdays and Wednesdays) to present their Ten Minute Rule Bill – at the high profile time just after questions and statements.

3.175 **The process:** Any backbencher can apply for leave to introduce a Ten Minute Rule Bill by registering their intention with the Public Bill office 15 sitting days before the slot they want. If successful there will be a short description of the Bill on that day's Order Paper and when called they can make a speech lasting no more than 10 minutes in support of the proposed legislation. Another MP can then speak against the proposal (for no more than 10 minutes). Although most Ten Minute Rule Bills are not even printed or reach second reading, they can attract publicity over a much longer period – perhaps because they are perceived as a more serious law-making effort than they actually are! David Taylor's Ten Minute Rule Bill to introduce an Older People's

Commissioner (along the lines of the existing Children's Commissioner) attracted sustained interest and publicity well beyond its only formal 'outing' in the Commons – its first reading was on 17 June 2003.

3.176   **Influencing the process:** As with other opportunities, MPs are open to suggestions for topics for a Bill. This procedure lends itself well to campaigns for law reform, in which it is essential to start to raise awareness, gather support and to think through the shape a desired law should take. It can be a great way to kick off or sustain interest in a campaign.

3.177   **Examples:** The flexibility of this technique is reflected in the range of issues MPs use it to raise. Examples from the 2003–04 session include: Cinemas in Rural Areas (David Rendel); Congenital Heart Disease (Exemption from Prescription Charges) (Ivan Henderson); and Doorstep Selling (Property Repairs) (Gordon Marsden). In 2003 David Atkinson MP used it to draw attention to the Traveller Law Reform Bill, a draft Bill very effectively used by the Gypsy and Traveller Law Reform Coalition to highlight the need for obligations to be re-introduced on local authorities to provide adequate sites.

Presentation Bills

3.178   **Summary:** These are very much like Ten Minute Rule Bills – the main differences being that MPs do not need prior permission to introduce them and that they do not get the opportunity to make a speech about the proposals.

3.179   **Timings:** Presentation Bills can be presented on any day that Parliament is sitting.

3.180   **The process:** An MP has to give notice of the short and long titles of the Bill to the Public Bill Office the day before.

3.181   **Influencing the process:** This type of Bill is simply another way to gain publicity for an issue or campaign. As they can be presented on any sitting day, they have the advantage that you can approach an MP and ask them to use it to coincide with an event such as a campaign launch.

Making use of ministerial statements in and beyond the courtroom

Pepper v Hart

3.182   Since 1993, lawyers have been allowed to refer to ministerial statements as an aid to statutory interpretation if they help to clarify an 'ambiguity' or 'obscurity' or to clarify wording, the literal meaning of which leads to an 'absurdity'.[21] The statement must be 'clear' and have been made by a minister or other promoter of the Bill during its passage through Parliament. There are significant restrictions on the statements to which reference can be made.

3.183 Since this case there has been discussion, in both Parliament and the courts about its proper usage, with no shortage of strong feelings either way. During a Lords debate on the Civil Partnerships legislation Lord Lester described himself as the 'guilty counsel who won the case' and advised use of the doctrine only 'in exceptional circumstances to construe legislation that was dodgy on its face'.[22]

3.184 As awareness of the doctrine has increased, backbenchers now more often seek to elicit explicit statements of intent from ministers as to the intentions underlying new legislation. In return, ministers and officials often display less willingness to give assurances about the meanings of provisions – lest statements come back to haunt them! Soon after *Pepper v Hart* was decided, Sir John Cope, a Treasury minister said during the passage of the Finance Bill 1994:

> 'The fact that the words of a Minister on such a clause as this might be used in court inclines Ministers to be much more careful and not produce examples that may prove to be illustrative but not particularly precise.'[23]

3.185 During the passage of the Human Rights Act, ministers were similarly cautious, perhaps in the context of their anticipation of the Act being much used. The Lord Chancellor at the time Lord Irvine of Lairg said that *Pepper v Hart* 'does not come free of risk'. He spoke of his 'grave reservations about giving legal advice' which 'will then be transmuted by the doctrine of *Pepper v Hart* into what the Government intended as a result of this provision of the Bill'.[24] He then confined his substantive response to a direct quotation from the relevant clause, without offering any further explanation. However, when ministers actively wish to encourage interpretation of a provision in a specific manner, they will refer to the doctrine in *Pepper v Hart* to signal that they are making a clear statement of intention that they wish the court to follow.

3.186 More than 10 years on from *Pepper v Hart*, a Commons select committee spent some time considering its implications in the context of pressures on parliamentary time. Sir Alan Hazelhurst commented:

21 *Pepper v Hart* [1993] AC 593, HL.
22 Hansard, HL Debates col GC131, 12 May 2004.
23 Hansard, HC Committee, cols 173–4, 10 February 1994.
24 Hansard, HL Committee cols 855–56,24 November 1997.

'I make the qualification about the effect of *Pepper v Hart*, that ministers now do need to get certain information on the record.'

3.187   He went on to recommend not that ministers should be given more time to speak but that there could be scope to add documents (eg to the explanatory memorandum of a Bill) that would have the requisite status to come within the doctrine.[25] Another member, Sir Robert Smith, pointed out that it was the 'probing interaction' between ministers and other members that was of most use to courts and that this was not replaceable simply by a memorandum or letter.

3.188   Lawyers have both sought to use the doctrine and equally poured scorn on colleagues for doing so. In *Re P* counsel referred to 'the usual hopeless attempt to obtain guidance from parliamentary debates under the rule in *Pepper v Hart* ...' Judges' views have been similarly varied. In another Lords case the Judicial Committee held unanimously that there was no ambiguity such as would justify recourse to the doctrine.[26] However, they went on to disagree about the circumstances in which it could be used. Lord Bingham thought only in exceptional or rare cases and only the meaning rather than the purposes of underlying policy; Lord Hope agreed that use should be exceptional but not confined to an Act's words rather than its policy. Lord Nicholls, however, took a more liberal interpretation, stating that it would not be rational to make a distinction between the meaning of words and statutory purpose when considering recourse to *Pepper v Hart*, whilst adding that as with any other external material it was for the court to decide what weight to attach to it.

3.189   None of these discussions have disturbed the continuation of the broad doctrine created by *Pepper v Hart*, and lawyers should bear it in mind, in case it is of use to them. Where an appropriate statement has been identified, there are procedures to be followed, which are set out in the Practice Direction (Hansard Extracts) reproduced in appendix 4. A brief summary of the argument and the extract/s should be served on the court and other parties no later than 5 working days before the hearing.

3.190   Paying attention to parliamentary debates can, in any case, be of broader value in clarifying the meaning and likely effects of a new law. A collection of statements made by ministers at each stage of the Bill's passage is a useful guide for how the law may take effect. But they also serve as useful reminders of how ministers *intended* the

---

25   House of Commons Select Committee on Procedure, Minutes of Evidence, 8 December 2004.

26   *Ex p Spath Holme Ltd*, 7 December 2000.

legislation would take effect and can therefore be used in campaigns literature and press releases, etc. The definition of 'public authority' for the purposes of the Human Rights Act has, for example been narrowly defined by the courts, although at the time ministers clearly intended there to be a wide definition. The Lord Chancellor said:

> 'More generally, the Bill provides for a wide interpretation of the term "public authority" because we want to provide as wide a protection as possible for the human rights of individuals against an abuse of those rights'.[27]

3.191 The effect has been to deny many vulnerable older people in receipt of private or voluntary sector care from the protection of the HRA, in spite of their suffering serious abuses (including neglect and malnutrition) which would appear to be just the kind of case that the HRA should catch. In this case the government is receptive to the need to tackle this legal loophole, but in others where there might be resistance it would be especially helpful to return to the government's original intentions. See para 3.17 for details of organisations' attempts to have the definition of public authority widened to aid this group.

3.192 From time to time groups publish comprehensive publications of all key ministerial statements. The Immigration Law Practioners' Association (ILPA), for example, has produced a number of compilations on immigration and asylum legislation and on the Human Rights Act 1998.[28] These are a good way to capture any useful statements as well as to give practitioners a feel for the general intentions behind the legislation.

Secondary legislation

3.193 **Summary:** Delegated – or secondary legislation as it is often called – is the collective term for a type of law that is made by ministers (and occasionally public bodies) under powers given to them by Parliament in primary legislation. It often takes the form of a statutory instrument and this general term (or SI) is often used interchangeably with 'secondary' or 'delegated' legislation. But it can take other forms such as: orders (which tend to give effect to a ministerial decision); regulations (which make detailed provision as to how an activity should or should not be carried out); rules (which apply to a specific area of activity); schemes and codes of practice and Orders in Council.[29]

---

27 HL Committee, Col 1262, 27 November 1997.
28 The Human Rights Act 1998: ministerial statements, compiled by Katie Ghose and published by Immigration Law Practitioners' Association (ILPA).
29 Orders in Council are made in the name of the Queen rather than a minister.

3.194   Secondary legislation is potentially as important to a client as primary legislation, yet opportunities for scrutiny or debate are severely limited. Parliament is asked to reject or approve the measures and will have nothing approaching the opportunities to shape or amend legislation that exists for primary legislation. For these reasons it is important for lawyers to be familiar with the political processes by which secondary legislation comes into being and to be aware of the limited opportunities for scrutiny that do exist.

3.195   There has been a steady increase in the amount of secondary legislation in recent years. Its original purpose was to allow detailed matters to be set down elsewhere – to avoid Acts of Parliament being unwieldy as well as to save parliamentary time. In addition, it was to allow the law of the land to be changed when necessary without always having to go back to Parliament for a new Act of Parliament to be approved. These reasons hold true, especially given how busy Parliament is, but many believe it has been chronically overused as a convenient tool for governments to leave matters to regulation that should properly be scrutinised under the full glare of the parliamentary spotlight. Members of the House of Lords have objected in particular to this general trend, raising concerns about powers being used inappropriately as well as about the significantly limited opportunities for parliamentary scrutiny of secondary legislation.

Case example: when is primary better than secondary legislation?

Race relations legislation
The government chose to use secondary legislation to incorporate the EU Race Directive requirements (which do not cover colour and nationality) to the existing primary legislation (which cover race, colour, ethnic and national origins). In effect this has led to the application of different rules on the burden of proof. So for example when a person complains about discrimination based on colour the tribunal is not obliged to make an inference that discrimination has taken place from facts on which you could infer that it has. But if the complaint is based on ethnic origins the tribunal has to make an inference on those circumstances.

This is a confusing situation and can lead to a significant difference to the tribunal's handling of a case and the outcome.

3.196 Secondary legislation rarely attracts the publicity that primary legislation does – starting with the beginning of the parliamentary year itself when the Queen announces proposed Bills to parliamentarians and the media but there is no mention of secondary legislation. This is one reason why campaigners often forget about secondary legislation, concentrating all their efforts on influencing Bills, forgetting about the important detail (sometimes large portions of a Bill) that will be contained in regulations. Another reason may be the impenetrable nature of the scrutiny of secondary legislation with its hard to remember rules about 'praying', motions and negative or positive procedures.

Monitoring the progress and influencing the process of secondary legislation

Points to consider:

3.197 • Is the government proposing to legislate for something that you think is too important to be dealt with by secondary as opposed to primary legislation?

   • If this is the case, is there any prospect of bringing about a change of mind? Any influencing needs to be carried out at a very early stage before the government has settled on a particular course.

   • Are there advantages in terms of timing for secondary rather than primary legislation? For example, is there a risk that no time would be made available for primary legislation in the Queen's Speech?

   • Further down the line, although the chances of getting an SI thrown out are remote, it is worth getting parliamentarians to engage with them as their interest will bring it to the minister's attention.

   • The chances of getting secondary legislation rejected are minimal but there is much value in monitoring their progress, content and seeking, where possible, to secure a debate and/or encourage parliamentarians to raise any concerns with the relevant minister.

What stage are the proposals at?

3.198 As with primary legislation, the earlier the influence is brought to bear the better. At a very early stage, the case can be made for an entire new law to take the form of primary rather than secondary legislation. For example, unsuccessful efforts were made to persuade the government that the age discrimination law (to come into force towards the end of 2006) should be primary rather than secondary.

3.199   Much later on in the process whilst a Bill is being examined by Parliament, the case can still be made for proposed delegated powers to be subjected to the positive rather than negative procedure.

3.200   Once at the stage of secondary legislation being presented to Parliament, your interest may be in encouraging the Opposition to secure a debate (this is possible for certain statutory instruments only).

3.201   **The process:** In contrast with draft primary legislation (Bills), most of which will be debated at least three times on the floor of each House in addition to scrutiny by a committee, draft secondary legislation receives at most one debate and often none at all, with many going through 'on the nod'. At this stage, whether or not the legislation is to be subject to the affirmative (or positive) or negative procedure is crucial. If it is the former, both Houses must expressly approve the legislation in order for it to become law (or to stay law), for those SIs which are 'laid' (ie a copy presented to Parliament) after they have been 'made' (signed by the relevant minister). Alternatively, for delegated legislation subject to the negative procedure, the presumption is that it will come into force, unless there is a protest registered against it.

Legislation subject to positive procedure

3.202   **These are 'positive' because Parliament has to expressly say 'Yes' to them before they become law.**

3.203   **The process:** A debate will be scheduled automatically. Sometimes this will take place on the floor of the House (when more than 20 MPs object to the minister's recommendation) but more commonly by a standing committee on delegated legislation which is open to all MPs to attend and speak.

3.204   **Timings:** If on the floor of the House, usually towards the end of the day. If in committee the debate will last a maximum of 1.5 hours (2.5 hours for Northern Ireland matters), although it may be curtailed earlier.

3.205   **Influencing the process:** You can brief MPs but need to bear in mind that only those members appointed by the committee of selection may vote. It would be highly unlikely that regulations would be rejected. However, it is just as important to get the minister's comments on the record as it is when draft primary legislation is being discussed. It is important to get across in your briefing the significance of the regulations and any points of clarification needed.

3.206   The Lords also have to give their approval and most will go though 'on the nod'. Typically they are dealt with on the floor of the House and on a different date from the Commons. As SIs cannot be amended there is no need for them to pass from House to House as with primary legislation.

Legislation subject to negative procedure

3.207 **These are called 'negative' because they will become law without any debate or vote unless action is taken to oppose them.**

3.208 **The process:** The legislation is laid before the House – either in draft or when already 'made' (ie in final form and signed by the relevant minister). There is then 40 days in which they can be opposed ('prayed against'). The motion has to be tabled by a frontbench spokesperson of one of the main opposition parties in order to have any real chance of being granted. The conventional form to register opposition is through an Early Day Motion (EDM) (for more information about EDMs see chapter 4).

3.209 **Timings:** For the purpose of counting the 40 days, include the day on which the instrument was laid but leave out periods when both Houses are adjourned for more than 4 days or when Parliament is dissolved or prorogued (the period immediately before the Queen's Speech).

3.210 **Influencing the process:** If you have taken an interest in a piece of delegated legislation that is to be subject to the negative procedure, you will need to check that a debate is to be requested. Often opposition spokespersons will be planning to do this anyway but not always so it is worth checking – and requesting them to do so. If there is no Opposition interest, it may still be worth encouraging a backbencher to table a motion opposing the regulations. Although backbenchers' requests are less likely to be listened to than the Opposition frontbencher, if they manage to collect a sufficient number of signatures to the EDM it is possible that their request might be granted.

3.211 In the Lords, there is the same opportunity for any member to pray against the regulations. A peer can secure this by requesting a 'no day named debate'; the whips will then need to allocate time for it, often during the dinner hour. If a debate is secured, the same considerations about briefing MPs and peers would apply as for positive regulations.

3.212 You could also add your voice to those calling for reform of these procedures to strengthen scrutiny of this type of draft law. Various recommendations have been made by the Commons Procedure Committee including: for substantial and complex SIs to be given pre-legislative scrutiny and for decisions on SIs not to be taken until the Joint Committee on Statutory Instruments has completed it consideration.

These have yet to be accepted and implemented.

3.213   **The Joint Committee on Statutory Instruments:** This Committee looks at all statutory instruments. Its focus is technical and includes: whether the authority conferred by the parent Act is within its proper boundaries or has been exceeded; any lack of clarity in the drafting and any other technicalities. It does not examine the merits of the legislation. For example, when it examined the regulations to outlaw discrimination in the workplace on the grounds of sexual orientation it published a report a few days before the Lords were due to debate the new law. It questioned whether the section of the law that proposed to permit discrimination where the employment was for the purposes of organised religion could be compatible with the EU Directive it was implementing.[30]

3.214   A report is issued but the committee has no power to stop a defective piece of legislation progressing; it can only make recommendations. The MPs from the committee form a separate group: the Select Committee on Statutory Instruments when secondary legislation on financial matters has to be examined.

3.215   **There are two other types of delegated legislation worth looking at: remedial orders and regulatory reform orders.**

The Human Rights Act 1998 and remedial orders

3.216   Human rights lawyers will be interested in the process by which legislation found to be incompatible with the Human Rights Act is rectified. Remedial orders are a brand new (but rare) type of secondary legislation introduced by the HRA 1998. Essentially they provide for fairly swift rectification rather than Parliament having to find time for the lengthier process of new primary legislation to effect the change.

3.217   The Joint Committee on Human Rights has the important role of examining both the proposals and then the draft order. After this period of consultation, the order goes through the same process as any other secondary legislation subject to the 'positive' procedure (see para 3.202 above).

3.218   Or the minister has the power to speed the process up, by laying an order that changes the law immediately – subject to both Houses approving it within 120 days. If there are objections, representations can be made to the minister within the first 60 days, allowing the minister time to lay an amended order to secure Parliament's approval within 120 days.

30   The Joint Committee's 21st report of the Session 2002–03, HC 96-xxi.

Regulatory reform orders

3.219　These are a new innovation and basically about getting rid of 'red tape' or over-burdensome rules and regulations. They allow ministers to amend or get rid of primary legislation that imposes 'burdens affecting persons in the carrying on of any activity'. The process is similar to that for remedial orders in relation to the Human Rights Act 1998. There is an extensive consultation period and both Commons and Lords committees scrutinise the proposals and subsequently the draft orders.[31]

3.220　In the 2005 Queen's Speech was a Regulatory Reform Bill which included plans to enable a greater number of reforms to be made by Regulatory Reform Order and to enable the implementation of uncontroversial law reforms by means of a new 'law reform order'.

Case study: ousting the 'ouster clause' – partnership work on the Asylum and Immigration (Treatment of Claimants etc) Act 2004

Illustrates: the effectiveness of lawyers and organisations working together to amend draft legislation.

Summary: Immigration and asylum Bills have been notoriously difficult to influence in recent years. With a hefty government majority backed up by Conservative support for tough measures, lawyers and others have tried and failed to moderate the scope and effect of new proposals. However, against the odds, lawyers, together with other campaigners, did secure a change to the Asylum and Immigration (Treatment of Claimants etc) Act 2004 which helped to weaken one of its worst elements.

Background: There was scarce warning of the proposals dramatically to curtail appeal rights in immigration and asylum cases, removing any role for courts above the High Court to scrutinise decisions. A short government consultation was issued in October 2003 but this did not contain full details of what was proposed. The Bill's introduction and first reading were on 27 November 2003.

31　In the Commons the Regulatory Reform Committee; in the Lords the Delegated Powers and Regulatory Reform Committee.

Partnership working: The Immigration Law Practitioners' Association (ILPA) co-ordinated the work of many lawyers and organisations on the Bill, as they have done for the other five Immigration and Asylum Acts in the last 10 years. Alongside them were many other lawyers, groups and networks who were vocal in their opposition to the proposals. The Refugee Legal Centre (RLC) was particularly active.

The issues: A number of the Bill's elements horrified immigration and asylum law practitioners and others. However the issue which attracted interest from a wider group – and which ultimately led to the Bill being changed – was the 'ouster clause' described by ILPA as a 'charter for lazy and unaccountable decision making'. The seriousness of the constitutional aspect brought together an unlikely alliance of lawyers and organisations who would not normally be obvious partners seeking to amend an immigration Bill.

The 'ouster clause': Clause 10 sought to get rid of any judicial scrutiny of the decisions of the newly proposed single tier Asylum and Immigration Tribunal. All decisions of the new tribunal would be protected from judicial review or appeal to a higher court. Instead there was to be a highly restrictive internal review and a discretion for the President of the Tribunal alone to refer the case to the Court of Appeal for an advisory opinion.

Arguments: The drastic nature of these changes and their implications for removing judicial scrutiny in other areas of law attracted opposition from a wide range of lawyers, including those who often acted for the Home Office in cases. They argued that in excluding a role for the higher courts, the proposals threatened the rule of law itself. The Chairman of the Bar Council at the time Matthias Kelly QC commented: 'The Bill snuffs out the concept of a right of appeal ... It has no place in any decent society'. Barristers from Matrix chambers called the proposals 'the most draconian ouster clause ever seen in Parliamentary legislative practice'.

Strategy: The overall plan and focus was to seek to amend the Bill, hopefully getting rid of the ouster clause but otherwise considerably weakening it.

Activities: Different activities and tactics were deployed. ILPA brought together lawyers for an initial meeting to 'dissect' the Bill and identify the key issues, as soon as it was published. They then organised a joint meeting with the British Institute for Human Rights (BIHR) which was well attended and which brought together a wide range of supporters and galvanised people to act.

Key tactics: The RLC commissioned an advice from Michael Fordham, a specialist in public law. This raised the gravity of the constitutional issues and the prospect of the courts considering the removal of the right to apply for judicial review to be unconstitutional. This could mean the new law itself being challenged if it were not amended. The legal opinion added considerable weight to the campaign.

Parliamentary work: Much of the parliamentary lobbying was carried out behind the scenes and on a cross-party basis. ILPA and others sought to engage with MPs from the three major parties, drafting amendments and preparing detailed briefings for the various parliamentary stages. Some Conservative MPs (including committee members) were sympathetic to the constitutional issues but reluctant to publicly be seen opposing an immigration Bill. Liberal Democrats were receptive and especially appreciative of lawyers' input as there were no lawyers from their party on the committee. Neil Gerrard was the only Labour committee member to be publicly sympathetic to concerns being raised and had spoken against clause 10 and other aspects of the Bill during second reading.

During the passage of the Bill, the Joint Committee on Human Rights conducted a short inquiry to which ILPA and others submitted evidence.[32] The Commons Constitutional Affairs Committee also examined the issue as part of an inquiry into asylum and immigration appeals, taking evidence from senior lawyers and putting their views to Constitutional Affairs minister David Lammy MP. He was asked:

32   Fifth Report HL35/HC304, 10 February 2004.

'How would you address the criticism, which has been supported by several senior members of counsel, that clause 10 of the Bill contains what has been described as the "most draconian ouster clause ever seen in parliamentary legislative practice"?'

The committee's report stated that the ouster clause 'provoked some of the most strongly worded evidence' received in the course of its inquiry and expressed deep concern about the proposals.[33]

It proved impossible to amend the Bill in the Commons but the key issues were debated. This helped build pressure for change and assisted peers who then opposed the proposals at later stages.

Media work: The campaign attracted some media coverage, principally in the broadsheets (including a *Guardian* leader). This helped to build up a 'head of steam', encouraging peers to take a stand when the Bill reached the House of Lords.

Turning points: The turning point in the campaign is said to have been forceful criticism of the proposals by loyal peer and former Lord Chancellor Lord Irvine of Lairg, as well as by the Lord Chief Justice Lord Woolf. Fearing the force of opposition (Lord Irvine was early to request a speaking slot in the second reading debate) and that it could lose important votes, it caved in. Lord Falconer kicked off the second reading debate by announcing that he would bring forward amendments to replace the ouster clause with a different system. He brought back the Bill in amended form in time for committee stage. The Bill's remaining stages were much quieter and it received royal assent on 22 July 2004.

Outcome: The government's amendments were welcomed by campaigners. ILPA welcomed the removal of the 'ouster clause' and related concessions including the restoration of the right of further appeal to the Court of Appeal and by implication to the House of Lords. However, they also highlighted the many

33 Asylum and Immigration Appeals, Second Report, 2 March 2004, HC 211-I and HC211-II.

remaining defects in the Bill and the lack of action to deal with poor quality decision making.

What appears to have secured the win is the government's fear that they would not secure a majority in the House of Lords and that their persistence might have put the entire Bill in jeopardy. There is no evidence that having heard the arguments they reconsidered the merit of the proposals themselves.

Principles of success

This case illustrates some key principles that should underpin any campaign:

- Unlikely alliances (in this case lawyers acting for 'both sides') can be powerful.
- The importance of tapping into other people's agendas (eg here, lawyers concerned with appeal rights outside immigration and asylum) and use them to your advantage.
- Who will influence the people you are targeting? Here, the government was clearly influenced by Lords Woolf and Irvine (another former Lord Chancellor Lord Mackay was also critical).
- You have to act quickly – there were only a few months to have an impact and some Bills get through both Houses in a matter of weeks.
- It helped the campaign that the Bill started in the Commons, allowing arguments to be marshalled and pressure to begin to build up. What would have happened had the Bill started in the Lords? Would campaigners have been ready?
- Information and research is an essential starting point for any campaign: here the legal opinion was crucial in persuading people of the importance of the issue and providing key facts and arguments for briefings.
- Detailed briefings were prepared by campaigners for all stages. However, some concede that they might have had even more impact if they had been shorter and in plainer, less legal English!

Case study: corporate influence over the content of the Financial Services and Markets Act 2000

Illustrates: The significant difference that can be made to legislation, even when it has begun its passage through Parliament.

Summary: Due to the efforts of those working inside and outside Parliament, the Financial Services and Market Act 2000 was the most heavily amended piece of legislation in the 1999–2000 session. It demonstrates the effect of 'strategic agitation' with corporate lawyers and their clients playing a leading role in influencing the legislative process. It is an interesting example of the engagement with the Human Rights Act 1998 by companies. And it shows how the publication of a Bill in draft form can give real opportunities for amendment.

Background: A week after its election, in May 1997 the Labour government announced that it would introduce comprehensive new legislation to achieve institutional reform of the system for regulating financial services. It followed this up with a draft law, published in mid-1998 which it then consulted on.

Partnership working: Law firms (among them City giant Clifford Chance), banks and peers (in particular the Liberal Democrat Lord Lester) and others worked together to challenge a perceived absence of due process in the Financial Services and Markets Bill 1999. They identified human rights issues, arguing that Article 6 of the European Convention on Human Rights, as incorporated in the Human Rights Act 1998, demanded provision for fair and transparent disciplinary processes where banks were to be sanctioned for misconduct.

Parliamentary work: Criticisms by lawyers and others (eg on the proposed offence of 'market abuse' and a role for the new sole regulator: the Financial Services Authority as 'prosecutor, judge and jury') led the government to set up a Joint Committee to scrutinise the Bill.[34] This took evidence from a range of witnesses including financial service providers and their representative

---

34   T Plews, 'UK Financial Services Act and Markets Bill revisited', *Futures Industry Magazine*, June/July 1999.

bodies, law firms and consumer groups. Responding to a number of the committee's findings, the government then introduced a redrafted Bill in June 1999.

On a smaller scale, the All-Party group on insurance and financial services also received representations from interested groups and its chair John Greenway MP contributed to the Commons debates.

However, concerns remained and lawyers worked hard, with parliamentarians and others, at all stages of the Bill's passage. Debates were characterised by detailed discussion of amendments (some introduced by the government in response to concerns already raised, others by backbenchers keen to probe the government's intentions or to challenge them on key clauses). Meetings took place 'behind-the-scenes' in-between debates, with parliamentarians and others seeking to secure agreement on key issues.

Outcomes: Overall around 1,000 amendments were tabled and a number of these were accepted by the government. In particular those lobbying on the Bill succeeded in persuading the government to take proper account of the Human Rights Act 1998. The new disciplinary system was seen as a significant improvement on the original proposals, although still lacking in some respects. The Bill finally gained royal assent on 14 June 2000.

Further information:

General

3.221   • To check an MP's voting record go to www.theyworkforyou.com.

Primary legislation (Bills)

3.222   • The Weekly Information Bulletin has full details of progress of each Bill, including Private Members' Bills: www.publications.parliament.uk/pa/cm/cmwib.htm.
  • The UK Parliament website has a section on Bills: www.parliament.uk/bills/bills.cfm.
  • For information about public Bills contact the Public Bill Office on 020 7219 3251/8.

- For a thorough guide to how to set out amendments to Bills when they are in the Lords go to: www.publications.parliament.uk/ pa/ld/ldamend.pdf.
- From 1988 the text of all Public General Acts is at www.opsi.gov.uk/acts.htm.

Secondary legislation

3.223
- You can check for progress of delegated legislation by going to the www.parliament.uk website and checking the Statutory Instrument List. They are also included in the daily 'Votes and Proceedings' and the Journal Office issues a list (with the number of 'praying days' left) each week.
- See the Weekly Information Bulletin for details of debates on SIs coming up the following week.
- Full texts of SIs since 1987 are at: www.opsi.gov.uk/stat.htm.

All about Parliament: the tools and techniques

continued

- Who's who in the UK Parliament?
- What happens when? Highlights of the parliamentary year
- Key campaigns tools: questions, debates and Early Day Motions
- Tips for using parliamentary procedures to win changes

Introduction

4.1 Parliamentarians are key targets for lawyers keen to reform existing laws or to see new ones introduced. The occasions on which they can completely override the executive may be few and far between, but they have a vital role in monitoring and scrutinising draft laws and proposals. They are also key 'agitators', able to bring issues to the attention of other parliamentary colleagues and ministers and through this help those outside Parliament with their campaigns.

What is this chapter about?

4.2 Parliament has its own annual cycle, working hours and a whole host of parliamentary procedures that can seem baffling to outsiders – and indeed to new members. Lawyers do not need to become experts in parliamentary procedure – this is the task of MPs and peers, who take to it with varying degrees of aptitude. As one MP told me 'what's written down isn't what happens anyway'. But campaigning lawyers do need to know how to engage with parliamentarians – how to capture their interest in issues – and they need to know enough about Parliament to be able to use this interest to maximum effect. This chapter is therefore about how to engage and build relationships with MPs and peers; how Parliament goes about its daily business; and how to use a 'toolkit' of techniques to secure change.

MPs and peers

MPs and their masters: constituency, party and country

4.3 As with anyone you seek to influence, you need to get to know MPs and to understand them. Most were people with ordinary jobs and lifestyles before they entered Parliament. Some may have been attracted by the prestige of public life but most will be genuinely keen to make a contribution. Many will at times experience a conflict between their own principles and beliefs and the direction in which their party is headed. Some will thrive on the rough and tumble of an adversarial political system whilst others will dislike the intensely partisan and confrontational nature of British parliamentary politics.

What do MPs do?

4.4   First and foremost – and as many won't hesitate to tell you – they are extremely busy. Dividing their time between their constituency and Parliament, and often feeling bogged down with a hefty case-load, they do not have much time to digest lengthy documents, have long meetings or draft amendments at short notice. Some say they have three masters: their constituency, their party and their country. A typical week for a backbencher will include some or all of the following: visits from a local business; showing a group of school children around Parliament; attending or speaking at one or more committee meetings; a hurried visit to the Table Office to seek advice on a question or parliamentary motion; media interviews; chairing or attending an All Party Group and/or backbench committee; attending a charity reception or meeting with a lobby group – and dealing with correspondence (including constituency casework) and telephone calls. This does not include time spent in the chamber, trying to speak or listen to debates or just hanging around waiting to vote. Meetings are frequently disrupted by votes – indeed if you go to meet with an MP you may occasionally find yourself alongside them whilst they run to the lobbies.

What are their interests?

4.5   Most MPs do not enter Parliament with a fixed list of issues in which they will take an exclusive interest for the rest of the time that they serve. Some will have existing interests or specialist knowledge in certain areas, but most will also be open to taking up causes that come to their attention, whether from national organisations or local or individual constituents. The power of one individual's story can help start a major campaign. Dr Lynne Jones, MP for Birmingham Selly Oak, took up the cause of trans people after being visited by a transsexual constituent. Prior to that she had not been aware of the problems faced by trans people or the legal reforms they urgently wanted to see. She went on to campaign for greater rights forming the all party Parliamentary Forum on Transsexualism. Conservative MP Roger Sims pledged similar support, again because of a visit from a trans person who had explained his problems to him – and Liberal Democrat lawyer Alex Carlile MP used his place in the 1995 Private Members' Bill ballot to take up the cause, to demonstrate his long-term commitment to the issue. He proved to be an excellent advocate for a very legal issue.

Policy and practice: getting word 'from the coalface'

4.6   MPs spend a lot of time helping individual constituents or particular groups in their constituency or region. Often these experiences highlight the need for action at a wider level. They help to show the implications and potential impact of a policy for hundreds, thousands or even millions of people in their everyday lives. However, an MP's constituency only gives them a sense of the issues affecting people in one part of the country. Getting word from those 'at the coalface' is therefore very important to MPs. As a lawyer with current expertise and knowledge of what is happening 'on the ground' – in housing, immigration or family for example, you will have valuable information to share with MPs. The lawyers in Parliament may be particularly appreciative of expertise from current practising lawyers.[1]

4.7   For senior lawyers turned politician, whose work in appeal courts has been continually to narrow down the issues, turning a human experience into a refined point of law which will be argued over in detail, the world of parliamentary politics can be a shock to the system. To succeed in the Commons the opposite needs to be done. A policy or plea for a new law or action must be given a human face – in order both to convince other politicians in the chamber or a committee room of the need for action but also to gain favour and understanding among the public.

MPs' value in campaigning

4.8   A core part of parliamentarians' value to outsiders is their access to ministers. MPs feed in their views in a variety of ways, formally and informally. Senior ministers' Parliamentary Private Secretaries are their 'eyes and ears' in the Commons. The whips and the Political Unit at Number Ten are other channels for ministers to hear about MPs' views. Ministers and sometimes the Prime Minister also keep in touch via backbench committees or groups (eg the weekly meeting of the Parliamentary Labour Party). And the archaic voting system that locks all MPs together

---

1   Neither the Commons or Lords information offices hold up-to-date figures of the number of MPs or peers who are lawyers. However, according to a publication by David Butler of Nuffield University there were 36 barristers in the Commons in the 1997–2001 Parliament.

whilst votes are counted gives invaluable opportunities to backbenchers to nab a minister for a quick word about an issue that is troubling them.

Engaging with MPs

4.9   • You need to identify parliamentarians with an interest or potential interest in your issue. It is better to develop good relations with a small number of MPs from each of the major parties than an acquaintanceship with a much larger number. As you build good relationships with a handful of MPs they will often be happy to give you informal advice on how best to progress a campaign or raise an issue.

• If you are in contact with an MP or peer they will want to know what you would like them to do, eg write a letter, table a question or call for an inquiry.

• You need to consider MPs' motivations in using the various parliamentary tools and techniques. They have to keep up their profile in their constituencies and putting down an Early Day Motion or securing an adjournment debate more-or-less guarantees coverage in their local press.

• When lobbying backbench MPs or peers affiliated to a political party, you also need to bear in mind where their party is at in the overall cycle of policy making between elections. For example, in the few months leading up to a General Election parties will be finalising the details of major policies.

Peers in Parliament: free agents?

4.10   Although the House of Lords operates like the Commons in some respects, in others it is quite different. Overall it is much less partisan and as a result debates are usually calmer and more considered. Membership comprises a mixture of life peers, hereditary peers and Bishops – around 700 in all. Numbers fluctuate, but there are generally around 700 peers[2] Following the 2005 General Election Tony Blair appointed a raft of new peers and for the first time since the party was founded almost a century before, Labour became the joint largest party with the Conservatives in the upper House. However, this did not alter the ability of the two main opposition parties (the Conservatives and Liberal Democrats) to outnumber Labour.

2 On 1 July 2005 there were 606 life peers, 92 hereditary peers and 25 Bishops.

4.11   In addition to the traditional patronage route which rewards service to a political party, the Appointments Commission is also responsible for appointing new peers. Heralded as the 'people's peers' in fact they are often experts in their field and/or already have a public profile. Many become active cross-benchers. Pressure from former MPs in particular has led the Lords to become more professionalised, improving its facilities and allowances for members, who if they attend every sitting day, receive around £15,000–20,000 a year, in addition to travel and accommodation expenses if they live outside London. However this is not enough to employ researchers as MPs do, and peers therefore rely heavily on outsiders for briefing and support.

4.12   As in the Commons, much important negotiation takes place behind the scenes. Peers will have discreet chats with Lords ministers, eg in peers' lobby.

Engaging with peers

4.13   Peers' participation in Lords' business varies tremendously. Around 350 peers (half the membership) attend regularly or fairly regularly and of these perhaps around half will play an active role. You therefore need to identify carefully who your key targets are.

- For lobbyists, there is the great advantage in the Lords of around 180 cross-benchers – independent peers who have deliberately chosen not to align themselves with one of the parties. On many issues they will co-operate with members of other parties.
- Remember that it can sometimes be easier for a peer to raise an issue than an MP. For example, all amendments tabled at committee stage in the Lords are discussed (in the Commons only some are selected) and a peer can introduce a Private Members' Bill at any time (there is no ballot). In addition peers have no pressures from a constituency to satisfy. However, there may be less publicity to be gained from activity in the Lords.
- The House of Lords has been partially reformed (with a reduction in the number of hereditary peers) and further reforms are likely, although there is no consensus in Parliament about what these should be. Abolition of the remaining hereditary peers seems likely, however, although this could be done gradually as peers die. No Bills to introduce reforms were included in the 2005 Queen's Speech; instead the government pledged first to set up another joint committee, with many predicting that again it would be unlikely to reach consensus.

Parliamentary business

4.14   In both Houses parliamentary time is divided into government-led business and discussion and time that can be used for backbenchers or the Opposition to raise issues. Both give ample opportunities to non-parliamentarians to ensure their issues are raised and the government of the day challenged. If you look through the verbatim record of debates in Hansard on any given day, you will see lots of examples of how individuals and organisations outside Parliament use these opportunities to air their concerns and influence government and the political parties. Familiarising yourself with the basic procedures is the best way to identify reactive and proactive opportunities to find out information, highlight issues of importance in your field and make a case for change.

4.15   The table below shows the different types of parliamentary business in the House of Commons.

Business in the House of Commons

Type of business	Description and examples
Addresses	The Queen's Speech
Government Bills	All stages and debates of Bills
Private Members' Bills	All stages and debates of Private Members' (ie backbench MPs) Bills
Secondary legislation	Presentation (and in some cases debate of the legislation)
Private Business	Private Bills
Government motions	Budget debates or to seek approval of procedural changes
Opposition motions	Day-long debate on topic chosen by Opposition party or a 'no confidence' motion
Adjournment debates	Debate requested by backbencher
Estimates	Debate on a select committee report related to the government's request for resources to run the state
Money Resolutions	Motion to authorise government expenditure
Ways and means Resolutions	Motion to authorise the raising of a tax or a charge (eg the Budget debates)
General category	Includes: Questions, statements, business statements, applications for emergency debates, presentation of public petitions

4.16 The House of Lords dubs itself 'one of the busiest parliamentary chambers in the world'. Business is divided up as follows: law making; holding the government to account; committees and judicial activity. It spends roughly 60 per cent of its time on legislation and 40 per cent on scrutiny (of this 20 per cent on debates; 15 per cent on questions and 5 per cent on statements).[3] As in the Commons there is a combination of business – Bills or motions for which the government must have Parliament's approval, and time spent on topics for discussion rather than decision.

A year in Parliament: what happens when?

4.17 **Summary:** Election years apart, the parliamentary year (a 'session') starts in late November or early December with the State Opening of Parliament and ends the following year just a few days before the next State Opening. A 'Parliament' is the full term that Parliament sits between General Elections.

4.18 **Key milestones:** The year kicks off with the State Opening and Queen's Speech which sets out the government's legislative plans for the year. Shortly afterwards, on the second Thursday of the session, is the ballot for MPs seeking to pilot their own 'Private Members' Bill' through Parliament. The Chancellor's Pre-Budget Report follows shortly afterwards, in November or early December. It is partly consultative and trails key announcements and plans for income and expenditure which are detailed in the Budget which follows in March or April. Legislation is needed to enact many of the measures included in the Budget and so the Finance Bill starts its passage shortly afterwards. It is also followed by a social security upratings statement which announces the new rates of pensions and benefits, etc.

4.19 From November/December onwards, each Bill in the Queen's Speech starts its passage – most in the Commons but some in the Lords – as well as some additional government Bills not included in the initial programme. From December onwards, a number of other Bills (ie Private Bills and Private Members' Bills) will also start their passage. A few public Bills in draft form will go through 'pre-legislative scrutiny', a device introduced to allow consideration of legislative proposals before they start their formal passage through Parliament. See chapter 3 for more details about this process. Secondary legislation

3 'The work of the House of Lords', March 2003.

will also be presented, and on occasion debated, at various points during the session.

4.20   Every year, in July the Chancellor announces the results of the spending review – how much cash each department will have to spend over the next 3 years (starting the following April). For more information about spending reviews see chapter 2. Summer recess typically kicks off in late July. Both Houses return for 2 weeks in early September until the party conference season commences, in the third week of September. With the tour of seaside resorts over, Parliament returns in mid-October for the final weeks of the parliamentary year which comes to an end with 'prorogation' – a period of a few days during which parliamentary business is suspended. The new session is then marked by the State Opening and Queen's Speech.

4.21   Prorogation is less significant than it used to be, as governments can now carry over Bills into a new session without having to start all their stages afresh. However, all other business starts from scratch; unanswered questions need to be re-tabled and any motions (eg Early Day Motions) cease to have any status.

4.22   The main recesses or holidays take place at Christmas (from around 19 December to 7 January), and summer. There is also a Whitsun recess which coincides with the late May Bank Holiday and lasts for 2 weeks in late May/early June. Parliament also rises for shorter breaks to coincide with school half term holidays. Breaks aside, Parliament sits continuously until summer recess.

4.23   Election years can mean a longer than normal parliamentary year. In 2005, for example, Parliament ended on 11 April, just a few days after Prime Minister Tony Blair sought the Queen's permission to dissolve Parliament, for a 5 May election. It resumed after the election on 11 May for MPs to be sworn in and the State Opening and Queen's Speech took place on 17 May, ready for a long session right the way through to November 2006 (with no prorogation or Queen's Speech in the autumn as in non-election years).

Tips:

4.24   • It is now common practice for key dates in the parliamentary calendar (including recess dates) to be announced well in advance, making it easier to plan events and lobbying activities.

   • To get a feel for the business the Commons covers in an entire parliamentary session (and for some information about the Lords) have a look at the 'Sessional Information Digest' produced by the

House of Commons Library in January each year. This gives a comprehensive summary of the passage of Bills; information about committees' work and reports for the year and a list of consultations issued by the government. It is available from the Stationery Office or go to www.publications.parliament.uk/pa/cm/cmsid.htm for digests from previous years.

A week in Parliament: what happens when?

House of Commons

4.25   **Summary:** The parliamentary week was shortened as part of the reforms aimed at modernising Parliament. Since then MPs have returned from their constituencies on Monday afternoons. Most Fridays are now 'constituency Fridays' when Parliament does not sit, allowing MPs to return to their constituencies late on Thursdays. Parliament does sit on a few Fridays spread throughout the year.

4.26   **Key points:** The truncated week has shortened the amount of time campaigners have during a week to make contact with parliamentarians. The shorter sitting hours have meant that Parliament empties out after 7.30 pm, making evening meetings and receptions less common. Overall, there are fewer opportunities to make contact at Westminster but arguably more opportunity to have access to MPs when they are in their constituencies. MPs themselves disagree about the changes and late night sittings on Tuesdays until 10.30 pm were temporarily reintroduced in 2005.

4.27   **Tips:** Every Thursday, the business for the following week is announced (in the 'Business Statement') by the Leader of the House at 12.30 pm or a little later if there are important ministerial announcements to be made first. The Weekly Information Bulletin is the most comprehensive source of information about what is happening over the next week in Parliament and is published on the Internet as well as in hard copy.

House of Lords

4.28   **Summary:** The House of Lords sits from Mondays–Thursdays and some Fridays towards the end of a session. Thursdays are now handed over exclusively for general debates (including backbench debates) rather than government business.

4.29   **Key points:** The House of Lords has more traditional hours than the Commons, although in keeping with its civilised approach to business, late night sittings are often interrupted by an hour-long dinner break!

4.30   **Tips:** In addition to the Weekly Information Bulletin which includes some upcoming business in the Lords, you can also check for future business at www.parliament.uk./about_lords/minutes_and_order_paper.cfm.

A day in Parliament: what happens when?

> **'Order, order'**
>
> The Speaker has a high-profile and important role both in controlling proceedings and also in the general running of the House of Commons. Aside from the fixed opportunities (eg for a minister introducing a Bill and the opposition spokesperson to respond) they have absolute control over who speaks in debates, taking into account a range of factors, including the need for party balance. Other crucial powers include selection of amendments to be debated and voted on and the power to limit the length of backbenchers' speeches and decide when to call a halt to a debate for a vote to be taken.
>
> In the House of Lords the role of presiding officer is fulfilled by the Lord Chancellor but they have none of the Speaker's powers – order is reliant on members regulating their own conduct.

House of Commons

4.31   **Summary:** On Mondays and Tuesdays business on the floor of the House starts at 2.30 pm and ends at around 10.30 pm. On Wednesdays business starts at 11.30 am and usually goes on until 7.30 pm. On Thursdays business starts at 10.30 am and goes on until 6.30 pm. On the few sitting Fridays business starts at 9.30 am and ends by 3 pm.

4.32   Business away from the floor of the House takes place outside these hours, with standing committees typically sitting on Tuesday–Thursday mornings between 8.55 am and 11.25 am and then again from 2.30 pm. Select committee meetings take place at various times – often at 9.30 am or at 2.30 pm. Westminster Hall sits on

Tuesdays and Wednesdays from 9.30 am to 11.30 am and from 2.00 pm until 4.30 pm and on Thursdays from 2.30 pm to 5.30 pm.

4.33   **The daily business:** From Monday to Thursday parliamentary business follows a similar order (although starting and finishing later on Mondays and Tuesdays). The sitting starts with prayers (read by the Speaker's chaplain) for which members must stand and turn to the wall. This is used by many as an opportunity to reserve a seat for the rest of the day. These are followed by a few minutes of Private Business (eg a Private Bill) and then question time (which lasts an hour or longer if an urgent question has been granted). On Wednesdays Prime Minister's Questions take place from 12.00 pm for half an hour. Ministerial statements come next (eg announcing a new policy initiative or outcome of an official inquiry) followed by an opportunity for the minister to be questioned. There are then slots for the following: introduction of new MPs; requests for urgent debates (if granted, which is rare, these usually take place the next day); personal statements (eg resignations); points of order (in theory about parliamentary procedure but in practice often used to make a political point).

4.34   'Public business' now commences, first with the 'preliminary business' and then the 'main business' which will take most of the time. Preliminary business comprises the presentation and first readings of government Bills; government motions related to procedure (eg to allow a Bill to go through all its stages in one sitting); motions to allocate tasks to standing committees and finally, on Tuesdays and Wednesdays, the more stimulating business of a backbencher presenting their idea for new legislation in the form of a Ten Minute Rule Bill.

4.35   The main business of the day includes government and Opposition business such as the stages of government Bills and notices of motions that allow for substantial debates. At 10.00 pm on Mondays and Tuesdays; 7 pm on Wednesdays; 6.00 pm on Thursday; and 2.30 pm on Fridays, the main business ceases and any major votes are taken (this is called the 'moment of interruption'). After this, public petitions can be presented. The last business of the day is then the opportunity for a backbencher to lead a half hour 'adjournment debate' on a topic of their choice.

4.36   On Thursdays the Business Statement takes place immediately after question time (or after any ministerial statements). On Fridays business is dominated by the passage of Private Members' Bills.

House of Commons

7 April 2005

Prayers

Private business

Oral questions to the Secretary of State for Trade and Industry

Oral questions to the Secretary of State for Women

Bills

Serious Organised Crime and Police Bill: Consideration of Lords amendments

Education Bill: Report stage and third reading

Crossrail Bill (Motion)

Statutory Instrument (motion for approval without debate)

International Organisations Bill: second reading and remaining stages

Adjournment debate (Anthony Wright MP) on proposals for the A47 between Great Yarmouth and Acle

House of Lords

4.37   **Summary:** The Lords sit from 2.30 pm on Mondays–Wednesdays, usually finishing by 10 pm. On Thursdays they sit from 11.00 am, finishing by 7 pm and on sitting Fridays from 11.00 am until mid-afternoon. The Lords is experimenting with conducting government business from Monday to Wednesdays with backbench debates on Thursdays, bringing its hours more in line with the Commons and making it easier for members to carry on with work outside Parliament. Committee meetings and other business away from the floor of the House takes place outside these times.

4.38   An important difference from the Commons is the publication of speakers' lists in advance of debates (on the government whips' website). These are a good tool for lobbyists as they are published in advance (members can continue to add their names up to the day of the debate) enabling you to target your briefings. Members not on the list may get the chance to speak, but only after everyone on the list has spoken (and if they have been brief).

4.39   **The daily business:** The Lords follow a similar order to the Commons with prayers followed by the introduction of any new peers. Starred (oral) questions follow and then any business statements (eg about procedures for that day's debates). Ministerial statements are delivered next – these are usually a repetition of a statement already made that day in the Commons. Up to 40 minutes for questions and clarification open to all peers is allowed following a statement. The main business then begins – with private legislation followed by any procedural matters. Public Bills, secondary legislation and select committee reports are next – with the legislation, as in the Commons, often forming the main part of the day's business. The final business is unstarred questions – ie debates. A dinner break is common from 7.30–8.30 pm, often to give those debating Bills an hour off. During this time the House will continue sitting, often dealing with secondary legislation.

4.40   Wednesday 16 March 2005 gives a good flavour of a fairly typical day in the Lords. There were three oral questions: on the implementation of the proposed duty on schools to promote equality of opportunity for disabled children; on accommodation and support for young people who, on release from custody, are unable to return to their families; and on any steps being taken to protect the independence and impartiality of the broadcasting media in the run-up to a future general election. These were followed by debates on the Consolidated Fund (Appropriation) Bill) whilst the Charities Bill was dealt with in grand committee. After this were two topical debates, one on the Tomlinson Report,[4] and the case for a diversity of routes into post-19 education (introduced by Baroness Sharp of Guildford) and another on the economic, political and security developments in Iraq since the intervention in 2003 by United Kingdom armed forces (Lord Garden). Finally, secondary legislation was dealt with including a Regulatory Reform (Trading Stamps) Order 2005.

---

4   The Final Report of the Working Group on 14-19 Reform, an inquiry chaired by Mike Tomlinson.

How does the Commons work?

4.41   The Commons has a large staff carrying out a variety of functions. The Clerk's Department (managed by the most senior official, the Clerk of the House) has a number of offices. These comprise the Table Office (handles parliamentary questions and Early Day Motions); the Public Bill Office, the Private Bill Office and the Delegated Legislation Office; the Committee Office and the Overseas Office. In addition, a Legal Services Office advises the Clerk (and indeed the House itself) on certain legal issues, eg freedom of information. A Journal Office compiles the daily permanent record of proceedings and the Vote Office supplies official documents to MPs.

4.42   MPs rely heavily on the Commons offices to help them carry out their roles. Some (eg the Table Office) are very strict about dealing with members only; others are less so and more willing to speak to staff or people working outside Parliament.

4.43   The Committee Office is the largest office, with around 300 staff. It now includes the Scrutiny Unit, an important innovation introduced into the Committee Office at the end of 2002. It helps select committees in their work, in particular to achieve more effective scrutiny of departmental estimates of spending – a role that Parliament has traditionally been weak on as well as to scrutinise draft legislation. Committee Clerks bid for the Unit's time.

4.44   Editors of the Official Report (Hansard) are responsible for a verbatim account of everything that is said on the floor of the House, in standing committees and in Westminster Hall (and of the answers to written questions). Parliamentarians can make minor corrections but may not alter the substance before it is printed.

Whips and whipping: party discipline in the Commons

Whips are a key part of Parliament and can be as fierce as they sound! They are the enforcers of party discipline and can be ruthless when faced with a member who threatens to step out of line. They issue the weekly paper 'Whip' which instructs MPs as to when they are required to attend for votes, etc. They also have a communications role, making sure that MPs' views are fed into the parties' leadership and vice versa. They have an important organisational role, ensuring that business is arranged and completed, meeting weekly with the Speaker to agree the following week's business. They are integral to the 'usual channels', the informal discussions that take place between Leader and Shadow Leader of the House, and government and Opposition whips on a range of business. Being given a whip's job is often a sign that an MP is 'on the up' and may become a Parliamentary Private Secretary (PPS) or receive a ministerial brief next time round. In turn whips keep an eye on performance and loyalty and feed in their views on fellow MPs – a kind of 'talent spotting'.

In spite of the more consensual approach, whips are nonetheless active in the Lords. Party members receive the whip weekly, indicating the key votes they will be expected to attend for. By agreement, votes are scheduled between 4.00 and 7.00 pm when peers are most likely to be present. The governing side has a roster of peers to ensure that it has enough members to get its business through (bearing in mind that unlike in the Commons no one party commands an overall majority). The government whips office provides support to the Chief Whip in securing the passage of Bills through the House of Lords and acts as a channel of communication between the government and the opposition parties on parliamentary matters. All the whips offices (and the Crossbench Convenor) perform an important co-ordinating role, sharing information among their respective groups.

Parliamentary procedures, tools and techniques

4.45 The next section looks at the opportunities for MPs and peers to raise issues on the floor of the House through questions and debates, and then at business that takes place 'in committee' – away from the main chamber. It covers questions, debates and committees.

Questions – House of Commons

4.46 **Description:** Questions asked of government by parliamentarians. Confusingly, oral questions are more like mini-debates rather than a simple question and answer. Any MP can ask questions of ministers from any government department or of the Prime Minister – either orally or in writing.

4.47 **Purpose:** Oral questions are a tool for raising an issue and often used as a very public way to attack or support government policy or the Opposition. Written questions on the other hand can be used to elicit detailed, factual information.

4.48   **The process:** Questions can be provided in any legible form. They must relate to matters for which a minister has responsibility, seek information or press for action rather than express opinions (not enforced in relation to oral supplementaries), have a 'reasonable factual basis' and not have been answered already in the current session. And if a minister declines to give the information, in general 3 months must elapse before it can be asked again.

4.49   Since devolution special rules have applied to matters devolved to the Scottish or Welsh executives (eg they must relate to matters covered or to be covered by legislation introduced in the UK Parliament).

4.50   **Oral questions:** Question time takes place close to the start of parliamentary business on the floor of the House (straight after any private business). There is a rota for oral questions, with ministers from each department answering them every 4 weeks. Questions can be tabled on any sitting day (or non-sitting Friday) in writing or by email no later than 3 sitting days before the relevant slot (5 days for Northern Ireland, Scotland and Wales). On the last sitting day they go into a random computer shuffle and the lucky top 25 MPs will have their questions printed the next day (for a department taking up the whole of the 55 minute question time slot; fewer will be printed for departments with shorter slots). The number of MPs listed who are likely to have the chance to ask them varies (from around 5–15); the remainder that are printed receive a written answer. Others can be re-tabled for written answer. Convention is that questions are addressed to the senior Commons minister of a department (usually the secretary of state).

4.51   Oral questions tend to be general – giving the MP an opportunity to come back with a 'supplementary' question that is topical and relevant on the day it is being asked (but which must relate to the subject of the original question). Oral questions to the Prime Minister usually take the form 'to list his/her engagements for the day' – enabling a topical supplementary to be asked. This means that many of the questions are highly topical and fiercely politicised debates between the leaders of the major parties (who the Speaker will invariably call to intervene).

4.52   In order to equip ministers to respond effectively, civil servants will research each question or issue and provide a short written briefing with key facts and figures; any potential potholes and lines to take as well as background on the MP (including any constituency interests they may raise). Eager to please backbenchers on the government side are often happy to receive a 'handout' question supplied by Number Ten or the whips on the day of Prime Minister's questions.

4.53 **Campaigning value:** Questions can be a powerful weapon for backbenchers to use. MPs often use questions to pursue a constituency matter, a subject of particular interest or for party political purposes. For campaigners, questions can be invaluable, providing opportunities through sympathetic MPs to bring an issue directly to a minister's attention; to attract publicity for a campaign or to elicit detailed information. If a question is followed up by letters from constituents, debates and media coverage a minister may well think an issue worth responding to. Questions need not take much time to draft – or for an MP to table – but drafting an effective supplementary question will take an MP a good deal longer. Paul Flynn MP advises fellow members to divide it into three: something to grab everyone's attention, a powerful new point followed by an unanswerable question![5]

4.54 **Urgent questions:** These are a type of oral question or debate which must, in the Speaker's opinion, be urgent and relate to matters of public importance. Applications can be submitted to the Speaker at various times in the morning of any sitting day. If successful, the minister is summoned and the MP called to ask their question immediately after question time or at 11.00 am on a Friday. Around 10 of these questions might be allowed in any one year.

4.55 In addition to these, the statement made by the Leader of House every Thursday about forthcoming parliamentary business is actually the answer to an Urgent Question (put by the Shadow Leader). The statement is followed by questions about upcoming business although these sometimes stray into more political or policy matters.

4.56 **Written questions:** Unless required on a specific date, the government usually answers *ordinary written questions* within a week of being tabled. Any number of written questions can be asked. Or MPs can table *questions for answer on a named day* (maximum five questions on a single day) specifying the date required in the form (but a minimum of 3 sitting days required, including non-sitting Fridays). Answers may be refused on the basis that it would involve 'disproportionate cost'. However an ingenious MP may find a different way to ask the same question which does not attract this response!

4.57 **Campaigning value:** Written answers may provide facts about the effects of a current policy (eg numbers taking up a new benefit) or formal confirmation of information that might be suspected but not yet publicly available. They can provide information useful for establishing the likely costs of a new reform campaigners are keen to see

5 *Commons knowledge: how to be a backbencher*, Seren, 1997, p37.

brought in – or of an existing initiative. They can be enough to provide new publicity for a long-running campaign. With the help of a committed MP, a series of questions can be asked on one topic over a period of time that will build up a dossier of useful information.

4.58   **Tips:** Most MPs are receptive to being asked to table questions – especially on an issue of interest to them and some make extensive use of the facility. They can be emailed or posted suggestions – in the standard form that MPs obtain from the Table Office (or on a plain sheet of paper with the heading: TO ASK THE SECRETARY OF STATE FOR X [eg HEALTH] and the question/s listed underneath). An accompanying letter or note should give a brief explanation as to why the question is worth tabling.

4.59   **Drafting tips:** Questions need to be drafted precisely in order to elicit the required information. Lawyers' drafting skills can be useful here. Each question needs to make sense and clearly convey the information that is being sought. They should not be legally or technically worded – if the wording needs to be altered or made more technical the staff at the Table Office will advise accordingly. Don't forget that the MP tabling the questions for you or the campaign you are working on will need to understand the question – and they may well not be an expert on the issue!

4.60   **For oral questions useful wordings are:**
- what plans he/she has to do x;
- what recent representations he/she has received on x;
- if he/she will make a statement about x.

4.61   **Examples:**
- On 22 March 2005 Stephen McCabe MP asked the Secretary of State for Health: 'If he will make a statement on charging of patients in the NHS'.
- On 15 March 2005 Sir Nicholas Winterton MP asked junior minister at the Department for Constitutional Affairs David Lammy MP: 'If he will make a statement on the progress of the draft EU framework services directive relating to the provision of legal services in the EU'.

4.62   **For written questions useful wordings are:**
- if he or she will make a statement about x;
- how much x cost and if he or she will make a statement;
- what he or she estimates x to cost;
- what criteria were used to do x or make x decision.

4.63 **Example:** Andrew Turner MP asked the Chancellor of the Duchy of Lancaster 'If he will make a statement on the steps he has taken to co-ordinate Government policy in relation to the impact of divorce law and family breakdown on children's educational attainment; what his objectives were in so doing; and what the outcome was of his actions'.

Questions – House of Lords

4.64 **Description:** As in the Commons, questions asked of the government by parliamentarians, with the important difference that they are not divided up into slots for each government department and there is no equivalent to Prime Minister's questions.

4.65   **Purpose:** To elicit information or to highlight and debate an issue.

4.66   **The process:** 'Starred' questions are questions for oral answer that do not give rise to a debate (and are marked with an asterix on the Order Paper). Four starred questions are allowed on Mondays and Thursdays and five on Tuesdays and Wednesdays. The peer asking a question gets one supplementary and it is then thrown open to others. As questions can be tabled up to one month in advance, they risk being less topical than in the Commons. For this reason, the Clerk now has the responsibility of ensuring that a certain number of questions are topical – having been drawn only 2 working days before they are to be asked.

4.67   **Written questions:** Peers can table up to six written questions a day and they are usually answered within a fortnight. As well as writing to the peer, the minister's reply is also published in Hansard.

Debates

4.68 **Debates can be divided into those initiated by the government or Opposition parties and those brought forward by backbenchers.**

    They tend to follow a similar format: an MP or peer is called to move a motion (usually making a short speech); the main question for debate is then proposed. The debate then shuttles between each side of the House and during this time amendments may be suggested. Westminster Hall has provided an additional forum for backbench MPs seeking debates on issues of their choice.

Making use of parliamentary debates

4.69   For outsiders, debates offer valuable opportunities to raise the profile of an issue as well as to elicit information or a response from the government. Interest groups make frequent use of parliamentary debates as a tool to raise awareness of an issue in Parliament and through this with decision makers, the media and the public of their particular issue or campaign. Adjournment debates which specifically give backbenchers the chance to air a topic of their choice, give outsiders the best proactive opportunities to raise their issues. But other debates initiated by government or Opposition also give opportunities to brief MPs and have your concerns put across. As well as appreciating short, incisive briefings for upcoming debates, MPs are often receptive to suggestions for topics for future debates.

4.70   **Briefings:** As with all communications with MPs and peers, briefings need to be clear, succinct and on one side of the paper only. A front page should summarise any background in one or two paragraphs and the key points with supporting evidence and contact details if further information is needed. Parliamentarians often appreciate being given an additional tailored briefing – perhaps one or two key points that only they have been given – that might be of specific interest to them and which they can raise during the debate or specifically with the minister. See appendix 1 for a briefing template.

Westminster Hall: a parallel chamber

Westminster Hall began sitting in 1999 and was intended to be a forum for less contentious debates and for matters that there is no time to discuss on the floor of the House. Open to all MPs it is purely a debating chamber (no votes are taken) and as such offers ample opportunities to backbenchers to air their views on a variety of issues. Most of its time is taken up with opportunities for backbenchers to request adjournment debates on topics of their choice. On six Thursdays in each session, the Liaison Committee (which brings together Chairs of the select committees) chooses select committee reports for debate. On some Thursdays there will also be debates on a topic of the government's choice.

House of Commons

Government debates leading to a vote

4.71 **Summary:** The government has the power to initiate debate on and seek approval of the House on a variety of issues, in addition to debates about proposed legislation.

4.72   **The purpose:** This is a 'catch all' category, allowing the government to seek approval of the House on matters that would not otherwise be covered (eg by debates on legislation). It includes the debates that follow the Budget and the Queen's Speech.

4.73   Following the Queen's Speech both Houses devote several days to debating, in general terms, the various measures proposed, divided into subject areas. If you are interested in a particular Bill it is worth following these or briefing a parliamentarian on a particular topic.

4.74   **The process:** Debates on a substantive government motion are usually announced during the Leader's Business Statements on a Thursday and take place the following week. In addition to the main motion, there will usually also be amendments tabled by the Opposition. The Speaker has the absolute power to decide on the amendment or amendments that will be debated. After the secretary of state responsible for the policy area has spoken for 30–45 minutes, the Opposition spokesperson will be given an opportunity to respond, before others are allowed to air their views. Junior ministers from government and Opposition wind up the debate before votes are taken, both on the main motion and the suggested amendment.

Opposition Day debates

4.75 **Summary:** These debates give Opposition parties the opportunity to devote the best part of a parliamentary day (20 days per session) to challenge the government on a particular issue.

4.76   **The purpose:** They are used by the Opposition to challenge the government on topical and often highly controversial issues.

4.77   **The process:** Most Opposition Days are allotted to the official Opposition, the party with the largest number of seats after the governing party. But some are given to the leader of the next largest party who by convention shares these with the other minority parties. In 2002–03 for example, the Liberal Democrats had four Opposition Day debates and the Ulster Unionists and Democratic Unionist Party one each. The Opposition tables the substantive motion and the government an amendment. The Opposition spokesperson speaks first with the secretary of state responding before the debate opens up to others. However, just as with government-initiated debates, the government then gets the last word, with a minister making the last speech before the votes. The Opposition can choose to cover two topics, allowing around 3 hours for each debate.

4.78   **Examples:** The Opposition's choice of topics over the course of a year reflect the chief political pre-occupations of the time. Over the course of the 2002–03 session for example, there were five debates called by the Opposition on different aspects of the Iraq war (including the humanitarian contingency plan and the military situation) and four on pensions (including state pension reform and 'Fairness and security in old age'). Other examples are the criminal justice system and student finance.

4.79   **Briefing MPs:** As Opposition Day debates are lengthy (up to 6 hours long) you may be able to brief an interested MP on one or two aspects from your specialism. They can also be a good opportunity to brief newer MPs who will be trying to make their mark.

Debates initiated by backbench MPs

Adjournment debates

4.80   These are a simple way of having a general debate without a substantive question on which the House comes to a decision. There are three types of adjournment debate open to backbenchers: daily (at the end of the day's business); emergency debates; (under standing order number 24) and debates taking place on the last day before a recess. Daily debates are the most significant for outside groups. The Speaker's Office deals with the applications but will usually run them past the Clerks at the Table Office (who have more procedural expertise in this area).

Daily debates

4.81   **Summary:** Short debates giving MPs the opportunity to raise issues on a topic of their choice.

4.82   **The purpose:** These debates give backbench MPs the opportunity to raise any topic of their choice and call the relevant minister to account. They can use these daily debates to raise constituency matters (eg 'Walsgrave Hospital Trust and Dr Raj Mattu'); topical matters (eg 'the International Court of Justice ruling on the Israeli Security Wall'); or a general issue (eg 'community sentences for young offenders').

4.83   **The process:** There is a half-hour adjournment debate at the end of each day's sitting. Applications are made in writing to the Speaker by the end of Wednesday for the following week. They must relate to a matter for which a minister has responsibility and must not involve a call for legislative change, except incidentally.

4.84   Thursday's subject is chosen by the Speaker (eg selecting someone who has been consistently unlucky in the ballot or has an urgent constituency matter to raise); all other days' topics are selected by ballot. The MP whose debate it is speaks first for around 15 minutes, leaving around the same amount of time for the minister to respond. Other MPs can intervene briefly with the consent of the MP and the minister responding. MPs wishing to speak must apply to the Speaker in writing beforehand. A draft list of speakers is drawn up (by the Speaker and his or her deputies) but not published (unlike in the Lords) – on the basis that this would encourage people to wander in and out of the Chamber or not to attend at all.

4.85   In addition, MPs can apply for the two one and a half hour debates and three half-hour debates that take place in Westminster Hall every Tuesday and Wednesday. They enter the ballot on the Wednesday for the following week but can only enter either for the longer or shorter debates, not both.

4.86   **Examples:** Adjournment debates are a powerful way to directly engage a minister in a constituent's experience. The former MP for Leicester West Greville Janner QC was approached by the parents of a young man who had died in Portugal. Their distress had been added to by the lack of information the Portuguese authorities had given them about the circumstances of their son's death. A debate on a Friday morning with just a handful of MPs present (and the parents in the gallery) was an effective way to secure a Foreign Office minister's engagement in the issue and encourage him to take action on the family's behalf.

4.87   **Briefing MPs:** Many groups use adjournment debates (or their equivalent) as part of a sustained campaign, as they offer a direct opportunity to bring a matter to the attention of a minister. MPs will often be willing to apply for an adjournment debate on a topic of interest to an outside group – and to carry on applying until they are lucky with the ballot. If the topic is picked, they will expect a full briefing and/or a draft speech. You may need to do this at fairly short notice as they will be announced on Thursday for the following week (although sometimes business is announced further ahead).

Emergency debates

4.88   **Summary:** There is provision (under standing order number 24) for an MP to request an emergency debate on a topic they believe merits very urgent consideration.

4.89　**The process:** If the Speaker gives permission, the MP can make an application for an urgent debate by making a speech (lasting no more than 3 minutes); following this if the Speaker accepts the case, then a 3-hour adjournment debate will take place (normally on the following day). It is extremely rare for debates of this nature to be granted (for example there were none in the 2003–04 session). But even if the MP is not successful, they will at least have had 3 minutes of 'prime time' (after statements) to make a case for something they feel passionately about.

Last day before recess debates

4.90　**Summary:** Time is set aside just before a major recess to give further opportunities for adjournment debates.

4.91　**The purpose:** Further opportunity for backbench MPs to raise similar topics as they would in an end-of-day adjournment debate. They are often although not always used for constituency matters.

4.92　**The process:** They differ from ordinary adjournment debates in that the Deputy Leader of the House replies to the MPs rather the relevant departmental minister.

Government debates on motions for the adjournment

4.93　**Summary:** Another type of adjournment debate, these are used when the government does not wish the subject to be put to a vote – for example when they wish to allow their own backbenchers to voice dissent but without the trouble of an embarrassing vote against them; to allow debate about a non-contentious issue or to 'test the water' in relation to a possible new policy.

4.94　**The process:** The subject is announced during Business Questions on Thursday. The format is the same as on a government substantive motion but with no vote at the end.

Examples: Debates about European Community documents.

The sub-judice rule

4.95　Matters awaiting adjudication by a court (ie in a criminal case once a person has been charged and with civil matters once arrangements for the hearing have been made, eg set down for trial) cannot be referred to during parliamentary debate. Appellate proceedings are defined as active from when an application for leave to appeal is made. There are important exceptions to this: first it does not apply to judicial reviews of ministerial decisions; second it can be disregarded if 'in the opinion of the Chair a case concerns issues of national importance such as the economy, public order or the essential services'; and third it does not prevent reference to a current case during a debate on legislation if it is clearly relevant to that legislation. The rule applies both to proceedings on the floor of the House and in committees (including select committees).[6]

House of Lords

4.96 Thursday is now the main day for general debates in the Lords and offers lots of opportunities, both to discuss major topical issues like Iraq as well as specialist issues of concern. By using a 'take note to', 'to approve' or 'to call attention to' motion, important matters can be discussed without going to a vote. These kinds of debates are shared out between all the parties. Rather than being the responsibility of a frontbencher, quite a few are then secured by a backbench peer by agreement within their own parties.

4.97 The Lords also allocate some time to discussing select committee reports.

4.98 Following a ministerial statement there will be an opportunity for questions and brief discussion. However, these are always delivered after they have been announced in the Commons.

Specific opportunities for backbench peers

No day named debates

4.99 These are a device for a backbench to request a slot – eg for a short debate or to pray against regulations. These requests will appear on the Order Paper as 'no day named' until the whips have allocated them some time.

Unstarred questions

4.100 **Summary:** Unstarred questions are in effect mini-debates rather than questions and last for up to one and a half hours (rather like Commons adjournment debates).

4.101 **The process:** They can be tabled for any sitting day and take place at the end of the day's business (or during the dinner break). The

6 'The Sub-Judice Resolution', 11 May 2000, *Handbook of House of Commons procedure,* 3rd edn, 2002, p84.

member initiating the debate will make a fairly substantial speech; other peers will follow and the minister winds up. A variety of topics are covered. As in the Commons, the participation of a relevant minister can make them an effective way to raise an issue.

4.102   **Examples:** On 15 June 2004, Baroness Massey of Darwen asked: 'Her Majesty's Government what their response is to the British Medical Association report Adolescent Health, with particular regard to obesity and sexual health'.

4.103   On 12 November 2004, Baroness Harris of Richmond asked: 'further to the report from the Select Committee on the European Union, Handling EU asylum claims: new approaches examined (11th report, HL Paper 74), what progress they have made in developing their proposals for regional protection areas and what view they take of the proposals of the United Nations High Commissioner for Refugees for the determination of asylum claims on an European Union basis, including the establishment of European Union reception centres'. In effect Lady Harris used the unstarred question to present a European Union select committee's report on handling EU asylum claims, before she stood down as chair of one of its sub-committees.

As well as unstarred questions, backbench peers also have a few Wednesdays per session (up until spring recess) to request a debate of up to two and half hours.

4.104   **Briefing peers:** Similar guidelines apply as for briefing MPs.

Committees

4.105   Parliamentary committees can be divided into two types: cross-party and partisan. Select committees and All Party Groups operate on a cross-party basis, as do standing committees, the one-off committees whose principal role is to scrutinise a specific piece of legislation. The Commons and the Lords have their own set of select committees but also run some together ('joint committees'). The Conservative and Labour parties have their own set of partisan, backbench committees that are only for their members.

Select committees

4.106   **Summary:** A number of select committees scrutinise the work of a particular government department. The other, non-departmental committees are mainly concerned either with other public bodies; issues that cut across all government departments; with specific legislative responsibilities or with the running of Parliament itself.

4.107   Five select committees look across all government departments, dealing with cross-cutting matters. Ten committees deal with procedure and administration.

4.108   The departmental committees in particular deliver their work through a number of inquiries each year, taking evidence from ministers and a variety of external witnesses including lawyers and reporting their findings and recommendations to Parliament. This section focuses on the committees that will be of most interest to lawyers.

4.109   **The purpose:** Select committees have developed into powerful groups that can hold the government to account, scrutinising and questioning the operation of particular issues, systems and laws. Their importance lies in the focus on a particular issue with detailed analysis, the expertise they are able to draw on from external witnesses and the interest that is stimulated by ministers being grilled by the committee. They have also become more streamlined in recent years, with core activities that they must all fulfil (eg scrutinising draft Bills). Committee findings are usually listened to by government and are sometimes acted on – particularly if the findings received unanimous support. Against this committees are sometimes criticised for not being strategic enough, eg in their line of questioning of a tricky witness. Some people argue that this can limit their impact and may even lead to independent (often judge-led) inquiries being set up because select committees have failed to 'do the business'.

Departmental committees

4.110   Departmental committees of especial interest to publicly funded lawyers will be the Health select committee (whose remit includes community care issues); Work and Pensions (whose remit includes welfare benefits); Education and Skills; Trade and Industry; Office of the Deputy Prime Minister: Housing, Planning, Local Government and the Regions; Home Affairs; Environment, Food and Rural Affairs; and Treasury. The Constitutional Affairs select committee will be of general interest with its focus on issues relating to the legal system as a whole.

Legislative committees

4.111   All five legislative select committees will be of interest to lawyers. The Joint Committee on Human Rights has developed a high profile and reputation for influence. It is a very active committee, with a general remit to consider matters relating to human rights in the UK. As well as conducting inquiries into specific issues, it also examines every government Bill shortly after its introduction and gives an opinion as to whether its enactment would pose potential breaches of human rights. It also looks at any proposals for and drafts of the remedial orders that result from a finding of incompatibility with the Human Rights Act 1998. It has six MPs and six peers and significantly has no in-built government majority. It is aided by expert legal advisers. Its highly influential reports include 'The Case for a Human Rights Commission'[7] and 'The Case for a Children's Commissioner for England'.[8]

4.112   For information about the other four legislative committees (The Joint Committee on Consolidation Bills; The Regulatory Reform Committee; The Joint Committee on Statutory Instruments and the Tax Law Rewrite Committee) see chapter 3.

Cross-cutting select committees

4.113   The European Scrutiny Committee is one of the five 'cross-cutting' select committees. It is vitally important, looking not only at EU policies, spending and draft legislation but also at institutional matters. See chapter 5 for information about this committee. The other committees in this category are: (i) The European Audit Committee which focuses on the impact of government departments' policies on environmental protection and sustainable development; (ii) The Liaison Committee (chairs of all the permanent select committees) which seeks to improve the work of select committees as a whole and whose most high profile activity is now its twice-yearly sessions with the Prime Minister; (iii) The Public Accounts Committee (PAC) which works closely with the Comptroller and Auditor-General, the chief controller and auditor of public spending with responsibility for examining value for money;[9] and (iv) The Public Administration Committee. This is an important committee for lawyers to know about as it considers the Ombudsman's reports and often helps give them clout by drawing general lessons from the particulars of the cases she or he has looked at and making recommendations accordingly. In the other part of its role the committee

---

7   Sixth Report of Session 2002–03, HC 489-I.
8   Ninth Report of Session 2002–03, HC 666.
9   The PAC examines the accounts of each government department, taking evidence from accounting officers but also looks more widely at value for money issues, often examining and supporting reports made by the Comptroller.

examines wide ranging matters affecting the whole of government, such as freedom of information and House of Lords reform.

Internal committees

4.114　Of the internal committees, lawyers will find the following of most interest:

- The Modernisation of the House of Commons select committee is a Labour initiative created in 2001 and unusually chaired by a Cabinet minister, the Leader of the House. Many of its recommendations (eg on the parliamentary timetable) have been put into effect.

- The Committee of Selection has the task of choosing which MPs will serve on committees. Its domination by whips rather limits the number of independent minded MPs who will be chosen to serve on committees.

4.115　In addition to the joint permanent legislative committees, both Houses sometimes set up a joint committee to deal with a specific Bill. An example is the joint committee which was appointed to examine and report on the Draft Children (Contact) and Adoption Bill. Or a joint committee may be set up to deal with a specific issue – for example the Joint Committee on Lords Reform set up in 2002.

4.116　**Membership:** Backbench MPs are appointed to select committees shortly after a General Election and serve a full Parliament (unless they resign, or are promoted to be ministers or frontbench spokespersons). Numbers vary, with most departmental committees having 11 members, in close proportion to party strengths in the House. The Chairs may be government or Opposition MPs but overall the numbers of each will reflect party numbers. They are in a powerful position to stamp their mark on their committee and inevitably gain some status from their role. Most committees have the power to set up at least one sub-committee. Some develop into real champions and experts whilst others remain more pedestrian in their approach.

4.117　Each committee has a small team of staff, headed up by a clerk who is responsible for overall smooth running and including subject specialists as well as part-time specialists who can provide the necessary expertise for specific inquiries. The select committee for the Department for Constitutional Affairs has a staff of seven, including a Media Officer and Committee Specialist. Additional support is provided by the Scrutiny Unit, whose staff can help in particular with scrutiny of departmental expenditure and of draft legislation which can be complex and may have to be carried out at fairly short notice.

A recent innovation is a team of media officers based in the Committee Office, headed up by the Communications Adviser to the Commons. In small teams, they each service a number of committees.

4.118   **The process:** Each departmental committee and some of the others run a number of inquiries in each session. They rely on evidence from experts to inform their inquiries. A schedule will be drawn up and individuals or organisations invited to give evidence. In addition the committee will sometimes undertake study visits at home or abroad. It is rare for a witness to be requested to give oral evidence unless they have already submitted written evidence which they can then expand on. The length of written evidence will often be specified. Lawyers are frequent visitors to select committees, often as representatives of networks or organisations, such as the Discrimination Law Association. Their evidence is useful because it derives from the 'coalface' – the experience of using existing laws and policies everyday. But lawyers may also be invited to give evidence because they can provide valuable advice about what kind of legal framework or laws are likely or unlikely to work in future.

4.119   The inquiry will culminate in the production of a report, with the Chair seeking, but not always succeeding, in achieving unanimous recommendations. For departmental select committees the government has 2 months to provide a response to a select committee report. Some reports are debated in Parliament.

4.120   **Examples:** The week beginning 17 January 2005 gives a snapshot of the variety and importance of the issues considered by select committees and of their potential interest to lawyers.

- Celia Conard, a family law practitioner gave evidence to the Constitutional Affairs Committee for their 'Family Justice: The Family Courts' inquiry.
- The Education and Skills Committee was continuing its inquiry into the green paper 'Every Child Matters' and took evidence from organisations including the NSPCC and the Children's Rights Alliance for England.
- The European Union's Constitutional Treaty was being examined by the European Scrutiny Committee by Martin Howe QC and Professor Alan Dashwood, Professor of European Law at Cambridge University.
- The Welsh Affairs Committee was focusing on the Police Service, Crime and Anti-Social Behaviour in Wales.
- The Foreign Affairs Committee had summoned junior Minister Bill Rammell MP to question him on the Foreign and Commonwealth Human Rights Annual Report 2004.

- The Home Affairs Committee was taking evidence from journalists in the context of its inquiry into 'Terrorism and Community Relations'.

4.121 Committees make much use of lawyers' (and sometimes judges') evidence. In 2004–05, the Health select committee examined the contentious issue of the funding of long term residential care. In the final report committee members quoted extensively from evidence from Mackintosh Duncan, the Law Society and Solicitors for the Elderly. They referred to Mackintosh Duncan solicitors' observation that none of the sets of eligibility criteria that they had seen being used were 'in accordance with the Coughlan judgment' and called these 'very serious charges which the Government must answer'. The committee went on to make a robust recommendation that the new national eligibility criteria 'must be explicitly Coughlan-compliant, ensuring that all people whose primary need is for health care will receive fully funded care, even if this requires a fundamental revision of the definitions and terminology of the criteria'.[10]

4.122 The Constitutional Affairs Committee took a lead in criticising the government's plans for a new Supreme Court, taking evidence from many senior members of the judiciary including the Lord Chief Justice and members of the Appellate Committee of the House of Lords.

House of Lords select committees

4.123 There are a smaller number of select committees in the Lords, covering issues in a cross-cutting fashion rather than by department as in the Commons. But they too can have an impact. The European Union Committee is a weighty body, with seven sub-committees. See chapter 5 for more detailed information. Other key committees deal with Economic Affairs (with a sub-committee that examines policy aspects of the Finance Bill); and the Constitution (in particular reporting on any constitutional implications of public Bills). One-off Committees are frequently set up – often sitting for one session only.

4.124 Returning to the week of 17 January 2005, in the Lords the Economic Affairs Committee was considering the economics of climate change and no less than four of the European Union Committee's sub-committees were meeting. Topics included a new Council regulation concerning trade in products that could be used for torture or inhuman treatment with DTI minister Nigel Griffiths being called to give evidence, and current development in European foreign policy. The

10 House of Commons Health select committee, NHS Continuing Care (HC 399): 6th Report, 2004–05, published 5 April 2005, para 103.

Science and Technology sub-committee was taking evidence from Commission officials on energy efficiency.

4.125   A Liaison Committee which includes the party leaders and cross-bench equivalent (the 'Convenor') and a few backbench peers governs the general workings of Lords committees and decides when and whether to set up any new ones.

4.126   **Membership:** Select committees are run in a similar fashion as in the Commons, with clerks and specialist staff. But members of most Lords committees have to wait longer for the government to respond in writing to their reports – up to 6 months.

Influencing the process

Suggesting topics for enquiry

4.127   • The clerk to any committee can always provide information about current inquiries and who they are seeking evidence from. Or you can go on the email update list and receive regular information, such as the announcement of a new inquiry and/or call for evidence. If you have an idea for an inquiry you could write to or email the Chair (or if you think that one of the committee members may be particularly interested – approach them first), setting out the reasons and requesting a short (20-minute) meeting to explain further.

• Or you could make initial contact with the Clerk or Special Adviser to ask about upcoming inquiries and to seek their advice about how to make a suggestion. It's worth thinking several months ahead and anticipating an interesting topic for enquiry as the committee will tend to plan its work well ahead.

Preparing to give evidence

4.128   • You can assume a degree of engagement as MPs tend to request to be on committees in which they have an interest. However, they will have widely varying degrees of knowledge. They are often receptive to suggestions for topics or questions to be put to witnesses by committee members which will then help you prepare. If you are not successful in being called to give evidence you may be able to feed in key points via another lawyer or organisation that is being called.

• For a detailed guide to giving evidence go to www.parliament.uk/ commons/selcom/witguide.htm.

Tips:

4.129
- Check up on the background of members in advance.
- Get advance notice of the most important areas of interest to committee members.
- Think about what expertise and knowledge you bring to the inquiry that other witnesses will not have.
- Prepare your most important three points that you need to get across, whatever the questions. Think about what you would be happy to see highlighted from your evidence in the committee's final report.
- Read any transcripts available of evidence already given in the inquiry, to give you a sense of the committee's areas of interest and any obvious gaps.
- Check if you will be giving evidence alongside other witnesses at the same time – this is increasingly common, with, for example, non-governmental organisations being grouped together – and make contact beforehand to check on the evidence they are likely to give.
- Remember that committee members are unlikely to be familiar with technicalities, eg of how a family court works or the immigration appeals system. Work out clear and easy ways to make your points and practise them on a non-lawyer beforehand.
- Submit written evidence early – before the deadline – as committee staff will start drafting the report as soon as evidence starts to come in.
- You can use any quotes from your evidence in the final report in your lobbying efforts – to point out to the government the select committee's support for your proposals.

House of Lords

4.130 The same basic guidelines apply as in the Commons.

- For a current list of House of Lords select committees go to www.parliament.uk/parliamentary_committees/parliamentary_com mittees26.cfm.
- For detailed guidance on submitting evidence to a Lords Select Committee go to www.parliament.uk/directories/house_of_lords_ information_office/ctteepartic.cfm.

The political parties: policy-making and activities in Parliament

4.131   Each party has its own way of operating within Parliament. Processes also vary according to whether a party is in Opposition or government. In Opposition for example, MPs elect the Labour Party's Shadow Cabinet. It is useful to put the parties' activities in Parliament in the context of their overall policy-making policies. For more details see the box below.

How do the political parties make policy?

The Labour party

Under the party's constitution there are four key structures: conference; the National Executive Committee (NEC); the Parliamentary Labour Party (PLP); and the members (affiliated unions and individuals).

The NEC is the party's governing body, responsible for its overall direction and policy-making process. The National Policy Forum (NPF) oversees the development of party policy which ultimately influences the manifesto. NPF membership comprises the NEC and some additional elected members representing the constituency parties, MPs, MEPs, trade unions and councillors.

The NPF oversees a rolling programme of consultation called 'Partnership in Power', introduced in part to increase members and non-members' direct involvement in policy-making. This process involves the NPF gathering submissions from local Labour parties, community groups, individuals and NGOs. There is a 'Joint Policy Committee' chaired by the Prime Minister with a membership of ministers and NPF members. Documents on different policy areas are prepared, discussed and amended by a number of policy commissions (made up of representatives of government, NEC and NPF members and operating under the Joint Policy Committee). After debate and approval by the NPF these are the policy documents that will be submitted to conference.

Conference remains, in theory, the sovereign decision-making body of the party but the practice is often different. The leader of the Labour party (in a particularly strong position when in government) may seek to persuade or overrule other parts of the party.

There is some cynicism about the policy-making process. However, in July 2004, at the NPF meeting prior to party conference, the unions were able to exert significant influence over the manifesto, winning concessions on a wide range of proposals (including 4 weeks' paid holiday for every worker). Known as the Warwick Agreement, this suggests that there is room in the policy-making process for a variety of views.

Influencing the policy-making process

- It is certainly worth making a short submission on a relevant issue via the Partnership in Power process as an organisation or specialist group of lawyers. The programme works in two 'waves': non-members can only contribute to the first year documents which are more consultative and focus on identifying challenges and solutions. (In the second year these documents take into account the first round, but are only circulated within the party.)
- Some MPs advise that it is not that effective to lobby individual members of the NPF as by the time they get key documents (many drafted by members of the Number Ten Policy Directorate) it will be too late to change their content. However, others argue that they are a worthwhile group to influence as although they may not have any real power they do have substantial access to ministers or shadow ministers.
- In 2003–04, the party used a new series of discussion events (under the banner 'Big Conversation') to add to the existing process and stimulate debate with wider groups of citizens. Some of these were organised in partnership between the party and external groups including NGOs. Although the 'Big Conversation' events officially wound down about a year before the 2005 General Election, the party indicated its keenness to carry on running such events in a similar format.
- More generally it is worth, especially in view of the Warwick Agreement, seeking to influence policies via the unions.
- It is worth making contact with the relevant policy staff at Labour headquarters, whose duties include drafting documents and collating submissions. Their power is limited (especially when Labour is in government) but they can be useful.

For further information see www.labour.org.uk.

The Conservative party

Policy making generally is a process conducted by both the parliamentary Conservative party and Conservative Central Office. In 2005 the party was continuing a policy renewal process which included conducting policy reviews in specific areas (eg health), consulting across the board and producing policy documents.

The Conservative Policy Forum (formerly the Conservative Political Centre), seeks to engage party members in policy development, seeking views on key issues of the day. It operates at both national and local level (with local groups receiving briefs on a range of issues, to aid discussion). Members' responses are passed onto the relevant senior politician, via the party's Research Department.

Influencing the policy-making process

- There are a number of ways in which non-party members can influence the policy-making process. It is worth making contact with the relevant policy people at Conservative Central Office (especially when the party is in Opposition) as well as with parliamentarians.
- It is important to note that in the wake of the party's defeat in the 2005 General Election, discussions were on-going into many aspects of the party's direction, structure and processes. The arrangements for choosing a new leader, following Michael Howard's indication that he would step down were in flux and it seemed likely that other aspects of the party's organisation (including policy making) would also change.

For further information see www.conservatives.com.

The Liberal Democrats

The Liberal Democrats retain a high degree of involvement of party members in the development of policy. Federal policy is formally made twice a year, when elected representatives from constituency parties assemble at their party's conferences. Conference representatives elect a Federal Policy Committee that takes responsibility for producing policy papers, and election manifestos. Smaller, policy-working groups produce papers for discussion and development as well as the final versions setting out agreed policies.

Influencing the policy-making process

- The policy-making process is open to outsiders having influence. It is worth identifying the key figures in the party, both at the headquarters and parliamentarians, with a specialism or interest in your area and making contact with them.

For further information see www.libdems.org.uk.

House of Commons

Partisan committees

4.132 **Summary:** The Labour and Conservative parties have well-developed structures, based on committees or groups. They are in many ways under-used by outside groups who will tend to focus efforts on the more public, cross-party committees. But they offer valuable opportunities to engage with junior and senior parliamentarians and in some cases to influence policy at a very early stage. There are also groups of 'factions' within each party (eg the Bow Group in the Conservative party or Tribune within the Labour party). If you are meeting an MP it is worth checking out any affiliations.

The Labour party

4.133 The Parliamentary Labour party (all Labour parliamentarians) meets every Wednesday morning. Ministers (and sometimes the Prime Minister) or shadow ministers attend to discuss issues and field questions from backbench colleagues. It is a vital way in which backbenchers can make their views known to more senior colleagues (and vice versa). Sympathetic MPs can be asked to raise an issue at this meeting – an effective way to flag concern and glean the Prime Minister's or other's views. Or after a PLP meeting you can ask MPs about the issues 'of the week' that are concerning MPs.

4.134   The Chair of the PLP is a respected role held by a senior backbencher. The PLP has an executive committee ('The Parliamentary Committee') – in government the Prime Minister and other senior ministers and in Opposition the Shadow Cabinet. Although journalists do not attend PLP meetings the contents of more lively discussions are often leaked. For example, at the first meeting after the 2005 General Election some usually loyal backbenchers told the Prime Minister of their anger at the 'flak' they had received from constituents over the war in Iraq. This was widely reported on broadcast news and in the press.

Departmental groups

4.135   Backbench groups shadow each government department, giving colleagues a chance to share information and discuss policy, strategy and presentation. Under a Labour government these departmental groups are a major way for backbenchers to call senior ministers to account. At the very least ministers will give members a chance to air their views, even if they do not ultimately act in a way that members want. They will often attend meetings, reporting regularly on their department's activities and consult on draft proposals and Bills. Ministers tend to take more notice of a backbencher writing as a member of a backbench committee than in a general capacity. They are particularly useful for putting issues on the agenda of the party at a very early stage, well before legislation is being considered and to discuss possibilities with ministers for the manifesto. Since the Labour government faced heartfelt opposition over the introduction of 'top up fees' for students, ministers have been particularly keen to engage with backbenchers via the committees. In addition to a committee for each department there is also a Women's Committee which, again, will be open to suggestions for briefings or meetings from outside groups. Age Concern and the Fawcett Society engaged this committee in consideration of its joint women and pensions campaign, providing speakers for a meeting and asking for members' support in pressing ministers to engage with its proposed reforms. There is also a set of regional groups which meet regularly, again often with ministers in attendance, and focus on issues of particular concern to their region.

4.136   **Tips:** If you have a topic that fits into the remit of a particular committee you can approach the Chair, Vice-Chair or Secretary to suggest a meeting and provide briefing or a speaker. Meetings will often involve the relevant secretary of state or an external speaker.

The Conservative party

4.137   The main formal organisation for backbench Conservative MPs is the 1922 Committee (called after the year it was founded) which they are automatically members of. Peers are invited to attend, but when in government ministers do not usually attend unless invited. It meets weekly and like the PLP is an important way for backbenchers to get their views across to senior people in the party (via the whips who always attend). The Chair of the committee is an influential senior MP tasked with representing backbenchers' views to the leader. This role is formally reinforced by his or her seat on the Conservative Board (the governing body of the party), as the representative of the parliamentary party. It can be a powerful forum for MPs to unite against the party leadership. Like the PLP, the 1922 Committee also has an executive committee but it is quite different in membership, comprising the Chair, Vice Chairs and a small number of backbenchers.

Subject and area committees

4.138   Rather than a system of one committee for each government department, backbenchers can participate in one or more of the four policy groups (home, foreign, economic and environmental affairs). In Opposition these groups are chaired by the relevant Shadow Cabinet members. They are therefore an excellent way to seek to influence policy making within the party.

4.139   There are also regional or area committees, bringing members together to discuss certain issues and again, in government, providing a useful way to engage with ministers.

4.140   **Tips:** As with the Labour party it is a good idea to identify participants in these groups and to make contact with them, with a view to raising your key issues.

Liberal Democrats

4.141   In the Commons Liberal Democrat MPs also have a weekly meeting (Wednesdays) to cover similar matters to the other parties (eg forthcoming business). But they do not have a formal committee structure.

4.142 **Tips:** Due to the relatively small number of MPs compared with the other two major parties, most of them have frontbench responsibilities which obviously creates a different dynamic from those parties with large numbers of backbenchers.

4.143 The other parties also have weekly meetings to discuss business, but their small numbers rule out any kind of formal committee structure.

House of Lords

4.144 The House of Lords overall is far less politically partisan than the Commons. Nonetheless most peers are members of a party. Parties tend not to have formal backbench committee structures, with backbenchers working together and with frontbenchers as needed for particular proposals or legislation.

All Party groups

4.145 **Summary:** There are hundreds of All Party groups on just about every topic imaginable, from adoption to back care through to traveller law reform and youth hostelling. They are divided into subject groups and country groups.

4.146 **Purpose:** They are principally debating fora, a way for parliamentarians to increase their knowledge or awareness of a particular issue. Through this specialist knowledge, backbenchers hope to have some influence. Like backbench committees, they are also a way of engaging with ministers who will usually be happy to attend relevant meetings. There are two types of group: All Party Parliamentary Groups (APPGs) and All Party Associate Groups (APGs). Groups have to have at least ten members of the governing party and ten from other parties. The membership of associate groups gives voting rights to non-parliamentarians.

4.147 **Membership:** Any MP or peer can join. Groups tend to have a Chair and often a number of Vice or Co-Chairs from different parties. The level of participation by post-holders varies widely. They often allow individuals and organisations to attend their meetings. It can be useful for an organisation to arrange for its users or people with direct experience of the topic in question to address the group.

4.148 **The process:** All Party groups vary widely in terms of their level of activity. Most have regular meetings with outside speakers and some also organise receptions, dinners or joint events with other groups. A few have newsletters or email updates. But almost all find it a challenge to secure consistent and reasonable numbers of attendance at all their sessions – a reflection perhaps of the numerous demands on parliamentarians' time (especially since the shorter parliamentary week was introduced) with many meetings taking place at the same time. Even when a minister is attending or with a high quality external speaker it can be difficult to attract more than a handful of MPs or peers. Indeed outside observers (allowed by many groups) often outnumber parliamentarians. However, they do offer an opportunity for parliamentarians to focus on a subject area, a positive feature of a job which demands a bit of knowledge on many topics. For this reason, many outside groups find it worthwhile to invest some time in them, using them as a platform or focus within Parliament for their cause.

4.149   **Tips:** If your topic or issue fits within the remit of an All Party group it is worth approaching the officers to request an opportunity to address a meeting or to brief them. Many groups are administered by an external organisation (eg the APPG on Disability has secretariat support provided by RADAR and Alcohol Concern provides a similar role for the All Party group on Alcohol Misuse). If there is a Secretariat it is worth speaking to them first to find out about their plans for the forthcoming programme and to ask how your issue might fit in. Many peers are very active in all party groups – for example Lord Ashley is the Chair and driving force behind the All Party group on Disability.

4.150   There are many groups of interest to lawyers – including those on Adoption, Constitution and Citizenship, Domestic Violence, Homelessness and Housing Need, and Equalities. See one of the parliamentary guides – eg the PMS Parliamentary Companion for a full list.

Attending a meeting

4.151   • If you do attend an All Party group meeting as an outside speaker make sure you know what is expected of you in terms of time available and subject matter, and if there are other speakers in addition to you.

• If you can provide a short (eg two side) briefing or relevant report beforehand the members may be happy for this to be circulated with the minutes, which go to all members, not just those attending the meeting. New research is always of especial interest.

• Remember that members' levels of knowledge and their particular interests will vary widely. They will often be influenced by their 'postbag' or constituents' interests as experienced in their weekly surgeries and will want your views on these.

Early Day Motions

4.152   **Summary:** Written motions or 'calls to action' tabled by one or more MPs ranging from the fun ('Wales Rugby Grand Slam Victory') to the very serious or seriously challenging ('Army Deaths' or 'Tuberculosis and HIV in Africa'). They only exist in the Commons.

4.153   **The purpose:** Published in the blue pages of the Vote Bundle that arrives on MPs' desks daily they are a popular campaign tool – used by individual MPs and through them outside groups to draw attention to and gather support for an issue, but are almost never debated in the House. Guaranteed to create local media coverage in an MP's constituency they can also be a useful hook for national coverage, in particular when more than 100 members have added their names. Some people voice scepticism about the effectiveness of EDMs, particularly as there are so many of them (around 1,500 tabled each session). However, there is no doubt that they are a useful and easy way to engage MPs– and through them decision-makers and the public in an issue and to attract publicity. Used creatively they can help launch a campaign or keep its momentum going. The fact that they can be tabled instantly gives them added value. In 2005 John Mann MP tabled a motion about the discontinuation of certain drugs for Alzheimer's sufferers from the NHS, also taking the opportunity to publicise the Alzheimer's Society planned lobby of Parliament on the issue. For all these reasons they remain a well-used tool in most campaigners' toolkits.

4.154   **The process:** EDMs must begin with the words: 'That this House'; must not exceed 250 words and must be handed in to the Table Office. Other MPs can then add their names to the motion. As long as names keep being added, it is reprinted weekly until the end of the session when it falls. Amendments can also be tabled.

Tips:

4.155   • An EDM with cross-party support will tend to have more impact – and will also certainly register more strongly with the government if a substantial number of their own MPs have signed up to it. You need to try to get cross-party support before it is tabled by securing the signature of at least one MP from each of the major parties. This will then encourage MPs from different parties to add their support.
   • Ministers and Parliamentary Private Secretaries (PPSs) never sign EDMs – you can check an MP's status on the Parliament website before asking an MP to sign an EDM. Some MPs refuse to sign EDMs as a matter of principle, seeing them as a waste of time.

- Before a frontbench spokesperson signs an EDM they will sometimes need to check that it is in line with party policy.

4.156 **Examples:** An EDM calling on the government to reform the pensions system to make it deliver more for women highlighted a new Age Concern and Fawcett Society report entitled 'One in Four', which drew attention to the quarter of single women pensioners living in poverty.[11] Being able to inform supporters just a few weeks later that one in four MPs had added their names to the EDM was a nice touch.

Petitions to Parliament

4.157 **Summary:** Another vehicle for citizens to make a point and ask for some action to be taken on something within the power of the House of Commons to grant.

4.158 **The purpose:** Another way to express an opinion and more effective at gaining publicity than for any other purpose.

4.159 **The process:** The petition has to be worded in a certain way but there are no rules about the number of signatures needed. Any MP may then present a petition, either informally by putting it in the green bag behind the Speaker's Chair (the origin of the phrase 'it's in the bag') or formally, just before the parliamentary day is about to end (with an adjournment debate) when there is the opportunity to introduce it and read out the text. They can only be presented by MPs not peers. In addition MPs sometimes go to Number Ten to present the petition, which can help attract publicity for a cause.

Other ways of raising issues

Letters to MPs or correspondence between MPs and ministers

4.160 **Summary:** Letters to MPs or peers and correspondence between parliamentarians and ministers.

4.161 **The purpose:** An effective way to clarify government policy; have information put on the record; or to continue debate started on the floor of either House.

4.162 **The process:** MPs and peers write to ministers for a range of reasons, ranging from an individual constituent's problem through to a detailed policy matter in which the member has a specialised interest or on behalf of an organisation on a specific issue.

11 Launched on 2 February 2004.

Requesting MPs to write to a minister

4.163   If you or a representative of an organisation you belong to writes to an MP about an issue, they will often forward it to the relevant minister. The minister will then send back a fairly standard reply or a response from an official which will be faithfully sent back to you by the MP. However, if an MP writes directly to a minister, they will usually respond personally.

4.164   Either way this may feel like (literally) a paper exercise, but with a sufficient number of letters, the 'drip drip' effect will be taking hold. Letters to ministers are one way in which they sense that people are concerned about an issue. A number of letters on the same issue, but expressed in different ways and with a range of experiences, will have an impact. Although postcards are becoming discredited as a campaigning tool for failing to convey a range of views and experiences the sackloads of cards Gordon Brown received about the Jubilee 2000 Drop the Debt Campaign were said to have had an impact.

MPs and peers in correspondence with a minister

4.165   During debates on a Bill, the minister will sometimes offer to respond to a member in writing or invite the minister to write in the first instance, making their point in more detail. This is particularly likely to happen: (i) where the minister is not entirely sure of the response they wish to give and want to consider before making a commitment; and/or (ii) where they may wish to give some ground but would like to give it further thought – perhaps with a view to making a concession at the next stage of the Bill. You can assist the MP or peer you are working with by providing a succinct summary of the points (with any useful case studies) or if they wish, a first draft of the letter. The replies are usually predictable; but occasionally they are invaluable. Lord Janner of Braunstone gained valuable information in correspondence with Foreign Office ministers which spurred on his campaign to reveal the scandal of 'Nazi Gold' – gold that was stolen from victims of Nazi persecution and sold by Germany to other countries.

Tips for letters to MPs or peers:

4.166   •   Keep it brief – a one-sided letter is always best. More detail can go in a short accompanying briefing. Parliamentarians are extremely busy – and if you spend half an hour in a committee session you will see most of the contents of that day's post going straight in the bin.

- If you cannot say what the problem is; who it affects and how; and what the solution is (and the cost) in three bullet points, you probably need to think through in more detail what it is you want.
- Tailor it to the individual. For example: 'I know that you spoke strongly in the debate last week against the proposed abolition of trial by jury for x groups. For this reason I thought you would be interested to know about the evidence that myself and x other lawyers have collected about the impact of the new proposals'.
- Include key facts that are likely to be new to the member and can easily be used in a debate. 'We estimate that if the government presses ahead with its plans as many as x thousand suspected criminals will be denied the right to trial by jury in the first year. The cost of this could be x'.
- Make it clear what you are asking the parliamentarian to do, eg write a letter, table a motion or a question, etc.
- If there is a link with the MP's constituency be sure to highlight it.
- Request a short (20-minute) meeting to offer a further briefing. Many MPs in particular feel themselves to be so busy that they will instruct their staff to find out more information about why a meeting should be necessary!
- If you are asking others to write in support of a campaign it is not advisable to give them a template letter but rather to suggest some key points that they can add to – preferably with their own views and experiences. Personal letters tend to have more impact, and stave off the impression that a formal lobbying outfit rather than genuine concern is at stake.
- Include your contact details, clearly marked.

Tips for briefing MPs and peers:

4.167
- You must 'know your brief', research your contacts and have information tailored to them, eg if you are contacting an MP who is a member of the Work and Pensions Select Committee think about their interests – is there an inquiry that relates to one of your current concerns or is there a new inquiry they might wish to conduct? Don't forget that you will have useful information to share – provided that you can present it in a digestible format – maximum two-side briefing accompanied by a one-side letter is more than enough to start with.
- The vast majority of MPs and more than half of peers are on email. The rest need to be posted briefings (House of Commons London

SW1A OAA; or for peers: House of Lords London SW1A OPW; or for those members who use the Attendants' Office at the House of Lords by fax to 020 7219 5979). Members make arrangements for mail to be forwarded to them during breaks.

- Organisations sometimes get caught out when they hand deliver or courier bulk mailings for MPs (eg to make sure a briefing arrives in time for a debate). These are sometimes turned away so it's best to ring in advance.
- As only a small proportion of peers are active, there is therefore never any point sending a briefing to all peers. However, on some occasions (eg Queen's Speech debates) it is worth mailing all MPs.

Tips for meetings with MPs and peers:

4.168
- The most important thing to be aware of is time – you may have been promised half an hour or an hour but if the MP is running behind or is called to a vote it may well be much less. You need to be able to get your points across succinctly. Do offer them further information in writing – and take the opportunity to find out about their interests or the particular angle they are coming at an issue from. It's a good idea to ask for advice on how to progress your cause or campaign – they may have tips as to how to engage with a minister or frontbench spokesperson or to get other MPs or peers interested.
- Even if you have sent in information in advance, do not expect them to have read or remembered it (although you may be pleasantly surprised!). It's a good idea to take extra copies.
- Campaigners sometimes get so carried away by the merits of what they are proposing that they forget the basics: who will it affect; why does it matter – and crucially what will it cost? If you meet an MP or peer these will be the questions they will ask. Indeed even before you meet them you may have to justify why your cause is worth their time.
- For example, they may want to know out of the general population if certain regions or groups will be affected – such as women or a particular minority ethnic group. And they will want to know how much a proposal might cost: less than £5 million between £5 and £10 million, tens of millions or billions of pounds? What would be the costs and benefits – would more expenditure on one benefit or a certain procedural law reform actually save the government money? And what evidence do you have to back this up? Sometimes it's difficult to be sure about costs – you could ask a sympathetic MP to table a written question to help get you this information.

- MPs are available for meetings at various times. Peers tend to be more likely to be available for meetings in the afternoon and early evening (ie when the Lords is sitting).

Further information

4.169
- The best single source of information is the parliamentary website: www.parliament.uk.
- The House of Commons Information Office is incredibly helpful. Tel: 020 7219 4272; email: hcinfo@parliament.uk.
- The switchboard number at the Houses of Parliament is 020 7219 3000. You can contact members, their staff and other offices via this number.
- The House of Lords Information Office can be helpful but tend to grill you as to whether you have checked the website before calling! Tel: 020 7219 3107; email: hlinfo@parliament.uk.
- There is a Parliamentary Bookshop right under Big Ben (12 Bridge St) with a good range of books. Tel: 020 7219 3890; email: bookshop@parliament.uk. And for official publications, The Stationery Office has a number of shops (including one opposite Holborn Tube, 123 Kingsway, London); www.tso.co.uk or email: tsoservices@tso.co.uk.
- The Weekly Information Bulletin and the Sessional Information Digest can be found at www.publications.parliament.uk/ pa/cm/ cmpubns.htm (the Information Office's page) or via Parliament's home page. They include some information about the Lords (including future business).
- The daily working documents of the House of Commons are known collectively as the Vote Bundle (or the 'Vote'). They contain information on the business of the House for that day, the transactions of the previous day's sitting (Votes and Proceedings) and notices for future days.
- In the Commons the Order Paper lists today's business; the Lords equivalent is called the 'Minute'. See the Parliament website for more information.
- 'Business of the House and its committees' is a brief guide published by the Clerk of the House. Aimed at new MPs it is useful also for non-parliamentarians as it gives full details of parliamentary procedures. You could ask a friendly MP to share their copy with you.[12]

12 Published January 2003.

- For lighter reading Paul Flynn MP has written an entertaining guide: *Commons knowledge: how to be a backbencher,* Seren, 1997.
- For background on your MP the best way is to 'google' their name (www.google.co.uk). A full list of MPs and details of which are on email/have websites is available from the main Parliament site and you can check their voting records at www.theyworkforyou.com. For background on peers the Lords website has a full list of members which links to biographies.
- Many committee sessions are now broadcast live over the Internet: www.parliamentlive.tv. Transcripts are also published on the website (on the sites of individual committees). For a list of current House of Commons Select Committees go to www.parliament.uk/parliamentary_committees/parliamentary_committees16.cfm.

CHAPTER 5

The European Union: influencing law and policy

continued

> - From partnership to Union: a potted history
> - EU institutions and how to engage with them
> - How to influence EU laws and policies at an early stage
> - How EU laws and policies are scrutinised by the UK Parliament
> - Lobbying in Brussels: the work of NGOs and other groups

Introduction

5.1   There are plenty of reasons for UK lawyers to be plugged into the EU and its institutions. Since joining the European Community in 1973, UK law has become subordinate to EU law, with the European Court of Justice (ECJ) becoming the highest court. Beyond this simple doctrine of supremacy, the ECJ has been hard at work, taking steps to ensure the 'applicability and superiority' of EU law across a growing number of member states (now 25). As the size and policy remit of the EU has grown, so has the quantity of new laws emanating from Brussels which either take direct effect or must be transposed into UK law and implemented.

5.2   As a result, knowledge of European law is an integral part of most lawyers' practices. Every lawyer needs to know of the relevant existing law in their field and to be aware of the possibility of challenges going to the ECJ and its role in providing rulings on questions of Community law that the domestic courts cannot resolve – vital given that there are still judges in the UK who object to receiving submissions on 'foreign' law! But lawyers should also be aware of the growing number of new EU laws on the horizon that will eventually take effect in the UK and impact on their clients. Co-operation between nations may have started with coal and steel but the European sphere has now extended to cover many areas of our lives: security, crime and justice, job creation and employment rights, agriculture, regional development, competition policy, safety standards and the environment.

5.3   Law is central to the European Union project: the citizens of 25 states would not be guaranteed certain minimum standards, rights or treatment without a legal order to enforce the Union's agreements. Even more fundamentally, whether the EU has 'competence' – or the power (or duty) to act is essentially a legal question and one that any Brussels-based campaigner will ask before embarking on action. This question is answered only partly by the Treaties that created the Communities (and now the Union) and is frequently tested in the ECJ. It is not a straightforward question as in some areas the Union has sole competence to act; in others powers are shared between the member states and the EU's institutions. This set-up means that before considering specific law reforms, campaigners will sometimes have to start from first base and lobby for the EU to be given 'competence' in their area – so that it can go on to legislate. The provisions to take action on discrimination (on race and other grounds) that were inserted into the 1997 Amsterdam Treaty are a good example of this (see para 5.129 for a case study of this).

5.4   As with domestic lobbying, lawyers have the opportunity to be proactive; to help create or influence EU laws and policies before they are fully formed and before they are faced with their effects in court. But in some ways the opportunities for influence are greater than in the domestic context. The EU operates by negotiation; so many member states cannot possibly agree with each other on everything all of the time and this leaves room for 'give or take' and shifting alliances to take advantage of. The Commission is very open to engagement with 'outsiders'. Parliament's increased legislative powers have made it all the more worthwhile to engage with MEPs who in fact have more chance than most MPs to scrutinise and alter draft laws (and on occasion to reject drafts). Unlike the domestic sphere, lawyers also have a role to play in altering the EU's own powers, duties and 'competence' to act.

What is this chapter about?

5.5   The European Union continues to expand in size. Decisions are increasingly taken at EU level. It is therefore all the more important for lawyers to understand the EU's unique set of institutions, political processes and conventions in order to influence its laws, policies and practices. This chapter gives a potted history of the EU followed by the key facts about the EU's current workings that will be of most interest to UK lawyers. It includes information about how to have influence at an early stage – both to promote your ideas for reform as well as to respond to policies being floated in Brussels, and further down the road at how to engage with scrutiny of EU proposals by the UK Parliament. Finally it looks at how lawyers can work effectively with NGOs.

From partnership to Union: a potted history of the European Union

5.6   Initial co-operation for economic purposes combined with the driving motivation to make war between France and Germany 'not merely unthinkable, but materially impossible'[1] led to partnership and a degree of union between very different states. This is not the place for a detailed history of how this came about. John Pinder gives a brilliant summary of developments between 1950 and 2001 in his book about the European Union.[2] But a description of the two major forces or schools of thought (federalism and inter-governmentalism) together with a short summary of how early co-operation led to the European Union of today, gives a useful framework within which contemporary efforts to influence institutions, laws and policies can be understood. It shows in particular how Parliament's powers have gradually increased, to give it joint law-making responsibility with the Council in most areas.

Two schools of thought: the federalists versus the inter-governmentalists

5.7   The inter-governmental approach can be broadly described as the belief that co-operation or otherwise must be based on the acts and negotiations between individual sovereign nation states. By contrast, the federalists have consistently pushed first for the European Community and now the broader European Union to develop its own institutions and procedures whose decisions will bind individual nation states. They have sought a kind of 'United States of Europe' with its own centralised government. According to Pinder the inter-governmentalists view governments as the key players in decision making – primarily pursuing their own interests, always motivated by the interests of their own nation state to the exclusion of the wider movement. For them institutions other than the European Council and the Council of Ministers lack the relevance or power to merit engagement. In contrast, the federalists see the development of a full range of shared institutions (courts, Parliament and an executive) with real decision-making power as the way forward, rather than co-operation only between individual

---

1   Robert Schuman, the French Foreign Minister who launched the European Coal and Steel Community on 9 May 1950, now celebrated as Europe Day.

2   J Pinder, *The European Union: a very short introduction*, Oxford University Press, 2001.

governments. They see some spheres of activity as genuinely outside the scope of individual nation states, who must co-operate to deal with them. They are also keen to develop institutions in which citizens have some control over decisions – the inter-governmental method 'is neither effective nor democratic enough to satisfy the needs of citizens of democratic states'.[3]

5.8   These divergent approaches dominated the development of the EU in its first half century, and continue today to determine its direction and its 'speed of travel' as well as the balance of decision-making power between its chief institutions. However, the picture is inevitably more complicated – with nations being 'federalist' on some matters and inter-governmentalist on others. In addition, whilst some politicians and citizens have signalled that the moves towards ever greater union should slow down, this does not mean that they have a wish to row back from the Union altogether.

The early days

5.9   Soon after the end of World War II, a partnership between six nations[4] marked the beginning of a long and ever-developing process of co-operation between a growing number of European states. The European Coal and Steel Community derived from the desire to put the 'raw materials of war' (coal, steel and atomic energy) beyond the control of any one nation.[5] It was formalised in a Treaty signed in 1951. Following its success, the same six states agreed in 1957 on the creation of a European Economic Community (EEC) and a European Atomic Energy Community (Eurotom).

5.10   The EEC, established by the Treaty of Rome, provided for a common market for the six founder states. It was founded on the principle of freedom of movement for people, capital and goods and services. After a period of distancing itself during the 1950s, during the 1960s Britain's attitude changed, and having been turned down twice (in 1963 and 1967) in 1973 she secured entry to the European Community.

---

3 Pinder, p7.

4 France, Germany, Belgium, Luxembourg, Italy and the Netherlands.

5 H Barnett, *Britain unwrapped: government and constitution explained*, Penguin, 2002, p163.

1986–2005: key developments

5.11 There have been numerous changes to the nature of the Community (now Union) that Britain belatedly joined. Each Treaty or Act has had three key elements: the strengthening of the institutions (in particular the Parliament's powers); the extension of policy areas in which the Community or Union can take an interest and make decisions; and provision for stronger economic union. A common thread has been allowances for some countries to take a slower route or opt out of certain provisions, without stopping others from forging ahead in closer co-operation.

5.12 **The Single European Act:** This law, passed in 1986, allowed for completion of the single market; widened the Community's areas of interest (including foreign policy co-operation); and significantly enhanced the Parliament's powers, by introducing a 'co-operation procedure' and a procedure mandating Parliament's assent to treaties of association and accession. Crucially, it introduced qualified majority voting in the Council for most of the single market legislation, ensuring that the legislative process could proceed at a much faster pace.

A three-pillar Europe

5.13 A common confusion when speaking about Europe is the distinction between the European Community (EC) and the European Union (EU). Essentially, the EU was brought into being by the Treaty of European Union 1992 (the 'Maastricht Treaty') which came into force in November 1993. The existing EC and its institutions and the other communities (the ECSC and Eurotom) merged to become a first pillar within the overall Union umbrella. The second and third pillars were new. They introduced co-operation in foreign and security policy (second pillar) and co-operation in justice and home affairs (ie internal security and freedom of movement but later renamed 'police and judicial co-operation in criminal matters') (third pillar). The division of the EU into three pillars reflected the tensions between the federal and inter-governmental approach. Member states held differing views about the extent to which matters should be dealt with by way of inter-governmental co-operation or agreement or by leaving them to be determined and enforced by the collective, Community institutions. Many states for example, were happy for the subjects of the third pillar to be dealt with by Community institutions (ie be in the first pillar) but Britain and others did not initially agree.

5.14 The second pillar on foreign policy and security, also emerged from differing views. France and Germany both favoured a common foreign policy but whilst France was keen for an inter-governmental approach, Germany preferred involvement of the Community institutions. Britain, as usual, preferred the inter-governmental approach. The result was another pillar with each state able to opt in or out of individual matters, rather than foreign policy being wholly incorporated into the Community's area of competence.

5.15   **The Maastricht Treaty:** This Treaty also included provisions setting out a timetable leading to full economic and monetary union, including the creation of a single currency and a European Central Bank; formalised the principle of subsidiarity and again extended the reach of the Community's fields of interest (eg to education and public health). Parliament was granted 'co-decision' powers in many legislative areas, which meant that its approval was needed for many EU laws to come into force. It was also granted the power to approve or reject the appointment of each new Commission.

5.16   **The Amsterdam Treaty:** This came into force in 1999 and made further preparations for enlargement. The European Parliament's power of 'co-decision' was extended to include most legislation and its powers in relation to the Commission were significantly enhanced, in particular by being given the power to approve the President (who has the power to accept or reject nominations for the other Commission members).

5.17   The third pillar (justice and home affairs) was brought within the competence of the Community, enabling the Community to legislate in areas such as asylum and the immigration of third country nationals.

5.18   The practice that had grown up of some nation states proceeding without or at a faster pace than others, was formalised by the Treaty, through a new process of 'enhanced co-operation'. With the difficulties of reaching agreement between an ever-growing number of members, this gave legitimacy to the practice of a group of states (a minimum of eight) choosing to proceed at their own speed on a certain issue.

5.19   Employment (in the form of the 'social chapter') was added to its scope when the new Labour government that came into power in 1997 decided to reverse the previous administration's insistence on an opt-out. The social chapter was an attempt to tackle areas of high unemployment and focused on encouraging co-operation between member states and sharing best practice.

> Intergovernmental Conferences (IGCs) are the forums in which Treaties are revised or created. Unanimity is required and a treaty must then be submitted to national Parliaments (and sometimes the electorate via referenda) for ratification. IGCs have developed not only into the main constitution-making forum within the EU but more broadly into arenas in which governments can advance different views as to the overall direction and approach of the union. A simple majority of the member states is required to convene an IGC.

5.20 **The Treaty of Nice:** This Treaty, brought into force in 2003, primarily focused on enlargement. With the vast expansion of the Union in mind, and no doubt thinking that unanimity could paralyse any decision making, the Treaty considerably extended qualified majority voting and also weighted votes. Other notable elements were the establishment of a European Security and Defence Policy and agreement on a Charter of Fundamental Rights.

5.21   **An EU Constitution:** The next significant development was the move towards a draft constitution for the Union. In 2001 the Convention on the Future of Europe was tasked to examine the existing Treaties and recommend changes. The process, which took place during 2002–03, was described by many as a genuine attempt at a more democratic approach to EU integration. NGOs and others in civil society worked hard to influence the process, lobbying MEPs and Convention Board members as well as politicians in their member states. The Convention decided to amalgamate and simplify existing treaties. However it also sought to make some important changes: creating a full time President of the European Council and a European Foreign Minister; increasing the role of national Parliaments in relation to draft laws and extending qualified majority voting to more areas. A draft Treaty was agreed by member states at an IGC in June 2004. It then fell to national Parliaments and referenda in each member state to approve or reject the Treaty.

5.22   Overall across the EU the constitution opened up major debates about fundamental issues including the future direction and role of the EU, the relationship of its institutions with citizens in the member states, and the place of member states within the EU. When French and then Dutch citizens voted against ratification in May and June 2005 the whole process was thrown into turmoil and EU leaders scrapped the 2006 ratification deadline. The French vote was interpreted in different ways: as a protest against their government in times of high unemployment; concern about the government ceding too much power to the EU and a fear of an ultra-free market economy that would undermine the French welfare state. Some immediately predicted the death of the constitution. Others spoke of a 'constitution lite', a cut-down and less controversial version that would have more chance of ratification. Others argued that some of the reforms contained in the original could be introduced by other means, like agreement among heads of state.

5.23   **Enlargement:** In May 2004 a further ten countries joined the EU, bringing its membership to 25. This has led to a raft of further issues and challenges, ranging from the practicalities of debate and decision making with such a large membership through to domestic legal issues such as the plight of asylum-seekers from the accession countries already in the UK who had housing and other support suddenly withdrawn from them on the day their countries joined the EU. Two more states, Bulgaria and Romania, are to join the EU in 2007.

Policy-making and the European Union

5.24   This section is about the types of EU law, the processes for developing policy and new laws; the role played by each institution and how to make your views heard.

Types of EU law

5.25   The Treaties are the principal source of EU law and give the institutions their law-making powers. The Treaty of Rome still provides the basis for the EU's decisions and responsibilities, although it has been substantially amended since it was signed in 1957 (especially by the Maastricht and Amsterdam Treaties – with the latter re-numbering many of the original articles). The draft constitution would have consolidated the Treaties, as well as adding some extra powers. Its likely demise mean that the Treaties remain the nearest thing the Union has to a written constitution.

5.26   The Treaty of Rome provides for three additional sources or types of EU law: **regulations** (binding in their entirety and directly applicable in member states, although sometimes requiring supplementary domestic laws for their full implementation); **directives** (which in effect lay down minimum standards, thereby giving member states a degree of discretion to decide the exact form the law will take and a deadline for its introduction); and **decisions** (binding only on specific governments or companies, etc). An important fourth source is the

case-law of the ECJ. Alongside these, you will sometimes hear of the Commission or Council issuing **recommendations** or **opinions**. To date these have had no legal effect but have sometimes been persuasive or signalled a new or developing policy which may lead to legislation at a later stage. However, recent case-law suggests that they may after all have legal effect.

5.27   Most people tend to be more familiar with directives than other forms of EU law – perhaps because the room for variation in how member states transpose the law leads to a fair amount of consultation and involvement, but it is vital for lawyers to be fully aware of the other types of EU law as well.

How are EU policies and laws made?

5.28   In chapter 2 we looked at how domestic policies emerge in the UK and in Chapter 4 at how the political parties develop policy. European policy making is less co-ordinated and more complex, essentially involving a series of negotiations and compromises between individual member states and competition for power between the key institutions. The tensions between federalism and inter-governmentalism have led to different ways of making policy (eg in the type of vote taken in the Council of Ministers or in the degree to which Parliament will be involved in policy making in a given area). Moreover any action in a particular policy area may be preceded by a lack of certainty or disagreement as to whether the EU has the power or authority to act. The latter is hard to imagine in a domestic context; it would mean every single government department being challenged on their authority to bring forward proposals in the annual Queen's Speech.

5.29   In spite of these complexities, there are some patterns to follow in EU policy and law making.

5.30   It is virtually always the Commission who initiates new legislation (within the Community pillar). Proposals for new laws come from numerous sources: European Council projects or strategies; legislation that falls from IGCs or new Treaties; from within the EU's institutions (eg the Council or the European Parliament exercising its 'right to request'); international agreements that require EU action; regional matters pursued by groups of member states, policies pursued by a particular member state; cross-national agendas like the environmental lobby; pressure from NGOs and other stakeholders and occasionally Presidency initiatives.

5.31   As the Commission works on a proposal it will be influenced by different factors, including think-tanks, public opinion, its own staff's engagement with the issues and of course by officials' interaction with the Council and the Parliament as drafts are discussed and amended.

5.32   However, both the Commission and the Council have had to cede some policy-making power to Parliament. 'Co-decision' is now the dominant procedure, meaning that in most cases both the Parliament and the Council must agree legislation for it to be passed. When other procedures are followed, Parliament's involvement varies but is still significant. The adoption of new policies or laws is also affected by the member state holding the Presidency, their degree of keenness to see proposals through the system (and the amount of resources they have invested in the Presidency). Of course even when policies are successfully adopted their implementation can vary widely across the member states.

5.33   **Significance of the three pillars:** To date it has been important to remember the distinctions between the first pillar (where the institutions hold sway) and the second and third pillars (where the nature of decision making is agreement between the governments of each member state).

5.34   It is the competence of Community institutions within the first pillar that will usually give you the opportunity to engage. Almost always it is only under the first pillar that EU legislation can be made. For this reason European legislation is technically 'Community legislation' although it is commonly called 'EU' or 'European' law.

5.35   To make policy or law under the second and third pillars, member states generally sign up to common positions; joint actions; declarations; common strategies; or international agreements. Here, influencing has to be carried out at member state level, and factor in that many decisions still have to be taken unanimously.

5.36   The distinctions used to be very important. However, an increasing number of policy areas have now been transferred into the first pillar. For example, in 1997, asylum, immigration, visas and other matters relating to free movement of persons were transferred into the first pillar. A sufficient number of states believed that a greater degree of parliamentary control (via the European Parliament) and judicial oversight (via the ECJ) was required in these important areas.

5.37   The third pillar is confined to criminal justice (and includes the criminal aspects of immigration). Britain has an opt out on all 'Title IV' measures – ie on EU agreements on asylum, immigration and borders.[6] However, it only exercises its opt out in relation to measures

---

6   Title IV of the Treaty of Rome contains measures on visas, asylum, immigration and 'other policies related to free movement of persons'.

which it considers interfere with its own border controls including namely legal migration. It opts into all illegal migration measures. Other member states have not allowed the UK to participate in the border agency, a matter which is now the subject of legal action by the UK.

5.38   Overall, most matters are now within the first pillar. Under the draft constitution Treaty, the pillars were to disappear and virtually everything was to be dealt with via the EU's institutions. Foreign and security matters were no longer to have their own pillar, but would have special arrangements 'protecting' them from full scrutiny by the Community's institutions. Although the Treaty may not be adopted in its original form, it is possible that changes along these lines will still be achieved in the near future.

How to have influence?

The importance of 'getting in early'

5.39   **'Get in early. EU policies are like supertankers – a small nudge early on can make a huge difference to the end position, but the later you leave it the harder you have to push to make any difference at all. Produce the first bit of paper and you have set the agenda'.[7]**

5.40   Years before they reach the UK courts, ideas for EU laws are discussed and formulated. By the time regulations reach the UK there is no scope for altering them; they do not require UK legislation in order to take effect. Although directives leave member states some discretion about the new laws they must introduce, by the time this stage is reached, the UK government may only have relatively limited room for manoeuvre or may indeed choose to transpose the law in a way that is undesirable. (Moreover, most directives are implemented in the UK through secondary rather than primary legislation, and as we saw in chapter 3, this considerably weakens Parliament's and lobbyists' ability to scrutinise the draft law.)

5.41   Provided that the EU has 'competency' or a legal base in your area of interest you then need to identify where the power or ability to influence lies within the main EU institutions. The applicable procedures and the balance of power will vary widely between the Council, the Commission and the Parliament, according to the matter in hand as well as the stage the proposal has reached. Within the target institution/s, who are the individuals in whom decision-making power or

7   M Stanley, *How to be a civil servant*, 2nd edn, Politico's, 2004, p71.

influence is vested? Different players will need to be targeted at different times. Contrary to how EU matters are often reported in the UK media, much decision-making power rests with the member states so sometimes activities should focus primarily on lobbying our own ministers and officials rather than anyone in Brussels. The best advice of all is to get in as early as possible – ie to influence a Commission official or a parliamentary committee rapporteur before they put pen to paper.

The main EU institutions

5.42   The EU or 'Europe' as many Britons (inaccurately) shorten it to is often described as complex and bureaucratic – including by its supporters. In some ways this is justified. Its institutions and procedures can seem jargon-filled and baffling. But in other respects this analysis is unfair. In terms of influencing there is a very simple way of looking at it. There are three main institutions you will be seeking to influence: the Council of the European Union and Council of Ministers; the Commission – a kind of European civil service; and the European Parliament. When you fail to achieve your goals through these, there is the ECJ to turn to. This basic structure has been in place for several decades, but the powers of each institution and balance between them has altered significantly and no doubt will continue to do so. There are clear and systematic processes for making law and policy (including consultations) and although they are unique to the EU, involve many of the same tools and techniques that you would use in seeking to influence domestic policy and law making.

The European Council

5.43   There are in fact two councils: first, the European Council which comprises heads of state or government and the Commission President; and second, the Council of the EU (or the Council of Ministers, its former official title). The European Council is at the top of the EU 'tree' although it is more of a forum than a formal institution, comprising the quarterly summits of heads of state or government plus the European Commission President. Foreign ministers and sometimes finance ministers also attend in addition to this core group. Ministers attend as representatives rather than delegates. It has a broad and high-level strategic and policy-making function, rather like the Board of any large organisation, described in the Maastricht Treaty as 'to provide the Union with the necessary impetus for its development ... and define the general political guidelines thereof'. It sets the general strategic and political direction and, rather like the UK government's Cabinet or similar structures, it deals with those matters that have to be decided at the highest level, or in areas of disagreement (ie matters left unresolved by the Council of the EU). This can lead to the problem-solving role taking precedence over the more long-term and strategic thinking, although most summit agendas will reflect a desire to cover both areas of responsibility. Major projects will often be launched at European Council meetings – March 2000 saw the announcement of the 'Lisbon strategy' with its ambitions to transform the Union into 'the most competitive and dynamic knowledge-based economy in the world' and the Copenhagen summit at the end of 2002 concluded negotiations on enlargement.

5.44   The European Council's links with and accountability to the European Parliament are reflected in its obligation to submit a report to the European Parliament after each meeting and to produce an annual report on progress achieved by the Union. In addition the Parliament's President has the right to address European Council meetings.

5.45   In spite of increased power on the part of the Commission and the Parliament the European Council retains the power to set the broad goals which determine the direction and content of the other institutions' decision making. The presidency system has allowed each President to make their mark, introducing major initiatives that then have to be seen through. However, this has to be put in the context of the Commission and Parliament's significant increase in decision-making powers.

The Council of Ministers

5.46   'The major control mechanism through which states give up autonomy in return for well-guaranteed access and influence'.[8]

5.47   **Role and functions:** The Council of Ministers (the 'Council') is the chief decision-making body with both legislative and executive powers. It operates within the overall direction set down by the European Council. The Council legislates (now usually jointly with the Parliament) – but in almost all cases only once the Commission has initiated a proposal (although it can with the Parliament instruct the Commission to investigate and present proposals in an area of its choice); co-ordinates the EU's economic policies; concludes international agreements;

8   Wolfgang Wessels.

and approves the EU's budget (with Parliament). In relation to the second and third pillars it develops the common foreign and security policy and co-ordinates co-operation between national courts and police forces in criminal matters – adopting 'common positions' or taking 'joint actions'.

The Presidency

When you hear about the rapidly changing (every 6 months) EU Presidency (held by the UK during the last half of 2005), this is a reference to being President of the Council of Ministers and of the European Council. Presidency duties include chairing meetings of the European Council and Council of Ministers; representing the Council in negotiations with other EU institutions; overseeing EU foreign policy and promoting co-operation between member states. The Presidency is a key time to engage with that particular member state. Organisations factor this into their plans, as if there are member states that need convincing about the value of a policy (or encouraged to oppose it) the Presidency is an ideal time to raise it. During a UK Presidency, both the Whitehall and Brussels-based operations will be 'beefed up' and each department will have a key contact with responsibility for co-ordinating Presidency-related matters. In addition to progressing matters already in train, the member state will also identify its own themes and priorities, organising events and activities on key policy areas. These offer opportunities for engagement and influence but groups need to act early and think ahead, identifying opportunities well before a member state takes up the Presidency.

5.48   The Council is a chameleon – meeting in different forms, eg as the Justice and Home Affairs Council or the Economic and Financial Council.[9] Participating ministers will vary from meeting to meeting, depending on the nature of business under discussion. The General Affairs and External Relations Council is made up of foreign ministers and as well as discussing foreign affairs also has a general co-ordinating role over the other Councils and prepares the European

---

9   The nine Council configurations are: General Affairs and External Relations; Justice and Home Affairs; Employment, Social Policy, Health and Consumer Affairs; Competitiveness; Transport, Telecommunications and Energy; Agriculture and Fisheries; Economic and Financial Affairs; Environment; Education, Youth and Culture.

Council meetings. The appropriate European Commissioner attends Council meetings.

5.49 The Council is often described as secretive and therefore difficult for outsiders to influence. Liberal Democrat MP Chris Huhne, when criticising the UK's decision to maintain the closed nature of EU ministerial meetings during the 2005 Presidency, claimed that the 'only two legislatures apart from the EU Council of Ministers that regularly meet in secret are those of Cuba and North Korea'. Certainly many of the Council's meetings (around 90 a year) are held in private and many of the Council's deliberations remain very secretive, in spite of efforts to make it more open. However, it is probably fair to say that the level of secrecy (or openness) varies. Officials and sometimes non-government expert advisers will attend meetings (although dinners will sometimes be confined to ministers only) and may share information more widely.

5.50 There are no guarantees that once a proposal has reached Council level it will be passed. It may be rejected, amended or no decision taken at all. Alliances between groups of member states are constantly changing, according to the issue at hand (or tactical considerations about where support might be needed for another upcoming matter). Common tactics include assessing where another state will exercise a veto, thus escaping any criticism from interest groups at home for blocking a measure. It is an interesting creation, both acting as a forum for national interests but also as a fully-fledged EU institution empowered to act for the Union as a whole.

How is the Council run?

5.51 The Committee of Permanent Representatives (COREPER) is an extremely influential group made up of ambassadors to the EU chosen by each member state to head up their 'embassy' or 'national representation'. COREPER ambassadors and their deputies (COREPER II) meet to discuss Council meeting agendas and prepare to brief ministers. Former Minister Alan Clark went so far as to say: 'Everything is decided and horse-traded off by officials at COREPER'.[10]

5.52 The next level down from COREPER is the working groups which are staffed by civil servants from the member states and the national representations. Both levels seek to resolve key points so that only major disputes are left for the next tier up to deal with. The Commission is fully represented at both levels. In practice matters may go to and

10 A Clark, *Diaries*, London: Farrar, Straus and Giroux, 1993.

from the various levels, with efforts made to narrow down the issues and areas of disagreement.

5.53   The UK's national representation is called UKRep (UK Permanent Representation to the European Union) and is headed by a Permanent Representative and a Deputy Permanent Representative. This group of officials (technically diplomats belonging to the Foreign Office) act as the arm of the UK government in Brussels and represent the UK in day-to-day negotiations. They can be a useful source of information about current Commission activities and the state of play of legislative proposals emanating from the Commission. They are organised around the various configurations that the Council takes.

5.54   In the UK the Cabinet Office has a co-ordinating role in relation to EU matters and Number Ten also takes a keen interest.

5.55   The member state holding the Presidency takes responsibility for organising day-to-day Council business, supported by a permanent general secretariat (and also drawing on its own national representation in Brussels).

Voting in the Council

5.56   There are three types of vote: unanimous, qualified majority voting (QMV) or simple majority. The main trend to be aware of is the shift from unanimity to qualified majority voting (QMV). The aim of this is to ensure that measures can be passed without blockage from just one nation, of increasing concern as the Union expands. QMV has gradually been extended to more and more legislation and other decisions (now covering about four-fifths of all legislative acts) where consensus is not reached. Simple majority and unanimity remain for some areas. Unanimity for example is required for the adoption of any measure which involves amendment of the Commission's original proposal against the Commission's wishes. QMV has shifted power away from the Council to the Commission as it prevents one or two vociferous governments blocking a proposal. The UK has ten votes (like France, Germany and Italy). The very existence of QMV voting changes the dynamics of negotiation and promotes consensus. For most measures the matter never reaches a vote. Member states do however retain the right to a veto on a 'vital' national interest.

Influencing the Council

5.57   This has to be achieved at member state level, and effectively involves lobbying the right officials and minister. However, securing the UK's agreement is not enough. They may agree with your policy calls but will be reliant on a number of other member states taking the same view to get their way. This reinforces the need for lobbying and influencing to take place across the member states, for example through an NGO operating at pan-European level.

The European Commission

5.58   **Role and functions:** Like the Council, the European Commission also has both an executive and a legislative role. The Council delegates a fair amount of work (including legislation) to the Commission.

- The Commission has the sole right to initiate legislation in most – but not all – cases.
- The Commission also has a broad policy-making role – in some areas explicitly provided for in Treaty provisions (eg competition policy) – but in others a general discretion to make new policy suggestions.
- Much of the Commission's management and/or watchdog role is delegated to member states and it is probably fair to conclude that any weakness as an executor is at least in part due to insufficient resources. In this capacity the Commission seeks to ensure that member states implement and apply Community legislation. Non-compliant states will be issued with a 'reasoned opinion'; if they continue to fail to comply the Commission takes the country to the ECJ and financial penalties can follow. The Commission is sometimes criticised for not carrying out this part of its role effectively enough.
- Finally, the Commission has a negotiating role, eg externally in relation to trade and internally in relation to agreeing the annual Community budget.

How does the Commission work?

5.59   There is now one Commissioner for each member state, each taking responsibility for a different policy area and serving for 5 years (unless Parliament decides to dismiss them earlier). For example, the current UK Commissioner Peter Mandelson has the trade portfolio. A cap of 27 Commissioners has been placed on any future arrangements. There is a Commission President (José Manuel Barroso's term runs from 2004–09) and a number of Vice-Presidents.

5.60   The Commission's work is split into 37 Directorates-General (DGs) and other services (eg the Legal Service), each headed by a Director-General who reports directly to the relevant Commissioner. Each DG has a cabinet, a group of officials working directly to them. Two DGs that will be of particular interest to publicly funded lawyers are Employment, Social Affairs and Equal Opportunities, and Justice, Freedom and Security.

5.61   'The Commission' refers both to the core 'college' of Commissioners but also to the 20,000 or so European officials who work for the institution.

Law-making: the Commission's role

5.62   For a lawyer seeking to influence the Commission, its most significant role is its power to initiate legislation – in virtually all areas unique to the Commission and not held by either the Council or the Parliament. It would be highly unusual for the Council ever to legislate other than on a Commission proposal. The Commission drafts specific measures as well as broader policy packages that may require several pieces of legislation. It can also make recommendations and opinions (see para 5.26 for more about these). Proposals go on to the Council and Parliament for consideration. It also has a more limited capacity to adopt Community legislation on its own initiative.

5.63   **The process:** The relevant officials will prepare the draft law (regulation, directive or decision) after consulting both internally and externally. The co-decision procedure now applies to most matters, meaning that after the Commission initiates the legislation, both the Council and Parliament will play a role in discussing, amending and eventually passing or rejecting it. Once adopted, the Commission will then have responsibility for ensuring effective transposition into national law (for directives) and implementation across the EU. See para 5.75 for more about the co-decision procedure.

5.64   **Open method of co-ordination:** There are many occasions when member state governments want EU-wide discussion or action but without going down the legal route which they feel may be burdensome or unnecessary. Since 2000 the 'open method of co-ordination' is the process by which this can be achieved, helping member states 'to progressively develop their own policies'. It is created by the Commission (and delivered by the relevant DG). A good example is health and consumer policy where member states were keen to learn more about different approaches being taken which might lead them to take action or formulate new laws, but with the advantage of having looked at what was already working (or not). Usual activities would include the establishment of benchmarks as a means of comparing best practice, guidelines and timetables and mechanisms for monitoring and evaluation.

Influencing the Commission

5.65 As it is in the Commission that ideas and policies are first formed and legislation initiated, making inroads and seeking to influence Commission officials at an early stage can reap large rewards. Unlike the Council the Commission operates in an open and transparent fashion and officials are generally pleased to engage with outside groups. Initiatives will then go to the Council of Ministers which is hugely difficult to influence, principally because proceedings are in secret. It can be difficult even to establish the officials who will be taking part, let alone the positions that will be taken by the member states.

Tips:

5.66 • You need to identify the Commission official/s handling your area/policy of interest. It is easy to identify the right people: the website gives details including the names and contact details, etc of team leaders, etc.

• Check also for key documents, including the Annual Policy Strategy (which marks the beginning of the annual policy cycle), and the Annual Work Programme which is published shortly afterwards (and is debated in the European Parliament). These documents may flag up proposals before they become the subject of detailed work.

• Like the UK civil service, the Commission often issues consultation papers (sometimes in the form of green papers) inviting comments. Across Europe responses are often not spread evenly (or may be skewed to one area or member state). They therefore offer considerable opportunity to get your views across. A green paper on future equality actions, for example, attracted a very large number of responses from German organisations concerned with discrimination against lesbians, gays and bisexuals and far fewer from groups concerned with other forms of discrimination.

• You also need to identify the British officials, based both in Brussels and London, who are best able to help your cause. It can be difficult to assess who is the right target as it could be any of the following: (i) UKREP (the civil servants who are seconded from their departments to serve for a period in Brussels); (ii) EU specialists from the relevant department in Whitehall; (iii) the Cabinet Office Secretariat; or (iv) 'mainstream' officials from the relevant department who are brought in to work on a project but do not necessarily have any EU knowledge. Remember that some of these officials will be working closely together.

Consultative committees: the Economic and Social Committee and the Committee of the Regions

5.67   The Economic and Social Committee (EcoSoc) is a representative body set up by the Treaty of Rome to 'assist' the Council and Commission. It expresses the opinions of 'organised civil society' on economic and social issues although it is not always in agreement about who is best placed to represent 'civil society'! Out of around 220 members, around 24 will be from the UK (from the not-for-profit sector, employers' organisations, trade unions, etc). Member states nominate members to serve on the committee for a renewable 4-year term.

5.68   Its key role is advising the Council of Ministers on draft legislation in certain areas. In some policy areas the Commission is legally bound to consult the committee – in others it has the discretion to do so. When it receives a legislative proposal from the Commission a small working group will get to work, preparing a draft report and amendments. Neither the Council nor the Commission are bound to take account of or act on its recommendations. However, the Commission will need support from as many stakeholders as possible to get its proposals accepted, so in practice it will at least consider the committee's views. The committee conducts a range of activities, including conferences and seminars. It may run particular events during the UK Presidency (eg EcoSoc planned a conference on ageing and migration as part of the 2005 UK Presidency).

5.69   The Committee of the Regions is an EU advisory body set up many years after EcoSoc (in 1993). It is a consultative forum made up of representatives from regional and local authorities. It has a similar number of members as the Economic and Social Committee who are recommended by member states and approved by the Council of Ministers. Members tend to hold elective office either at local or regional level. In some areas the committee must be consulted (eg, economic and social cohesion); in others this is optional. However the committee (like parliamentary committees) has the power to initiate its 'own opinion' reports on matters affecting regional interests.

Influencing the committees

5.70   • Both committees can have an important agenda-setting role, flagging key issues and engaging EU institutions with them. It is worth checking who the UK members are for each committee if you are planning to do some lobbying in an area in which they will be taking an interest. For EcoSoc, member states tend to split nominees into three categories: employers, unions and 'other interests'. On many occasions the first two will vote 'en bloc' thus giving 'other interests' (who can include NGO representatives) a good bargaining position. It is worth noting that members of both committees will lobby MEPs so this can be another route to getting key points on the Parliament's radar.

The European Parliament

5.71   **Role and functions:** The European Parliament has come a long way since it was created to be a 'supervisory and advisory' body.[11] In 1979 it became a fully-fledged Parliament when the first direct elections were held and most members from then on sat only in the European Parliament rather than having a dual mandate. Since then its powers have gradually increased and it is now in effect a co-legislature (with the Council) and has a significant role in scrutinising the Commission. As the Community's areas of competence have grown, so has Parliament's scope and remit. There is not the same alignment between the political make-up of the executive and the Parliament as in national parliamentary systems (Commissioners are unelected and as a whole do not reflect particular party strengths). But the power over the Commission suggests that over time the institutions may become more aligned.

Law-making

5.72   • Around half of all legislation is now made jointly by the Council and Parliament and is subject to Parliament's approval before it can be passed (ie subject to the 'co-decision' procedure).

Supervision, scrutiny and control

5.73   Parliament's other major role is to scrutinise and hold to account other EU institutions. In this context its powers have also been noticeably strengthened.

•   Parliament now has the power to approve appointment of the Commission's President and each new group of Commissioners as a whole. With a two-thirds majority of votes cast, it can also pass a motion of censure, requiring mass resignation of all

11   The Treaty of Rome.

Commissioners. The Parliament flexed its muscles in 1999 when scandal broke out about mismanagement and corruption. Parliament unearthed dubious practices, set up an independent investigation and when it became apparent that it was willing to deploy the two-thirds majority required, the Commission 'jumped before it was pushed' and resigned en masse.

• The Parliament can take other institutions to the ECJ for infringements of the Treaties.

Authority over the EU's budget

5.74   • The Parliament has joint control (with the Council) of the Community half of the EU's budget (everything except agriculture). Council has to agree the broad parameters, but Parliament allocates the exact sums to be spent on each area.

Law-making: the co-decision procedure

Co-decision: a summary
Both Parliament and the Council read and discuss the draft legislation twice (called 'readings'). If they fail to agree a text, a conciliation committee is formed (with representatives from each side) with a view to reaching a compromise which is then formally agreed at a third and final reading. However, if this is not possible, the proposal falls.

5.75   Co-decision is now the procedure for all cases except for European Monetary Union. Its significance is that it gives the Parliament the power to stick to its guns and ultimately veto a proposal it does not agree with.

5.76   When the Council receives a proposal from the Commission, it is sent via COREPER to one of the Council Working Groups for close scrutiny. Much detailed negotiation takes place at this level. If required, the Economic and Social Committee and/or the Committee of the Regions may also be consulted at this point. At the same time the Commission submits its proposal to Parliament which communicates its opinion.

5.77   The Commission can make amendments at any time before the Council has acted on it. This often occurs when Parliament takes a view and suggests amendments, although at the same time, officials may also be suggesting alterations to the original text.

5.78   If the Council substantially alters what the Commission proposed, you may well be able to persuade parliamentarians that the Commission was right and that the proposals should revert to the original. With the ammunition of Parliament's views, the Commission is then more likely to be able to stand firm and argue for the original. After Parliament has adopted a report with amendments it goes back to the Commission which recommends to Council which amendments should be accepted.

5.79   The Council can then either agree with the Parliament's amendments and agree the law – or, it will adopt a 'common position' and seek Parliament's views on this. Parliament then communicates its view – either approving it; rejecting it outright; or proposing amendments. The Commission then delivers its opinion to the Council. On the basis of this, the Council may approve the suggested changes, in which case the measure becomes law. However, if at this stage the Council and Parliament are still in disagreement, the process goes to conciliation giving each side the chance to negotiate 'face-to-face'. A Conciliation Committee brings together 15 representatives from each institution (Council members acting by QMV; the Parliament by simple majority). This is 'breakpoint' – failure to agree means that the law falls; approval by the committee sends the measure back to the full Council and Parliament for approval or rejection (by way of a third reading and vote).

Other law-making procedures

5.80   The importance of the other law-making procedures has declined with the increase in co-decision. For a few measures the Parliament only has the right to be consulted – eg in relation to some immigration and asylum matters. It can give its opinion, requesting amendments to a proposal but ultimately can only delay its adoption rather than stall it indefinitely.

5.81   Co-operation used to be the normal mechanism for many areas but has now been overtaken by co-decision. Although Parliament had to be consulted and could propose amendments it could ultimately be overruled by the Council.

5.82   For some vitally important areas, the Council can only act with Parliament's assent. Examples include the conclusion of international agreements or applications from prospective member states.

5.83   **Initiating new laws:** In addition, although the Commission retains the right to initiate legislation, Parliament can take a more entrepreneurial approach, by ensuring it has representatives at key Commission meetings and by producing 'own initiative' reports to which it seeks the

Commission's and Council's response. And it can make recommendations to the Commission for new legislative proposals (eg arising from the Commission's annual plan which Parliament always debates).

Who's who in the Parliament?

Key leadership roles

5.84   Formal office-holders are the President, Vice-President and 'Quaestors' – all elected at the beginning of and halfway through each 5-year Parliament. The President has a wide-ranging external and internal role and much choice over which duties to carry out himself and which to delegate to Vice-Presidents. Quaestors are in charge of administration and finance. Collectively this group form the Parliament's 'Bureau'.

5.85   Other key leadership roles to be aware of are the leaders of the Political Groups and of party delegations; and committee chairs, co-ordinators and rapporteurs.

5.86   The President and political Group Chairs come together as the 'Conference of Presidents', the key decision-making group that takes internal responsibility (eg for Parliament's agenda, for drawing up membership and remit of committees and delegations) as well as being in charge of external affairs (eg relations with other Parliaments). They take on board suggestions from the committee chairs who meet regularly (as the Conference of Committee Chairs) and from the delegation chairs.

MEPs: their role and activities

5.87   MEPs' day-to-day work reflects the Parliament's chief functions as set out above. Much of their time is spent debating and voting on legislation and on monitoring and scrutinising the Commission – questioning both officials and politicians (Commissioners). This is the key difference from the UK Parliament, where MPs will be scrutinising the government and often attacking representatives from the other party/ies!

5.88   Of the 732 MEPs, 78 represent UK constituencies. It is hard to generalise about MEPs' day-to-day work: some spend more time in plenary sessions, others engage in committee work; some focus on their Political Group, whilst others are more concerned with their region and/or national party.

Political groups

5.89   Working life for MEPs is dominated by the eight official, trans-national political groups rather than the member state they are from. The two largest groups are the European People's Party (Christian Democrats) and European Democrats (which includes Conservative MEPs) which has 268 members and the Socialists Group (which includes Labour MEPs) which has 202 members. The next largest group is the Alliance of Liberals and Democrats for Europe (which includes Liberal Democrat MEPs) with 88 members. There are seven political groups altogether plus a number of 'non-attached' MEPs.

5.90   Each group exerts discipline (eg through the whips) but this is less strict than in national Parliaments (there is no governing majority to be whipped to follow or oppose).

5.91   Richard Corbett MEP describes the Groups as being of 'central importance in the work of the Parliament. It is the Groups that play the decisive role in choosing the President, Vice-Presidents and committee chairs. They set the parliamentary agenda, choose the rapporteurs and decide on the allocation of speaking time. They have their own staff, receive considerable funds from the Parliament and often influence the choice of the Parliament's top officials.'[12]

5.92   Each Group chooses how to organise itself, generally with a 'Bureau' comprising a Chair, Vice-Chairs and other officers. In larger groups these will include members from each national component of the Group, including the leader of each national party delegation. The elected Group Chair is the leader, taking part in the external dealings, including informal negotiations with other chairs. Their staff numbers depend on the Group's size, and may range from around 15 to 150 officials (mainly with temporary status). Smaller, working groups will meet to discuss legislative proposals.

5.93   Group meetings take place once a month in Brussels (during 'Group week'). They cover a range of business, in particular preparations for the forthcoming plenary sessions as well as the Group's activities which might include publications, conferences, visits from Commissioners or national party leaders. In the same week are Group working parties and national party delegations.

National delegations

5.94   Within each group are the national party delegations, members from a nation state, usually from the same party. These are a vital link to national parties, although individual members vary widely in terms of how much time they spend on party business. Many national parties have sought to increase the integration of MEPs which can be difficult

12   R Corbett, F Jacobs and M Shackleton, *The European Parliament*, 5th edn, John Harper Publishing, 2003, p59.

given the different cycle and issues they are working on. The European Parliamentary Labour Party (EPLP) is Labour MEPs' national delegation. The EPLP Leader sits on the National Executive Committee, the EPLP has representatives on the National Policy Forum and when in government ministers from each department link with a British Labour MEP from the relevant parliamentary committee.

Party federations

5.95　　Outside the Parliament the main groups have a corresponding 'European party federation' bringing together the various national parties and led by a President and Secretary-General. A key activity of these is the organisation of summits which take place just before heads of state meet in the European Council and involving heads of government, party leaders, political Group Chair and Commission members. Some federations have sought to extend MEPs' influence by also having pre-Council summits.

5.96　　An interesting feature of the Parliament is the power it gives to those who wish to come together outside the political groups (eg a coalition involving members across Groups), usually in an ad hoc manner. A certain number of members can take action such as tabling an amendment in plenary or nominating a President.

5.97　　**The culture:** In spite of being split into broad political groupings, the European Parliament is certainly more consensual than the UK Parliament, a major feature being the lack of a divide between government and opposition and a vast array of national, regional and sectoral interests. No group has an overall majority and in order to reach the numbers needed for many decisions Groups have to go into coalition with others that may be some way off their political views – working with those to the left and the right. The make-up of coalitions will in addition vary according to the issue (eg those preferring inter-governmentalism over federalism may come together on certain issues) and sometimes not be on left-right lines at all. The prevalence of committee over plenary work also helps to foster a different kind of atmosphere to the 'bear baiting' that is common sport on the floor of the UK Parliament (although less so in its committee work) with a greater emphasis on discussion and compromise. In addition proportional representation is the normal way for representatives to be elected. Finally, for the Parliament to be effective its members have to reach agreement in order to negotiate with the Council to get a desired outcome.

Levels of operation

5.98 MEPs will find themselves operating broadly at three levels: First, in seeking to influence their own political Group, they will be working with members from many different countries, in a range of languages, seeking to achieve common positions. Second, they will need to persuade members of other political groups to 'come on-side', targeting different groups according to the issue. Third, they will have in mind the need to negotiate with and influence the Council. MEPs will also have their own national party committees or working groups.

> The Parliament sits in Brussels (for committee sessions and some plenaries) for about 3 weeks per month and in Strasbourg (in plenary) – for about one week per month. Its administration (General Secretariat) is carried out in Luxembourg. A typical cycle involves a week in Strasbourg followed by 2 committee weeks in Brussels and then a week for Political Groups to meet (and prepare their positions for the following week's plenary session). Demands on Parliament's time have led to greater flexibility, with plenaries held during 'committee weeks', committee sessions during Group weeks and time allocated for more conciliation committee meetings. Fridays are kept free so that members can return to their constituencies.

Key activities

5.99 MEPs can exercise their scrutiny role in a number of ways. There are regular opportunities for oral and written questions – to both Commission and Council.

5.100 Again, as in the UK Parliament, procedural rules can be used by members for their own devices, perhaps to highlight a constituency matter, to register a protest or to prolong a debate. Since 2002 however, there has been a weekly slot to allow this kind of activity (although confined to one-minute speeches) without resorting to procedural devices.

5.101 Questions are used both to extract information and to draw attention to a specific issue.

5.102 Tabling a motion for declaration or a written resolution is a little like an MP putting down an Early Day Motion. It can be a useful technique to flag an issue and used as part of a wider campaign.

5.103 Making an 'explanation of vote' takes place after votes and therefore often to few members but are still a useful way to draw attention to an issue.

5.104   Many MEPs make full use of the tools and techniques open to them as parliamentarians. In the 2003–04 session, Claude Moraes MEP's activities included: a written declaration, calling for more rigorous implementation of the disability elements of the Employment Directive by employers and governments; speaking in plenary about the need for a comprehensive disability directive; speaking at inter-group meetings; tabling an array of oral and written questions to both the European Council and the Commission. In the UK he and other Labour MEPs met with Home Office ministers to discuss issues including immigration where the degree of EU co-operation and competence is increasing. As Labour's Employment and Social Affairs spokesperson he played an active part on the relevant parliamentary committee and wrote a report for the committee on immigration which was later adopted by the Parliament.

Committees

5.105   The European Parliament is dominated by committee work; there are 17 permanent committees covering internal policies and 3 covering external policies (eg international trade). They review the chief areas of Community activity and report to the main plenary sessions. They carry out most of the legislative scrutiny. Key committees of interest to publicly funded lawyers are: Legal Affairs; Constitutional Affairs; Employment and Social Affairs; Environment, Public Health and Food Safety; Women's Rights and Gender Equality; and Civil Liberties, Justice and Home Affairs. The strengthening of Parliament's role and the introduction of the co-decision procedure for most areas has added to the workload and importance of the Legal Committee, among others.

5.106   Parliament also has the power to set up temporary committees and committees of inquiry to investigate alleged contraventions or maladministration in the implementation of Community law or ad hoc issues of urgency (eg foot and mouth disease or the committee on the challenges of an enlarged Union).

5.107   July (immediately after the June elections) is when the number, size and remit of each committee is decided. Two and a half years later (halfway through the session) there is another opportunity for changes including to post-holders, but without wholesale change. The Political Groups then negotiate which of their members will be on each committee. As in the UK Parliament, the strength of the various political groups is reflected. Most MEPs will sit on one committee as a full member and another as a substitute, although there is not too much practical difference between the roles. Groups get to choose committees to chair (and vice-chair – three per group) according to a system of proportional representation. Each Political Group has a series of co-ordinators to cover the committees, each acting as a specialist in and spokesperson for the committee's subject area. These roles are an excellent opportunity for parliamentarians who wish to build on or develop a specialism in a key policy area. Their tasks include discussing committee agendas and who is to have a 'rapporteurship' and to allocate tasks to members of their own groups.

5.108   **Role and activities:** Most committee business centres on discussing draft reports and opinions with the bulk of the work being the consideration of draft legislation (or other documents). A Council or Commission proposal will be referred to the relevant committee (and sometimes to other committees but only for an opinion – they will not have a vote). But in addition committees are free to take the initiative and draft a report on a subject of their choice, in relation to which there is no formal consultation of Parliament. The balance of legislative and non-legislative work will vary widely between committees. Once a report or opinion is to be prepared a rapporteur is appointed who takes responsibility for a number of tasks from preparation of the initial discussion and text through to presenting the committee's opinion and recommendations in plenary. For important reports Groups will appoint their own shadow rapporteurs.

5.109   After an introduction by the rapporteur other members of the committee are able to give their views. Commission officials (or Commissioners if the matter is deemed sufficiently important) will attend. They can be questioned by MEPs. There may also be Council or Presidency officials observing rather than taking part. Committee meetings are usually open to the public. Initial discussion is followed by a draft from the rapporteur who must strive to reflect the committee's (and not their Group's) views. At a further session, members, having seen the draft can vote on amendments or the resolution.

5.110   **Example:** The Legal Affairs committee has 49 members, 25 full and the rest substitutes. UK MEP members are Diana Wallis (EPP-ED); Arlene McCarthy (substitute, Socialist Group) and Malcolm Harbour (substitute, EPP-ED). The EPP-ED group holds the chair but two out of the three vice-chair posts are held by the Socialist Group.

5.111   **Influencing committees:** You need to identify key members (not only from the UK) and in particular the co-ordinators, rapporteurs (and shadow rapporteurs). Again, it is important to get in early, eg to be influencing the rapporteur before they start to draft their report.

Plenary sessions

5.112   There is a lot to pack into the plenaries and Groups and committees will negotiate for slots for their reports to be debated. There will also be oral questions, debates on legislative and non-legislative reports, requests for statements from the Council or Commission. Legislation at various stages will need to be dealt with – eg the Parliament must consider common positions from the Council (where the co-operation procedure applies).

5.113   The Parliament has the right to debate the Commission's annual plan for legislation.

Inter-groups

5.114   Like All Party Groups in the UK Parliament, there are inter-groups on all manner of issues ranging from Amici Curiae, to Health and Anti-Racism right through to Friends of Cycling, and the North Sea. As their numbers have increased, more rules and regulations have been introduced (eg to have three chairs from different political Groups), with some operating with official status, others unofficially. They are a useful tool for lobbyists as they offer an opportunity to engage with MEPs with a genuine interest in a specific field.

Ombudsman

5.115   A Parliamentary Ombudsman investigates complaints from EU citizens (or residents) alleging maladministration by Community institutions or bodies (apart from the ECJ).

Petitions

5.116   Any EU citizen or resident can petition the Parliament on an issue of EU interest or responsibility that directly affects them. The Committee on Petitions considers petitions and chooses from a number of options, including asking the Commission to conduct a preliminary investigation; refer it to another parliamentary committee for consideration; or exceptionally submit a report to Parliament to be voted on.

Constituency work

5.117   Like MPs, MEPS are approached by constituents, keen for help with specific problems (eg an accident that occurred in another member state or an employment question) or to query policies, laws or to lobby them on a cause. Given their regional base they will also have a range of people and organisations to keep in contact with, including businesses, unions, development agencies, colleges and schools, local and regional government and their local and regional political party offices. They will need to respond to matters of European legislation and EU funding. MEPs are increasingly proactive, often producing newsletters, websites and encouraging constituents to contact them about any EU matter within the remit of Parliament.

How to engage with MEPs

5.118
- Now that MEPs are organised on a list system you can contact any MEP responsible for your region. The constituency or regional links are very important to them.
- If you request a short meeting with one of your MEPs when they are in the UK (you can find them at www.europarl.org.uk/uk_meps/ MembersMain.htm), think about their interests and how these might dovetail with yours. Find out about the committees they serve on and areas of common interest. They will appreciate a short email rather than a detailed legal text.
- Ask your MEP/s to speak at a meeting – about how Parliament works and their key interests. If you can combine this with a photo opportunity this will be appreciated!
- If you are interested in finding out first hand how the institutions operate, some MEPs organise annual visits to Brussels for constituents.
- You need to bear in mind that the MEP/s you need to target may very well be from another member state. For example, a Polish or French MEP may be the rapporteur (responsible for writing Parliament's opinion) on the legal affairs committee. In this case you need to identify the UK MEPs on the committee and ask them to exert their influence. Or, you need to be able to use pan-European networks to reach these MEPs.
- On some policy matters, where there is a major impact on the UK, MEPs from different parties may be willing to come together for joint discussion or action. However, you would be wise to be aware of their opinions and feelings about each other before organising a meeting!
- For more information see www.europarl.eu.int – the European Parliament's website.

The European Court of Justice

5.119   The European Court of Justice (ECJ) is the supreme judicial authority in areas of 'Community competence'. Overall its role is to ensure that the principal base of EU law, the Treaties (as well as the other sources), are properly interpreted and applied. To enable it to do this it has a wide jurisdiction to hear various types of action including:

- adjudication on a member state's failure to fulfil an obligation (actions usually brought by the Commission);
- dealing with an action (brought by a member state, Community institution or an individual who is directly affected) to annul a measure (eg regulation or directive) adopted by a Community institution;
- reviewing a failure to act on the part of a Community institution;
- interpreting the Treaty and other sources of EU law for member states seeking guidance as to the proper interpretation of EU law. Cases are then sent back to the domestic court for a decision on the facts, applying the ECJ's ruling on the law.

5.120   One judge is appointed from each member state and serves for a 6-year renewable term. There are also eight Advocates-General who assess the cases and deliver preliminary opinions to assist the judges in their work. One of the judges serves as President of the Court.

5.121   Perhaps the ECJ's best-known feature is the length of time taken for cases to be heard and judgments given. As the areas in which the Union is competent to make law grow, this pressure can only increase. A Court of First Instance was created in the 1980s to deal primarily with cases brought by individuals and legal persons (eg in relation to competition policy) but despite this the ECJ still has a vast workload.

Ensuring the application of EU laws across the member states

5.122   In addition to the core doctrine of supremacy, the ECJ has effectively taken other steps to ensure the uniform application of Community laws across the EU. The strategy could be called supremacy plus! Most significantly, the Court has developed the concept of **direct effect** which allows citizens to rely on some but not all Community law provisions, in their own courts, if they are sufficiently clear and unambiguous. Citizens can invoke Treaty articles and regulations against the state and private bodies whereas directives can only be invoked against the state (although the picture is rather more complex than this).

5.123   The Court has also taken steps to plug the gap left by direct effect, of individuals not being able to rely on a directive in an action against another individual. Article 10 of the EC Treaty imposes a duty on member states to do everything they can to give effect to Community obligation and objectives. Creative use of this Article (and interpreting member states to include their courts) has developed **indirect effect**, which obliges the courts to interpret their national laws in line with a directive. An individual can rely on the directive in court and if all goes according to plan, and the court reconciles national law in line with the directive, the outcome will be as if they could have invoked the directive against their opponent.

Using the ECJ in campaigns

5.124   Although it is preferable to influence laws before they come into force, actions before the ECJ can be an important element in a campaign, just as legal challenges are used as campaigning tools in the domestic context.

5.125   The ECJ makes decisions of principle that have EU-wide effect. The Court has, for example, been proactive in its use of human rights law and establishing principles around the fundamental protection of human rights.

5.126   A number of high profile cases that are part of a wider cause or campaign are finally resolved in the ECJ (or in the European Court of Human Rights) and some are the subject of references (a ruling on the correct legal interpretation) before going back to the member state for resolution. For example, the ECJ ruled that the UK's failure to allow a woman (KB) who had worked for 20 years for the NHS and was a member of the NHS Pension Scheme to marry her trans man partner (and thereby allow him to inherit a widower's pension) was in principle a breach of EU law.[13] The ECJ said that it was for member states to determine the conditions under which legal recognition is given to changes of gender, and so the case was referred back to the national courts to determine whether a person in KB's situation could rely on Community law to nominate their partner as the beneficiary of a survivor's pension

5.127   Member states can be challenged in the ECJ for failing to implement a directive so as to achieve the desired result or to meet the deadline for compliance. Individuals also have the right to challenge a failure to comply (once the deadline has passed) and seek compensation, via the domestic courts.

13   7 January 2004, Case C-117/01.

5.128   As the above description of the ECJ's duties shows, Parliament can bring legal actions against the Council. Sometimes this is the most effective way of challenging legislation, as it does not require a victim or a reference from the domestic courts.

5.129–
5.145

Case study: EU-wide action to combat discrimination

In 2000 two new equality laws emerged from the EU: the Race Directive (RD)[14] and the Employment Directive (ED).[15] This case study looks at how the ED emerged and took shape in relation to age discrimination; how its transposition was handled in the UK; and the influence of age organisations and lawyers at key stages. It shows the importance of influencing Treaties and directives before focusing on how member states will give domestic effect to them.

What was the source or 'legal base' of the new laws?

The Amsterdam Treaty was signed on 2 October 1997 and came into force on 1 May 1999. It contained a significant change to existing Treaties: a commitment by the Union 'to take appropriate action to combat discrimination based on sex, racial or ethnic origin, religion or belief, age or sexual orientation' (Article 13).

Non-discrimination on grounds of gender or of nationality (of a member state) had been part of EU policy since the Treaty of Rome was signed in 1957. But it took 40 years for the foundation to be laid for further-reaching action on discrimination. Including a number of equality grounds in Article 13 was prompted in part by effective lobbying by NGOs working in the fields of racism and xenophobia (and on other areas). Age organisations, under the umbrella body Eurolink Age lobbied Parliament and worked hard to get the unanimous support from member state governments (necessary for agreement of any Treaty). They were able to demonstrate that the EU institutions themselves displayed blatant ageism which helped to build their case for new laws. In a sense age benefited from the stronger political commitment to other grounds and succeeded partly because there were no strong objections to its inclusion.

14   2000/43/EC.
15   2000/78/EC.

What happened next?

In November 1999, 6 months after the Amsterdam Treaty came into force, the European Commission published a proposal for a draft directive establishing a general framework for equal treatment in employment and occupation (the Employment Directive). In the same package of proposals to combat discrimination under Article 13 were: a proposal for a draft directive aimed at implementing the commitment to equal treatment between persons, irrespective of their racial or ethnic origin (the Race Directive); and a proposal for a Community Action Programme to combat discrimination.

NGOs' activities

Negotiations about the Commission's proposals started to take place, and UK government officials and NGOs were keen to input into the detail of the draft directive. Tactics included commissioning a UK discrimination lawyer Robin Allen to produce an alternative draft of Article 6, and circulating this opinion (and wording) to MEPs, which helped to secure a change to Article 6. This article was crucial, as it provided for wide-ranging exemptions (unlike other areas of discrimination).

The relevant law-making procedure was by consultation with the Parliament so it was important to influence MEPs who had the right to make their opinion known to the Council and to suggest amendments. MEPs engaged in a number of ways, including through a committee hearing in May 2000 to examine the potential of Article 13.[16]

Eurolink Age was not initially in favour of the directive, believing that it risked institutionalising ageism and was too limited in scope to have any real impact. It challenged early drafts, which it saw as focusing on the justifications for ageism, rather than steps to tackle it. The organisation feared that that this approach would encourage employers and others to focus on their power to make exceptions to equal treatment rather than on rooting

---

16 The hearing was held jointly by the Committee on Citizens' Freedoms and Rights, and Employment and Social Affairs on 25 May 2000.

out ageist policies and practice. However future drafts responded to some of these concerns and other commitments were made to action on ageism. As a result, Eurolink Age and a new not-for-profit pan-European Older People's Platform (Age) that it co-founded subsequently supported the new law.

Throughout this period NGOs had begun to stimulate greater awareness of age discrimination, making effective use of the International Year of Older Persons in 1999. Eurolink Age conducted a consultation on a Commission 'communication' on age issues.[17] They also produced a code of practice on age diversity (later used by the UK government for its own model). During this year the Commission committed to funding AGE, the new umbrella body.

All three proposals were adopted by a unanimous Council of Ministers on 27 November 2000. Council Directive 2000/78/EC established a general framework for equal treatment in employment and occupation.[18]

What did the UK government do?

Member states were given 3 years (to December 2003) to create new national laws except for age discrimination and disability discrimination for which an additional 3 years (to December 2006) were allowed. The UK government indicated early on that it would take advantage of the full 6 years, arguing that age was 'complex'. They committed to publishing the law 2 years before it came into force, to allow employers time to prepare, but then failed to stick to this timetable. This period was taken up with protracted analysis, consultation and indecision on the scope of exemptions to the new law (especially regarding the future of retirement ages).

Once the directive had been agreed, the process of influencing switched to the individual member states who were engaged in transposing it into domestic law.

17 *Towards a Europe of all ages – promoting prosperity and intergenerational solidarity,* COM (1999) 221 of 21 May 1999.

18 The directive outlaws discrimination on grounds of sexual orientation, religion or belief, disability and age, in employment and vocational training. It covers both the public and private sectors.

New laws were required in all four areas (sexual orientation, religion and belief, disability and age), some amending existing legislation.[19]

What did the UK government do in relation to age?

Consultation: The government set up an Age Advisory Group, bringing together representatives from employer bodies, unions, age organisations and others to advise them on the shape and content of the legislation.

There were initial consultations on other areas but none specifically on age until summer 2003 when the government published *Age matters*. A major issue raised by many organisations was for the scope of the legislation to be widened beyond employment (rejected by the government). They then consulted further, homing in on the most controversial issues (the approach to retirement ages and what might constitute 'objective justification' for employers treating people differently on the basis of age). However, in 2004 there was still no agreement within government about whether or not to scrap compulsory retirement ages and give people the choice as to when to retire. This caused further delay when the government set up a working group specifically to consider this issue. At the end of 2004 it finally decided to allow employers to continue to get rid of workers over the age of 65 on the basis of their age. Draft regulations were published in summer 2005 with a view to Parliament approving them in early 2006.

Legal expertise: Discrimination lawyers with a background in race, gender and disability helped inform the approach towards the 'newer' (in legal terms) areas of discrimination (age, sexual orientation and religion and belief). In 2003, Age Concern, Cloisters Chambers and the Discrimination Law Association brought together discrimination lawyers to look at the key legal issues and to identify areas where the government was on shaky ground and likely to find it hard to justify aspects of its proposals. The

19 The Employment Equality (Sexual Orientation) Regulations 2003 SI No 1661 and the Employment Equality (Religion and Belief) Regulations 2003 SI No 1660 came into force in December 2003. Amendments to the Disability Discrimination Act 1995 came into force in October 2004. Age legislation has to come into force by December 2006.

resulting report[20] was valuable in the coming months of discussion with officials over the detail of the law. For example, in relation to redundancy, the government originally argued that statutory redundancy pay would not be available to people aged over 65. The view taken by lawyers was that such provisions would not be justifiable and would amount to direct discrimination. The government later changed its mind and announced that redundancy would be available to people aged over 65. The seminar was also useful for identifying possible areas for future legal challenges (eg to the new law in the ECJ). Other groups were also active. The Employment Law Association ran a series of seminars on all areas of discrimination covered by the directives. The Discrimination Law Association brought together lawyers and NGOs to help inform its responses to the draft regulations (under both the Race Directive and the Employment Directive).

Legal challenges: During this period a legal challenge helped to highlight the issues. Two men, Mr Rutherford and Mr Bentley, both over 65, were fighting to receive the same employment protection (unfair dismissal and redundancy pay) as younger groups. In the absence of age discrimination law, the two men argued their case under the Sex Discrimination Act (on the basis that more men than women would be in work aged over 65). The men won their case at the Employment tribunal, lost before the Employment Appeal Tribunal and then took their case to the Court of Appeal. The hearing was held in March 2004, when the government was still undecided about the crucial issue of compulsory retirement ages. The case was particularly helpful in the long-running debate about retirement ages, helping Age Concern and other campaigners to make the case for scrapping compulsory retirement ages altogether (although as noted above, they were not ultimately successful). Although the two men lost their case, the judgments included useful material and analysis that are certain to help future cases and campaigns. Leave was granted to go to the House of Lords.

Monitoring member states in transposing the laws

The Commission has very limited resources to track member states' implementation across 25 states. For the equality directives

20   Age matters: legal issues, report from a seminar held on 11 September 2003.

a team of three officials in the Commission is expected to carry out this role. Naturally they outsource much of their work, which can provide some interesting opportunities for lawyers and NGOs to be involved. The umbrella group Age is playing an important role in monitoring the transposition of new age laws, in the run-up to the December 2006 deadline. Age is active in observing the variety of approaches, ranging from the addition of age to other grounds in a broader anti-discrimination law (France) through to a lengthier and more detailed approach (the UK) and reporting this back to the Commission. Through an expert group it delivers a range of awareness-raising and monitoring activities – and a European Network of Legal Experts (in the non-discrimination field) has been established to provide the Commission with a variety of information including a comprehensive report on the implementation and application of the Article 13 directives and regular 'flash reports'.[21]

Scrutinising the EU: the role of the UK Parliament

5.146 Ever since the UK joined the European Community in 1973, Parliament has had an important role in scrutinising a wide range of European issues. As the EU institutions are not answerable to national Parliaments, it is up to parliamentarians to call to account, and to influence ministers, in relation to their EU activities, in their capacity as national representatives in the Council of Ministers.

5.147 In general UK ministers cannot agree to EU decisions unless some form of parliamentary scrutiny has taken place. However, there are many who feel that the UK Parliament, like other national Parliaments in the EU, are often caught at the end of the process, seeking to influence decisions that have already been made. UK MPs and peers have been among those calling for EU scrutiny to become 'part and parcel' of Parliament's work, rather than seen as a discrete and obscure area for a few specialists.

5.148 The draft constitution included an important provision to enhance the role of national Parliaments: if one third of national Parliaments believed a law would be better delivered domestically than at EU level, the Commission would have to review it (making it extremely difficult to proceed).

21 The contract to establish and manage this single network has been awarded to a consortium MEDE European Consultancy/Migration Policy Group.

5.149   Backbenchers in both Houses can use the usual means of scrutiny to raise EU issues: including questions; debates on government business and on Opposition Days and in adjournment debates, and in select committee inquiries. There are general debates on EU matters, on the floor of the House, usually twice yearly before heads of governments meet in the European Council.

5.150   However, there also specific procedures for Parliament to scrutinise EU proposals before they are agreed. These are important – after all, the next time parliamentarians will see a draft directive, for example, will be when the resulting primary or secondary legislation is before the House. Scrutiny is conducted by the following committees: the European Scrutiny Committee and the European Standing Committees (House of Commons); and the European Union Committee (House of Lords).

The European Scrutiny Committee

5.151   **Summary:** A Commons select committee with a broad remit that scrutinises a wide range of EU matters and documents (around 1,000 per year) – including institutional developments.

5.152   **The purpose:** As with its equivalents in other member states, to highlight the most significant matters (politically and legally) coming from the EU and to seek to hold the UK government to account in relation to its activities as an EU member.

5.153   The Scrutiny Committee's guide splits the committee's work into five roles:

'•   to assess the political and/or legal importance of European Union documents, and to decide which should be further considered in European Standing Committee or on the floor of the House;

•   to be a source of analysis and information, by reporting in detail on each document it judges to be important (about 475 a year), and by taking the oral or written evidence it requires to come to a decision;

•   to monitor business in the Council, the negotiating position of UK Ministers, and the outcome;

•   keeping under review legal, procedural and institutional developments in the European Union which may have implications for the UK and for the House;

•   in co-operation with the equivalent Committee in the House of Lords, policing the scrutiny system to ensure that it works effectively and that the Government complies with undertakings to Parliament.'[22]

22 Scrutiny Committee guide. The European Scrutiny System in the House of Commons, European Scrutiny Committee, May 2001, pp8–9.

5.154 **Membership:** Sixteen members (cross-party) but appointed by the government rather than by the usual Committee of Selection. Large staff (around 16) including legal staff: Speaker's Counsel (European Legislation) and an Assistant Legal Adviser.

5.155 **The process:** There is a formal process (the 'scrutiny reserve') that has to be followed before the government can give its assent to the Council of Ministers that a proposal can progress. In some ways this is an effective control. The government must provide detailed information about proposals and give the committee time to respond accordingly. But it has severe limitations. First, the government has the discretion in some cases to go ahead before any parliamentary scrutiny has taken place. This is a broad category including where the minister thinks it is 'confidential, routine or trivial' or has other 'special reasons' (for the latter she or he must subsequently explain these reasons to Parliament). Second, and more fundamentally, even where scrutiny does take place, the process gives no guarantees that the government will take into account the committee's views, nor report back the negotiating position that it eventually takes at Council.

5.156 **The documents:** It is very important to note that the documents examined by the committee will come from different institutions (eg the Commission or the Council of Ministers) and will be at different stages. They will include draft regulations, directives and decisions; Commission consultation papers; and recommendations and resolutions from the Council of Ministers.

5.157 The committee will sometimes involve the other departmental select committees, seeking their opinion on a document under scrutiny. (See the flowchart on p233 for a summary of the scrutiny process.)

5.158 The committee will assess the government's evidence – provided in the form of an Explanatory Memorandum and indicate any queries or if more information is needed. They may either request this in writing or by inviting the minister to give oral evidence. The committee should not proceed to make any decisions until it is satisfied that it has all the relevant information. An Explanatory Memorandum will typically include the following: key facts including a description of the subject matter; who holds ministerial responsibility for it; the type of legislative procedure that will apply (this is very important for lobbyists as it will signal to you how much influence the European Parliament may have); its impact on UK law as well as the government's opinions about its policy implications. It should also include information about any consultation and the timetable for consideration of the proposal.

Is the document of political or legal importance?

5.159   These are broad categories, best defined by way of example. Essentially political importance would stem from a view that the matter has significant implications for the UK – perhaps for a key industry. Legal importance would include where there was doubt that there was a proper EU legal base for the proposal or concerns about its impact on existing UK law.

5.160   A vast number of documents come the committee's way and they need to be able to sort out the ones that could have real impact for UK citizens. If a document is deemed sufficiently important the committee will include an analysis of it in its weekly report.

Should the document be debated?

5.161   The committee can report on the issues raised but recommend no further action. Or it can recommend debate: in committee or on the floor of the House. The government can and almost always does refuse the latter. However, it has to consent to the former so this is what generally happens – and fairly swiftly so that the government can show it has 'scrutiny clearance' and the matter can proceed. Alternatively, for documents not deemed important enough to be recommended for debate, the committee may assess them as being relevant to another debate – either on the floor of the House in the relevant European Standing Committee. This means that the document can be referred to as part of the wider debate.

European Standing Committees

5.162   **Summary:** There are three European Standing Committees: (i) environment, food and rural affairs, forestry; transport, local government and the regions; (ii) treasury; work and pensions; foreign office; home office; constitutional affairs; (iii) trade and industry, education and skills, culture, media and sport and health.

5.163   **The purpose:** To debate certain documents referred to them by the European Scrutiny Committee.

5.164   **Membership:** Thirteen MPs (other MPs can take part but not vote).

5.165   **The process:** The government decides when documents referred to the committee will be considered. They will usually be announced at Business Questions on a Thursday. Once in committee, the relevant minister makes a short explanatory statement and answers MPs' questions for about the first hour. For the next hour and a half, debate takes place on a government motion (and any amendments proposed). This includes the opportunity for the relevant Opposition frontbencher to speak. After two and a half hours in total there is a vote.

5.166   Subsequently, a government motion (usually the same one as in committee but sometimes a different one) is presented to the House but there is no further debate only a vote. If positive, this marks the end of the scrutiny reserve process.

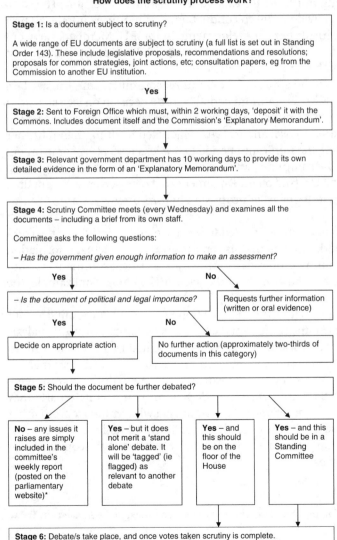

How does the scrutiny process work?

Stage 1: Is a document subject to scrutiny?

A wide range of EU documents are subject to scrutiny (a full list is set out in Standing Order 143). These include legislative proposals, recommendations and resolutions; proposals for common strategies, joint actions, etc; consultation papers, eg from the Commission to another EU institution.

Yes

Stage 2: Sent to Foreign Office which must, within 2 working days, 'deposit' it with the Commons. Includes document itself and the Commission's 'Explanatory Memorandum'.

Stage 3: Relevant government department has 10 working days to provide its own detailed evidence in the form of an 'Explanatory Memorandum'.

Stage 4: Scrutiny Committee meets (every Wednesday) and examines all the documents – including a brief from its own staff.

Committee asks the following questions:

– *Has the government given enough information to make an assessment?*

Yes   No

– *Is the document of political and legal importance?*   Requests further information (written or oral evidence)

Yes   No

Decide on appropriate action   No further action (approximately two-thirds of documents in this category)

Stage 5: Should the document be further debated?

No – any issues it raises are simply included in the committee's weekly report (posted on the parliamentary website)*

Yes – but it does not merit a 'stand alone' debate. It will be 'tagged' (ie flagged) as relevant to another debate

Yes – and this should be on the floor of the House

Yes – and this should be in a Standing Committee

Stage 6: Debate/s take place, and once votes taken scrutiny is complete.

* Occasionally the committee will publish a separate report about a proposal or topic.

5.167   On those occasions when the government does allow a debate on the floor of the House, it will choose a day and table a general motion, often signifying the direction in which it wishes to go. Before it does this it has to technically 'de-refer' the proposal from the relevant Standing Committee.

5.168   **Other activities:** In its monitoring role, committee members monitor Council business (eg through tabling parliamentary questions or summoning ministers to respond to questions in person). The committee has a wide remit to conduct general inquiries into legal, procedural or institutional developments in the EU. Members carry out visits to other EU institutions and visit the Presidency country just before it is about to take up office.

5.169   Thanks to the efforts of the Scrutiny committee, the Amsterdam Treaty lays down a minimum period before a decision on legislation can be taken by the Council of Ministers. The government endorsed the committee's proposal and in 1997 negotiated to strengthen it further by increasing the minimum period to 6 weeks (excepting some urgent matters). The committee was motivated to lobby for this through frustration at the UK (and other) Parliaments not being given sufficient time to scrutinise legislative proposals before they were approved or rejected.[23]

5.170   **How to have influence:** Aside from seeking to influence the committee's work, you will find its reports give useful factual information about upcoming proposals as well as good critical commentary, both about specifics but also about the wider EU agenda. For example, the committee issued a report analysing the next 5 years of work on justice and home affairs (the third pillar).[24] If there is a draft law relating to your specialist area, the document itself as well as the committee's analysis and explanatory memoranda will all be valuable. In terms of influencing its agenda and work, the committee will often invite external witnesses to give evidence. It is worth engaging with the committee – even if it fails to influence the UK government – as its reports may well be read by decision-makers or people with influence from other member states. But you need to bear in mind its limitations – that ultimately the government does not have to listen to the committee, or even report back.

---

23   Protocol on the role of national parliaments, annexed to the Amsterdam Treaty Cm 3780.

24   House of Commons European Scrutiny Committee, The EU's Justice and Home Affairs Programme for the next 5 years Twenty Eighth Report, 2003–04.

The European Union Committee

5.171   The House of Lords takes very seriously its role in scrutinising and reporting on EU matters.

5.172   **Summary:** The European Union Committee is a select committee which considers and gives its opinion of EU documents and other EU matters.

5.173   **The purpose:** Like its Commons equivalent (the Scrutiny Committee) the committee's main function is to scrutinise EU policy proposals, including legislation whilst they are still in draft form. However, it has a broader remit: 'to consider EU documents and other matters relating to the European Union'. It examines far fewer matters than the Commons committee but in a great more detail. A briefing paper produced by the committee describes some of its key activities as:

> 'contributing to the law-making process by detailed analysis of draft texts, by exposing difficulties and proposing amendments [and examining] the Government and its role in agreeing European legislation and, as part of that process, compelling the Government not only to think through what it has done but sometimes to account for it.'[25]

5.174   **The process:** The committee is tied into the scrutiny process, like its Commons equivalent. Once documents are deposited and the government has provided explanatory memoranda, the Chair will consider which are worth scrutinising in any detail. These will then be referred to the relevant sub-committee.

5.175   **Membership:** Eighteen peers sit on the main committee but many more are co-opted to sit on the seven sub-committees.

5.176   The sub-committees likely to be of most interest to publicly funded lawyers, will be: Social Policy and Consumer Affairs; Home Affairs and Law and Institutions. The other committees deal with financial matters and international trade; the internal market; foreign affairs and development and agriculture and the environment. They consider documents delegated to them by the main committee and carry out their own free-standing inquiries. Additional, ad hoc committees are set up from time to time.

5.177   Each sub-committee considers issues and documents. Many will simply be noted but others will be chosen for examination and oral and written evidence taken. Sometimes, rather than inviting a minister to attend a meeting, the committee will set out its views in a letter to the minister – useful when a decision is to be taken quickly. The

25 European Committee Briefing, April 2004.

committee's final reports are then approved by the main committee and within 2 months of publication the government undertakes to respond.

5.178   The main committee will, in addition to considering the sub-committees' reports, also hold regular meetings – taking evidence from key ministers (eg following European Council meetings) and from the ambassadors of Presidency countries. It also examines the Commission's Annual Work Programme.

5.179   **How to have influence:** The committee's make-up is heavyweight and distinguished and as a result the reports it produces are impressive and valuable. They are an excellent source of information and analysis about broader EU political matters as well as specific proposals and are often drawn on. For example, the committee's reports were used by the British members of the Convention on the Future of Europe to inform their input into the draft treaty.[26] As with the Commons committee they frequently invite non-parliamentarians to give evidence. The transparency of the process, with all documents in the public domain and much of the correspondence (eg with ministers) available on the Internet can be contrasted with the next stage when the Council of Ministers will deliberate in secret. It therefore offers a real opportunity to challenge the government on its negotiating position and to make its position more transparent.

5.180   **Examples:** The committee has conducted inquiries and/or produced reports into a range of EU measures on asylum and immigration matters. Examples include 'Fighting illegal immigration: should carriers carry the burden?'[27] and 'Handling EU asylum claims: new approaches examined'.[28]

Influencing EU matters: a role for lawyers

5.181   This section identifies the main routes open to UK lawyers who wish to become engaged with EU matters and highlights the influence they can have. It focuses in particular on lawyers' work with NGOs but also highlights other channels that may be useful.

5.182   Anyone trying to influence an EU matter has to remember that this involves engaging on an EU-wide basis – ie with all 25 member states (or a sizeable number of them). For UK lawyers it is not enough simply to have expertise in that capacity; knowledge of European and

26   Issued in 2003–04.
27   Fifth Report, 12 February 2004.
28   Eleventh Report, 30 April 2004.

international law is also needed and you will generally need to be linked (formally or informally) with a network or organisation that is operating across the member states. You need to factor in that the UK has deliberately made itself less of a 'player', for example by not yet adopting the euro and staying out of the Schengen agreement and that this makes it even more important for the UK to build alliances with other member states in order to have an impact.

Working with NGOs – how do they operate?

5.183   There are numerous NGOs and 'social movements' (looser alliances rather than established organisations) operating at European level. Many NGOs have a Brussels-based 'arm'. They are as difficult to classify as domestic organisations. However, they can broadly be split into three groups: 'those that were set up with help from the European Commission ... networks which were either created or moved to Brussels because they realised the increased importance of the EU and needed to find ways to influence European affairs; and a third group including large national or even international NGO organisations which made a decision to open a Brussels office'.[29] In addition, there is a Platform of European Social NGOs (Social Platform), an alliance of representative European federations and networks of non-governmental organisations active in the social sector.

5.184   Giampiero and Wilson point to the Liaison Committee of Development NGOs as an early example of an EU-funded initiative that helped many organisations to develop an EU perspective. There are numerous networks that fall into the second category, such as Solidar (NGOs working with the trade union movement). In the third group are organisations like Save the Children and Greenpeace which have opened Brussels offices. They also offer an alternative, issue-based classification of NGOS: development, social, human rights and environment.

5.185   **Funding:** A key feature of Brussels-based NGOs is that many are principally funded from the EU budget. NGOs will lobby around the Budget to secure funds for their cause and if successful, the Commission will, in allocating budgets have as part of the agreement some assistance to the Commission (eg by monitoring implementation of a directive by member states). However, allocation of funding is also useful evidence that the EU has power to act in that area – the EU

29   *European civil society coming of age,* Giampiero Alhadeff and Simon Wilson, Social Platform May 2002.

institutions would be reluctant to spend money on something not within the Union's competence. Another feature is that organisations will often come together to operate on a pan-European basis under an umbrella organisation, some whilst operating their own office as well.

5.186   **Activities:** NGOs are actively engaged in influencing and campaigning, focusing both on challenging the application or interpretation of existing law and policy, as well as in seeking law reform and engaging in policy at the very earliest stages of its development. They also use a variety of 'levers' to highlight their cause, push it higher up the EU's agenda and to push for concrete actions. Methods include engaging with 'European Years' (eg of Volunteers, or Disabled People), formal and informal networks and alliances or working around the Presidency in a particular member state. Much of what they do concerns the law, and this is why lawyers can be immensely valuable.

Lawyers and NGOs

5.187   A major route for lawyers to have influence over the EU is through NGOs.

5.188   **Advising on the EU's 'competence':** At the beginning of this chapter we looked at the importance of asking whether there was 'competence' – or does the EU have the power or a duty to act? As the EU's competence is not set down anywhere in a neat, agreed list, the question of its competence is a live one and inevitably defined through interpretation of the law (and tested in the ECJ). This is a whole level at which lawyers' input can be valuable, giving their opinion about the boundaries of what the EU and its various institutions is legally empowered to do.

5.189   **Advising on legal challenges:** There is an ever-increasing amount of EU law covering a wider range of policy areas that could possibly have been envisaged when the Common Market started up. Just as test cases can form an important part of a broader campaign in the UK, so in the EU, challenges to directives in the ECJ can also be valuable. A major difference from domestic test cases is that the European Parliament can mount such challenges. The European Council on Refugees and Exiles (ECRE), for example, succeeded in persuading the Parliament to take a case to the ECJ challenging the Family Reunion Directive which sets out the right to family reunification of people living legally in the EU, the conditions under which family members can join someone in the EU and their rights once an application has been accepted. The Parliament objects to its imposition of an integration test that all children over the age of 12 will have to sit before deciding whether they may join their parents. They argue that this breaches Article 8 of the European Convention on Human Rights (the right to family life).[30] As it was in the immigration and asylum field, the Council was only obliged to consult Parliament. It is interesting that Parliament has chosen to signal its dissatisfaction with the process and the outcome by taking the litigation route.

5.190   More generally, it can be very useful for people to understand what is or is not challengeable in the ECJ. Lawyers can help increase people's understanding of the ECJ's powers and remit, the circumstances in which a member state can be taken to court (or actions that might precede this) and the general parameters within which the ECJ operates. All these considerations can help inform an organisation's influencing strategy.

5.191   **Inputting into law reform:** Much influencing work at EU level is based on calls for law reform. Lawyers have a crucial role here in advising NGOs on what a law might achieve – and what it cannot do. Robust legal analysis and opinion is invaluable especially when combined with the excellent arguments and evidence that NGOs can bring. It can be a persuasive 'package' which is particularly important given that both the Commission and Council have their own legal services. A ready-made draft law (eg a Treaty article or directive) is a powerful lobbying tool. It helps NGOs to make their case when faced, eg with a Commission official's views on how a draft directive should be worded if they have a concrete alternative, rather than just a view on how it might be done differently. The nature of EU law making often gives scope to influence the remit or scope of a law as well as its detailed content. Once Article 13 of the Amsterdam Treaty was secured, for example, there were no guarantees that particular legislation would follow. NGOs and lawyers (and a certain political climate) helped to determine the remit and shape of the laws that ensued.

5.192–
5.195

Case studies

As with UK NGOs, there are opportunities to become involved on a formal or informal basis. When disability organisations (the European Disability Forum) were seeking to have the Amsterdam Treaty amended to include disability, they commissioned a group of lawyers for a legal opinion, to accompany the

---

30   Family Reunion Directive, agreed by member states on 22 September 2003.

economic analysis about the issue. These lawyers then went on to become a permanent legal sub group.

It can take years to effect change, and during this process legal analysis is essential. It took EURONET, the European Children's Network (which brings together many organisations including Save the Children and NSPCC) a decade to secure two references to the rights of the child in the Treaty establishing a constitution for Europe.[31] In the long process of securing agreement from all member states, lawyers' preparation of detailed legal texts about the benefits of including these references was invaluable. Lawyers were also consulted on the draft legal analysis produced by the charity on the Constitution. The campaign highlighted the limited scope of the reference to children in the Amsterdam Treaty and continued to argue for a 'legal base' for children. Alongside the hard-edged legal commentary the NGO was able provide a lighter touch, pointing out that animals' rights were spelled out in the Constitution whilst children's rights were not!

UK legal practitioners' associations and groups often engage effectively with EU policies. The Immigration Law Practitioners' Association (ILPA) has a European sub-committee whose members work on matters at all stages, often in co-operation with Brussels-based networks and NGOs. ILPA wrote an entire set of legislation intended as a prototype or guide for the Commission when it came to propose legislation in immigration and asylum under Title IV. Although they were not used directly by the Commission, they were a helpful lobbying tool. This illustrates the importance of lawyers' involvement at an early stage. Non-lawyers may not be able to articulate how legislation should be drafted, however by the time it comes to influencing Parliament and the Council the primary focus is the terms of legislation rather than the general themes or principles.

The European Council on Refugees and Exiles (ECRE) is an effective umbrella organisation of refugee agencies that works on the large amount of migration and asylum policy and law coming

---

31 Children's rights are included in the internal and external objectives of the draft; the inclusion of the EU Charter of Fundamental Rights also helped to strengthen children's rights.

> from the EU. They rely on detailed legal advice from lawyers (eg in the UK they work with ILPA and other individuals and networks) to enable them to lobby the Commission and Parliament effectively. In order to combat the UK proposal for external processing centres for asylum-seekers, for example, they relied on legal opinion that this would be incompatible with the Geneva Convention. ECRE runs a European legal network on asylum (ELENA), a forum for legal practitioners that brings together around 2,000 lawyers from different European countries.

Other routes to influence

5.196 Aside from, or often in conjunction with NGOs, there are other routes for influence. You can work through your own law firm, law centre or chambers. Some UK firms have done this successfully, using their particular specialism to make direct contact with the relevant Commission official. Or you may be able to develop links through a trade union, who are active in Brussels. Trade bodies are another route. Individual lawyers from the UK can make contact with their representative in Brussels (both the Law Society and the Bar Council operate from Brussels). You can raise key issues or proposals and ask what stage they are at and if the offices are seeking to work on them. The Council of the Bars and Law Societies of Europe (CCBE) is the representative organisation for the legal profession in the EU. They are not resourced for individual enquiries but their website (www.ccbe.org) has useful information including position papers.

Further information

5.197 • The OUP's 'A Very Short Introduction' series includes *The European Union* by John Pinder (OUP, 2001).

5.198 • One of the challenges of EU lobbying is keeping on top of key developments so that you can input at the earliest stage. There are a variety of sources to help you do this (listed below) but you also need to build up relations with officials (in the Commission, UKREP and other relevant UK-based civil servants) who may be able to share additional information. As usual, you need to think about information and analysis that will be useful to them.

The EU institutions

5.199 • Vacher's European Companion is a detailed guide to the EU insti-
          tutions (including listings of MEPs, Commission officials, etc).

       • For the European Union go to: www.europa.eu.int.

       • The Official Journal of the European Union (OJ), published daily,
          gives information about programmes, decisions and legislation.
          See the European Union website.

       • For the Foreign Office's website on Britain and the EU go to:
          www.europe.gov.uk. The FCO publishes a basic Guide to the
          European Union.

       • For the European Parliament go to: www.europarl.eu.int.

       • For the ECJ go to: www.curia.eu.int.

       • For the Commission go to: www.europa.eu.int/comm.

       • For information on Commission activities in Britain go to
          www.cec.org.uk.

       • For UKREP see www.ukrep.be.

       • For the UK Office of the European Parliament go to:
          www.europarl.org.uk.

The UK Parliament's role in European affairs

5.200 • For the UK Parliament's EU activities go to: www.parliament.uk.

       • Factsheet (L11) on European Communities Legislation is available
          at www.parliament.uk/factsheets.

       • A list of EU documents recommended for debate is published every
          Monday when the House is sitting by the Vote Office. A list of EU
          documents awaiting scrutiny is available from the European
          Scrutiny Committee.

       • The European Scrutiny Committee holds a full list of UKREP staff
          and their individual responsibilities.

       • Information about the House of Lords European Union Commit-
          tee is available at the Parliament website or email euclords@
          parliament.uk or telephone 020 7219 5791/3150.

       • You can download a guide produced by the Scrutiny Committee:
          'The European Union: institutions and legislation' from the
          parliamentary website.

NGOs/other sources of information

5.201 • The Euro Citizen Action Service is aimed at NGOs. See www.ecas.org.

       • The Local Government International Bureau publishes a European
          Information Service at www.lgib.gov.uk/eis.

CHAPTER 6

Having your say – in the media

continued

- How modern media operate; key facts to know
- Media management during a case or a campaign
- Tips for getting your points across
- Working with other lawyers to set the media agenda

Introduction

6.1   We live in an era in which the media's power or influence is much debated; we like blaming 'the media' for pestering people or worse; for distorting the facts or for spending too much time on things we are not interested in. At the same time very few people remove themselves from all contact with the press, radio or television. Most of us buy a regular daily newspaper, perhaps chopping and changing on a Sunday; tune in and out of radio and TV news bulletins; as well as check a favourite website for the latest reports on-line. We are increasingly a nation of 'grazers' when it comes to the media, used to the digital revolution which has brought instant access to hundreds of channels and feeling much less loyalty to any one publication or channel.

6.2   Lawyers have much the same habits as other citizens, with the addition of their own trade press. But they have a strong additional interest – in how the law or laws and the legal system as a whole are reported. They are also often in demand by the media – to comment on legal cases, issues or current campaigns. It is common to see lawyers on *Newsnight* or hear them on Radio 4: Imran Khan, solicitor for the family of Stephen Lawrence, the black teenager murdered in 1993, commenting on the Macpherson inquiry into racism in the police force, for example, or Louise Christian,[1] speaking about the British detainees in Guantanamo Bay. Representatives of legal campaigns groups such as Liberty are often given airtime or are quoted in the national newspapers. But journalists are also keen to have contact with other less high-profile lawyers, seeking help to place a case or legal development in context; or in exploring a legal angle to make something more out of an apparently ordinary story.

6.3   The courtroom has always been a rich source of stories. Andrew Marr describes the front-page story of the *Weekly Packet* for 30 August 1718 as follows:

> 'a court report from Dublin, about the conviction of a mob who attacked an informer against "Popish Priests" (and who were fined, imprisoned and whipped for their pains).'[2]

1   Senior partner at Christian Khan solicitors.
2   A Marr, *My trade: a short history of British journalism*, Macmillan, 2004, p65.

6.4   Nearly 300 years later, legal cases and courtroom dramas remain a rich source of media stories, including but not confined to celebrities.

What is this chapter about?

6.5   For reason of the natural interest that their profession and its daily work continues to attract, lawyers often find themselves in the media spotlight – or behind the scenes seeking to react to a report or to place a story. For citizens and journalists who want to understand the implications of a high profile case lawyers are useful commentators, able to look beyond one person's experience in the courtroom to analyse the bigger implications of a case or prospective new law for society as a whole. However, lawyers are rarely trained in the particular knowledge and skills needed to deal with the modern media. They are unlikely to have had the time to take a step back and think about how they might make the media work for them. This chapter is therefore about how to use the media as a tool for social change. It covers the basics: what is the media and how does it operate; what are the ingredients of a news story; engaging journalists in your cause or campaign; how to get your messages across and handle the media to your advantage – whatever circumstances you find yourself in. I also include a call to action. As a specialist you can work with other lawyers in your area to make the stories rather than be responding to someone else's agenda.

6.6   This chapter is a 'starter for ten' rather than a comprehensive guide. For more detail it is worth referring to Sue Stapley's excellent *Media relations for lawyers.*[3] The 'bible' on media law is Andrew Nicol QC's and Geoffrey Robertson QC's *Media law.*[4]

Modern media: the basics

6.7   • The media is a series of communication channels – and the most basic and age-old form of communication is storytelling. Everyone involved in the media has their eye on 'the story'. Alastair Campbell is reported to have got rid of every press officer who was unable to tell him what the main stories were likely to be in the next day's papers.[5]

---

3   2nd edn, The Law Society, 2003.
4   Sweet & Maxwell and Penguin, 2002.
5   Alastair Campbell was Tony Blair's first Director of Communications when he took office in 1997.

- Remember how broad and diverse 'the media' is as a concept. Media coverage can mean anything from two lines in a local freesheet through to a national television interview on *Newsnight*. It encompasses earnest polemics in 'Prospect', a light-hearted 'drive time' radio interview or an article in the *Law Society's Gazette*.
- The pace and timings involved in media work have changed, a reflection of the faster nature of modern communications generally. There is now a 24-hour news cycle which has increased the demands on journalists to find content for a continual diet of news. Overall this means less analysis and faster turn-around times. As channels compete to 'break' stories, there is an even greater need to switch the angle or do something slightly different with a story, such as find a new expert to make a comment. This gives lawyers more opportunities to be proactive and to place stories rather than waiting for a journalist to call.
- Traditional divisions, for example between tabloids and broadsheets are becoming less clear – with broadsheets adopting an alternative tabloid format and all publications becoming more engaged in the business of entertainment as well as traditional news. The 'cult of the celebrity' is reflected in the amount of column inches and TV and radio coverage given over both to genuine 'big names', as well as to recently created stars, afforded stardom through the media (eg created by appearing in reality TV shows). This trend is not confined to the tabloids or 'softer' publications or broadcast outlets; it is also reflected in the more serious or 'heavyweight' media.
- Linked with this trend is the seemingly ceaseless range of programmes and column inches given over to 'real people' and their lives, whether it be their 'problem children', inability to clean their homes or find a soul-mate.

Engaging with the media: what are your objectives?

6.8   As with any kind of influencing work you need to be clear about the purpose of your interaction with the media. It can be easy to respond to the journalist's agenda and forget to think how it will help client, case or cause by spending your time giving them information. I have identified six scenarios (at para 6.117) which may help you to think about your likely involvement with the media and pin down your goals. Depending on the scenario, you will have specific objectives, eg to enable a client to tell their side of the story; or to make the link between a specific case and its implications for a broader set of issues or campaign.

6.9   It helps to be specific: eg are you aiming to have one piece placed in a broadsheet to highlight a particular issue? Or are you aiming to have thought through some key messages or sound bites so that you are prepared to react if a case you are involved with attracts attention? How does media activity relate to your other tools and techniques for publicising a cause or campaign? For example, could your parliamentary lobbying lend itself to a particular kind of coverage and does it need to be tailored to achieve this (eg involving a high profile MP or famous peer)?

Who are you speaking to?

6.10   Having clarified your objectives, you need to consider who you want to communicate with. You need to remember that the media is a tool or a channel for communication. Given the choice, we might all prefer to have a megaphone or a direct line that could reach every citizen uninterrupted or mediated by anything else. From his first days in office Tony Blair tried to go 'direct to the British people', making public speeches, 'doorstep interviews' and providing regional and national press with signed articles.[6]

6.11   In the absence of such luxury, your communication will to some extent be mediated. There are three levels: the interviewer or journalist; the person reading, listening or watching and the others who may not be reading, listening or watching but who may be influenced by those who are. Lots of decision-makers listen to the *Today* programme which often helps set the day's news agenda. But ultimately politicians are interested in what the voters are reading and listening to and this encompasses a whole range of programmes and publications. Under Tony Blair's leadership, pre-breakfast daily reading for most ministers is the media summary prepared for them by 6 am – a political summary of the day's coverage.

6.12   You should always try to speak directly to the reader, listener or television viewer, whilst being mindful of the other players. A common mistake is to forget this and to start speaking to the wrong person – to a Radio Five Live audience as if they were the same as those who listen to Radio 4 for example. In everyday life you are unlikely to use the same language or arguments to speak to a QC, your 6-year-old niece or non-lawyer friend. Exactly the same principles apply when you are speaking to people via the media.

---

6   D Kavanagh and A Seldon *The powers behind the Prime Minister,* Harper Collins, 2000, p282.

Which medium are you interested in?

6.13 As well as being clear about the people who you are seeking to communicate with, you need to know who the intermediaries – ie the media – are. You need to identify the medium: broadcast (television or radio); print (newspapers, magazines and specialist press); and new media (the Internet) and be clear about the different rules and conventions that govern each. You then need to identify what kind of story you have. Is it a news story or a feature? Is it something for a weekly supplement to the main paper or material for a column (or both)? For television or radio, is it newsworthy or more appropriate for a discussion between experts? Are you looking at national, regional or local media? The vast reach of regional media is often forgotten and surveys suggest that regional newspapers 'are the most trusted print media'.[7] In addition a good regional story will often be picked up by the national media or a news agency.

Which journalist are you targeting?

6.14 Bearing in mind the various categories, who exactly are you targeting – is it the social affairs editor or one of the journalists 'in the lobby'? Above all, you must hang on to a broad idea of what 'the media' is, remembering that your own habits may be very different from the people you are trying to influence. Your choice of target will be governed partly by what you decide will be most effective and partly on what is possible. Your passion for the plight of a dispossessed group of tenants may merit a piece in 'Society Guardian' but not ignite those putting together a package for *Newsnight*. Depending on who you wish to speak to, 2 minutes on Five Live may be infinitely more valuable than a slot on *PM* on Radio 4. Ten million people read the *Sun* – and they could be the people most likely to be adversely affected by a proposed new law you are campaigning against. As a general rule you want your point or organisation to be included in the first four paragraphs of a story – most people read no further! If you stay focused on your objectives and who you are trying to reach you will have a good chance of making the right decisions – both on the reactive work that it is worth doing and in relation to the proactive coverage you hope to stimulate.

---

7 Research commissioned by the Central Office of Information and carried out by Dipsticks Research found that 71 per cent said they trusted the information contained in a sample 'advertising feature' in the regional press: *PR Week*, 24 June 2005, p3.

Above all, if you are making the running, you need to have a story – you can only develop the personal relationships that are so important if the journalist begins to see you as a source of their bread and butter: information, intelligence and good stories.

Lawyers' value

6.15   Lawyers are experts: in the law and judicial system in general and in their own areas. They are strongly partisan, wedded to representing their client's interests which makes them good value (sitting on the fence doesn't make for good listening, reading or viewing). They can also provide the bigger picture, the link between the individual whose case has made it to the headlines with others' experiences, by giving some answers to the questions that accompany major cases: does Diane Pretty's experience mean that a terminally ill person can never be assisted to commit suicide; does the experience of the 'McLibel two' mark a blow to the powers of companies who pit their weight against ordinary people seeking to exercise freedom of speech; how many other women are there like Sally Clark, who have been wrongly convicted of murdering their babies and imprisoned as a result? You will often hear a journalist asking a lawyer: what does this really mean; what happens next; or why does it matter? ('Mr Smith has been released from prison but what about the remaining 100 people with similar cases?)' Lawyers are good at engaging with the questions that a strong story naturally provokes and helping make sense of it.

6.16   Aside from specific cases, the law itself can also provide a 'hook' or part of the package that journalists will be looking for in order to run a story. Proposals for law reform – or a new law emanating from Europe – can provide extra material for a piece. Again, lawyers are in a good position to offer expert comment and, particularly with EU law making but also domestically, to translate some of the processes that people find baffling.

News

6.17   For lawyers, day-to-day news stories are where your main focus on the media will be. They are likely to provide your best opportunities for getting your points across as well as where journalists will most naturally think of approaching you for background or a comment.

The essence of news: telling a story

6.18 In a novel by Mario Vargos Llosa, an entire people's history is kept alive by professional storytellers who travel thousands of miles between the Machiguenga Indians of Peru.[8] By contrast, in the twenty-first century communication is almost instant; the millions who saw the planes crashing into the Twin Towers in New York on 11 September 2001 watched news unfold rather than just being on the receiving end of it hours later. However, although the pace at which information can be sent around the world may have changed dramatically, the content hasn't. People still want to know the basics; they want to be told a story that will help them make sense of what has just happened. For journalists the world over, these can be encapsulated in six basic questions – Who, What, When, Where, Why and How – that form the basic structure of a story. I return to the 'five Ws and the H' below.

What is news?

6.19 At its most simple it is something beyond the ordinary: an episode or event that will at least arouse some interest from the general public and at best inspire shock or horror. New, dramatic, major or unexpected (or all four): the Boxing Day 2004 tsunami; the first test tube baby; school shootings; and terrorist attacks are all 'hard news', defined by BBC political editor Andrew Marr as news which 'shapes our world, demands an emotional reaction and produces an almost physical thirst for more information', setting and dominating the news agenda, often for several days to come.[9]

6.20 Yet newspapers and airtime are far from filled with hard news: there are a limited number of stories that are so obviously of major and immediate life-altering interest. At the other end of the spectrum is 'weak' news: stories that are not genuinely new, but rather involve some re-telling or recycling of information. Between these two categories, is lots of time and space that needs to be filled with other stories, less dramatic than 'hard' news but with enough substance and interest to be a genuine news story.

6.21 News is a strange mixture of facts and values. Before a story has been selected as worthy of investigation – or further down the line for publication or reporting – someone has made a judgment about its value as a story. In its reporting or presentation, it is further influenced by the writer or presenter who will choose which information to

---

8 M Vargos Llosa, *The storyteller*, Faber & Faber, 1998.

9 A Marr, *My trade: a short history of British journalism*, Macmillan, 2004, p50.

focus on and how to present it. People may be able to agree that some-thing is 'new' (ie previously unpublished) or unusual but they will have different views about its 'value' – ie its weakness or strength as a story. Views will depend on the prevailing values of the publication, pro-gramme or news organisation which in turn rest on what it thinks its audience or readers want. Shocking new revelations from the life of a soap opera star will be high value to one paper but low value to another.

6.22   'Consumer news' is another fast growing category, which focuses on how developments affect ordinary individuals. It includes special features and supplements in the daily and Sunday newspapers, with a range of factual information and analysis (eg 'best buys'); radio programmes like *You and Yours* and *Money Box* (on Radio 4) and television programmes like *Working Lunch* (on BBC 2).

6.23   You need to put yourself in the journalist's shoes and ask yourself – from their perspective – 'what's the story?'. You may be fascinated by the intricacies of the largely unwritten British constitution; or out-raged by judges without a care for rough sleepers; or steeped in the unfairness of a benefit rule that no one else can understand, but you need to keep a grip on why anyone else would be interested. It is up to you to convince the journalist that there is a story, it is worth telling and that you are the right person to talk about it. The journalist will be making a judgment based on a number of criteria. For example, is the story part of a current 'news fashion', a topic receiving regular and renewed interest, like 'anti-social behaviour', immigration and asylum or travellers' rights. Or is it about to become the next big story? If so, any information you can provide will be more valuable. Has the infor-mation been reported in some form before or is it totally unpublished? Anticipating these considerations and others will help you to engage with a journalist. For their organisation more generally, you need to remember that the editor or board will be thinking about opportunities to shine – in an extremely competitive industry.

6.24   **The structure of a story:** The 'five Ws and the H' are the questions you would be bound to ask a friend who lets slip a surprise: 'Oh Steve's having an affair' or 'My best friend from school has got 6 months to live'. You would want to know the basics so that, curiosity satisfied, you can process the information; put it in context, and hopefully engage with your friend in an appropriate fashion, adding to the basic information you have already gleaned.

6.25   Most journalists are trained to structure a story in the shape of a pyramid, the most important information at the top and the least important at the bottom. This allows it to be cut from the bottom up.

Flick through a newspaper and spot the story that has been chopped. If it was written properly, pyramid style, it should still give you the information you are looking for, answering the questions Who, What, Why, When, Where and How.

6.26 You should use this structure too, both in drafting a press release but also when pitching a story. As a lawyer you are certain to have lots of detail; if you think about these questions before you speak to a journalist you will be well equipped to get the basics across. If there is time, the 'icing on the cake' can be added later.

Who's who in journalism?

6.27 Journalists are busy people operating in a highly competitive environment. If you can make their job easier, by providing them with a good story, or reliable and relevant information and intelligence they are likely to come back to you for more.

6.28 Most journalists are generalists but some develop specialisms. You need to remember that news journalists have to cover an incredible range of stories, picking up bits and pieces of information about an issue as they go. As a result you may have to supply them with some basic facts or statistics as well as your analysis. It's a good idea to have a list of key facts from your specialist area, either by drawing it up yourself or by looking at existing resources. The Refugee Council for example published an excellent leaflet, giving key facts and figures about refugees and the UK for use in the run-up to the 2005 General Election and beyond.[10]

6.29 Other journalists may be specialists (eg health or personal finance correspondent) but still have to cover a wide range of topics. Gaining coverage through a specialist correspondent can kick-start a wider interest. For example, a pensions story covered by a personal finance journalist may spark a political story that a lobby correspondent will cover. In turn this may be picked up and as interest develops, form the basis of future news stories. Or a newspaper may publish an interview with a politician, but use part of it as the basis for a news story.

6.30 As a general rule you can call the news desk and ask who you should speak to about your idea. They have a co-ordinating role and should be able to signpost you to the right person. Or you can call a

---

10 'Tell it like it is: the truth about asylum', published by the Refugee Council in partnership with the Scottish Refugee Council, the Welsh Refugee Council, Refugee Action and Student Action for Refugees (STAR).

specific correspondent direct. The publication *Editors* has full details of journalists' names, positions and contact numbers.

6.31   Broadcast outlets often have planning diaries that help them keep on top of potential stories. You can call ahead and ask to have something put into a planning diary. For example, you may know that judgment in a major case is expected on a certain date and would like to recommend yourself or another lawyer as a possible spokesperson. You may then be contacted nearer the time for more information or to be a spokesperson.

6.32   For information about a particular breed of political journalists based at Westminster see the box below.

6.33   Do not forget the power of those at the very top of media organisations: the senior managers and editorial boards. Convincing these people of the worth of a story makes it more likely that the people further down the ladder will cover it. The best way to get to this group is through high-profile figures including celebrities. In a legal context, think about the handful of lawyers who are household names or members of the House of the Lords who could play a behind the scenes role in engaging with these people to raise an issue or publicise a campaign.

Political stories: the 'lobby'

In addition to central lobby where citizens have the right to meet with and lobby their MPs, there is another lobby in the Palace of Westminster – but one confined only to MPs, security staff and accredited lobby journalists from recognised, major national news outlets. This group of political correspondents, who are based away from their organisations in an office in Parliament is part of a nineteenth-century 'lobby' system through which the government passes information onto the media. They are effectively a mini news team, a group of generalists who will be looking out for the political angle to a story (which usually means a row, crisis or a decision for the government). They will be interested in policy but also in personalities – many meaty policy issues have been reported in recent years as being about the 'Blair/Brown' divide.

All conversations between lobby correspondents and politicians are automatically deemed to be 'off the record' and will be reported as 'a senior minister said x'. However, lawyers speaking to a journalist should clarify the terms on which they are speaking at the beginning of a conversation. The Prime Minister's

Press Secretary continues to hold two briefings a day (at 11 am and 4 pm) for the 'lobby' but such has been the growth in mistrust between government and journalists that the government representative will in general be less frank, assuming that what he or she says may well end up out in the open. The same lobby system operates when the Prime Minister travels abroad, accompanied by the same, accredited group. Its secrecy is justified as a way to ensure that the truth gets out (without politicians fearing the consequences of sharing important information) but also attracts criticism on the basis that it is an old fashioned and somewhat arbitrary way to treat the transformation of vital information to citizens.

The ingredients of a good story: human interest

6.34   There are many types of information or comment contained in a typical story or report: eg eyewitness quotes; expert opinion; reported information from another publication. But it is people's stories or the 'human interest' that help bring to life the abstract or hard to grasp problem. They are often used in the media to captivate us and provoke a response. Ultimately news is about trying to make sense of the individual experiences and events that happen everyday and put them into some kind of wider context. Lawyers are well placed to help with this.

6.35   The media teams in any of the large charities spend much time and effort finding people willing to talk to the media about their own circumstances – visiting local groups and putting out frequent requests for help. Why? Because journalists like a human face for their story – and if they are undecided about the value of publicising a particular campaign – are much more likely to 'if case studies are available'. When Age Concern was running a campaign to reform the pensions system to make it deliver for women ('Let's make pensions work for women') it was Annie Brenton and Susan Grindrod, 56-year-old identical twins with very different entitlements to a pension – who ensured widespread broadcast and print coverage. The visual image was irresistible – and their stories beautifully illustrated the injustices in the system – that sisters born at the same time and identical in every other respect, could get such different amounts out of the pensions system. For a notoriously complicated issue it was invaluable to have a real story to help people unravel the issues.

6.36   At its most basic, a legal case is one person's story or experience, although often representative of many more. Lawyers have the most powerful weapons of all at their disposal – their clients, whose stories convey to the public – and to decision-makers – the reality of the law and its effects on them everyday. Yet precisely because they are busy dealing with their cases and doing their best for each client, lawyers often fail to capitalise on this valuable resource. Of course, many clients will, for a number of reasons, not wish to talk publicly about their situation. But others will be keen to – and not only for themselves but because, whatever the outcome of their case, they want others to draw some benefit from what they have been through. Some, although not wishing to be publicly known themselves, are pleased to have the details of their case shared – sometimes anonymously, if they feel that it might help others.

6.37   One step on from an individual's case is a collection of cases or stories which may enable identification of a trend. Coupled with a lawyer's analysis this can be a media story. Imagine a spate of 'lenient' sentences for those convicted of burglary in one region coupled with new statistics about prisons bursting at the seams. A criminal lawyer could supply some analysis, speaking about their experience of clients committing similar crimes but receiving very different sentences depending on where they live. This has all the ingredients of a good story, perhaps with the headline 'Postcode lottery hits the criminal courts'. With emotive topics such as burglary and other serious crimes, where media coverage can cause the public to become unnecessarily fearful about crime, it's important for people with expertise in how the system really works to add some perspective.

6.38   Another example might come from the family courts, where the interest group Fathers for Justice has hit the headlines with their stories of men being denied contact with their children. Here, lawyers' analysis of the factors behind the courts denying access to fathers and how different judges approach these difficult cases are important for people to know about. Sometimes a spate of cases are won or lost, with serious consequences, such as families facing eviction or asylum-seekers being removed to a particular country. Identifying the success factors or reasons for failure can be the basis for a story.

> **Case example: asylum-seekers and 'section 55'**
> During 2003 lawyers worked together to identify a tranche of cases of asylum-seekers who became homeless and destitute when new rules came in that effectively denied them support unless they applied for asylum at the port of entry. As lawyers took these cases through the courts they were successful in attracting media attention, including national broadcast coverage. Radio 4's Woman's Hour ran an item looking at the plight of women sleeping rough as a result of the rules. The coverage helped the campaign as a whole, which got the issue on the political agenda and eventually secured policy changes. See p317 for full details of the campaign.[11]

What are the different media and how do they operate?

6.39 As a lawyer it is useful to have a broad grasp of how the different media operate: their varied priorities; news values and different approaches to the 'stories of the day'. You need to know enough to be able to make good proactive and reactive use of the media. Your value to a campaigning organisation will be considerably enhanced by some experience and knowledge of how to handle the media.

Print

6.40 Newspapers (national, regional and local) offer lots of opportunities for reactive and proactive work. Magazines and specialist/trade press are also useful routes to publicity.

6.41 If you are planning proactive media work you need to think about what makes a news story and whether your material is strong enough or what else might be needed. Is it a national story or would it be better received as a local or regional story? Consider any major events happening in the wider world that might scupper any other stories or be preoccupying the journalist you are thinking of contacting. Remember that in many cases the journalist is on your side – keen to use your quote or information or to publicise your cause – but will find that

---

11 Section 55 of the Nationality, Immigration and Asylum Act 2002 resulted in thousands of asylum-seekers being denied housing and other support for failing to apply for asylum as soon as they arrived in the country.

their editor has other ideas and that for this reason the piece does not appear. It is always useful to get feedback – so that you know whether it was for this or for some other reason.

***

Case example: publicising your views
The *Independent* published a news story about plans to fine employers who fail to curb their employees' noise. Prominent in the piece was a sizeable quote from employment lawyer Martin Edwards.[12] He got across very clearly his worries about the full implications of the new regulations with a question: 'What if your work colleagues are consistently raucous or keep shouting messages or orders?' and pointed out that it wasn't only employers in the construction industry who were at risk, but also those managing discos or football grounds.[13]

***

Press (or news) releases

6.42   Press (or news) releases are the standard method for offering a story to print media and can be used with broadcast media as well, although some people prefer to prepare a short brief for the latter. They are typically used to highlight one issue, and can be sent well in advance, just beforehand or shortly after an event or report launch to highlight what was achieved. They need to contain just the right amount of information – enough for the journalist to write a short piece without any further material (although you hope it will prompt them to get in touch for more). They should follow the 'pyramid' principle: the most important facts and information from the top down and cover the 'five Ws and the H'. Other essentials to include are a quote and clear contact details.

6.43   If you have a good story and have produced a well-written and targeted news release, it should be picked up. You can telephone just before you send a release simply to flag it up and make a follow-up call once it has gone out (ideally to the specialist but if not to the news desk). But you should not pester journalists, who are deluged with hundreds of releases daily.

6.44   **Embargos:** You can 'embargo' your story – ie make a request that a story not be published before a certain date and time. This is a generally respected convention. It has the advantage of alerting journalists to a potential story and giving them the time to prepare whilst

12   Head of employment law at Mace & Jones in Liverpool.
13   The *Independent*, 29 March 2005, p13.

controlling the timing and maximising the chances of impact. You should clearly mark your news release at the top with details of the embargo. Or if speaking to journalists about a story you should make sure they are aware of any embargo.

6.45   Some organisations use on-line contact management systems (eg Mediadisk), a database of contacts and media outlets that is updated regularly. These are useful for drawing up target lists to receive press releases by email. Over time you can also build up your own lists of contacts. See appendix 5 for a template press release.

6.46   On some occasions you may want to issue a statement – a reaction to an event or comment that is already public – in order to try to get your views integrated into the story that will follow. A holding statement is used when you suspect that a story may get out by accident and you want to have something ready, often to help limit any damage it may cause.

6.47   **'Selling-in':** To 'sell-in' your story to the media, you should try to put yourself in the journalist's shoes. They will be looking for the type of story that their publication usually covers. They will want the strongest angle (often involving conflict) whereas this may not be what you want to emphasise – and they will be interested in the impact on people, rather than the process. You should be able to quickly summarise the story and establish if they would like further information. For example, an organisation launching a report on the plight of women prisoners might highlight a survey showing a sharp increase in the number of suicides since a private company took over management of a group of prisons. A journalist may be interested but feel that they do not have enough material. You can help by establishing what else they need and whether you can provide it: eg in this case information about the families of women who had died; background to the research; or ideas for someone in the Prison Service they might talk to.

Throughout the process you need to keep asking yourself 'what's the story' and 'how does this help me achieve my objectives'.

6.48   You always need to have something to give a journalist. But it does not always have to be a full-blown story; as you build up relations, you could share a useful lead or contact.

6.49   **Exclusives:** These are when you negotiate with one journalist for them to write a piece to the exclusion of it appearing more widely. There are obvious risks of putting 'all your eggs in one basket'; however it can work well and may secure a more in-depth and prominent piece that you will have had more input into than if it was covered by more publications.

Tips:

6.50 • In general it is better to contact journalists in the morning. By late afternoon most journalists working on daily newspapers will be on deadline. However, some regional newspapers come out at lunchtime, so these journalists will have a late morning deadline. For proactive work, journalists will be under pressure to have good ideas for the news list that will be discussed at their daily morning conference. If you can give them a good idea you may be half way to seeing it in print.

• A general guideline is that selling in on a Sunday for a Monday story can work very well (you will be competing against fewer stories).

• See para 6.77 below for guidance on media interviews.

Features

6.51 Coverage can be split into news and features, with 'features' used to describe a range of more in-depth pieces that explore and explain an issue in more detail than would be found in a news story. There are different types of features, eg profiles or interviews and comment/opinion pieces. However it is not a straight divide as there are genres that combine the two, such as 'news features' – longer news stories with more background and detail. Other genres that fall outside 'hard news' include diary items, reviews, lifestyle features, editorials, sketches and columns.

Comment and analysis

6.52 Newspapers are always looking out for stimulating commentary pieces on a topical issue and many run them daily. They need to offer fresh analysis or interpretation that will deepen readers' understanding of an issue. Comment pieces are a good way to engender some thoughtful discussion about an issue, and they often provoke readers to respond through the letters pages. They give you an opportunity to be partisan – to make your case, rather than rely on news pieces which will seek to put across others' opinions. They may be even more important, given that many people's knowledge of the issues will be from television or radio and therefore quite sketchy.

6.53 However, it is a very competitive market. Many comment pieces are produced by in-house writers, whilst the rest are generally written by well-known people. Lawyers who have established a name for themselves will definitely have a chance of publication, as will leaders of major organisations. For example, Louise Christian, a solicitor in many high-profile cases (including the victims of the Lockerbie, Marchioness and of many of the major train disasters) has had numerous articles published (eg one on the Belmarsh detainees[14]).

Tips:

6.54 • To have a chance of your comment piece being accepted, it needs to be topical, perhaps commenting on a recent political event or debate.

• You could suggest ideas for pieces to in-house writers, or if you are working with an NGO on a legal case or campaign, try to have a piece placed by their chief executive.

Letters

6.55 The letters pages can be a powerful channel and have the advantage of being a relatively speedy and time-efficient way to get your message across. They are often in a prominent position in a newspaper – eg in the *Times* straight after the news section – and often respond to a recently published article or previous letter. A group of prominent lawyers writing together or as part of a wider coalition of organisations such as trade unions or charities can add weight to a well-drafted letter and help increase its chances of inclusion. Make sure you know the deadlines for the publication you are targeting. They will vary for dailies, Sundays, regional, locals, etc.

Tips:

6.56 • Have a look at the length and style of a typical letter in the publication you plan to write to.

• Try to make it punchy; even if the content is serious it still needs a lively opening that grabs the reader's attention.

Columns

6.57 Most newspapers have one or more columnists, and they are often seeking material, intelligence or an interesting angle on an idea they have had. Columns are variable, in terms of purpose, style and content, ranging from social affairs commentary (eg Malcolm Dean in the

---

14 The *Guardian*, 17 December 2004.

Guardian) to the light-hearted descriptions of family life found in many weekend magazine supplements through to political columns.

Tips:

6.58 • If you build a relationship with a regular column writer they may be open to including material or a briefing that you offer them on a particular topic. Think about any events that you could invite them to (or to be involved with, as a Chair or Speaker). This can provide a valuable opportunity to get to know more about their interests and to start to build up a relationship.

Editorials

6.59 Editorials are the 'mouthpiece' of a newspaper, reflecting its core values and opinions on topical issues. It can be difficult to secure a direct mention but very valuable if your angle on a campaign or issue is picked up and appears in an editorial.

Legal sections/pages

6.60 Lots of publications have specific legal sections or supplements with a variety of reports, features and information about events, etc. The *Times*, for example, has a supplement on Tuesdays (and see www.timesonline.co.uk/law).

6.61 Sometimes the legal correspondent from the main newspaper is involved in the supplement; sometimes different journalists are responsible.

6.62 There are of course other sections in newspapers that, although of general interest, will often have legally-related stories or information about NGOs and charities. Examples include the *Guardian's* weekly 'Society' supplement and 'Public Agenda' in the *Times*.

Tips:

6.63 • These sections and supplements offer lots of opportunities for you and your organisation to promote your work. For example they sometimes have profiles or interviews with lawyers (and not only those at the top of the profession). You could have a session with colleagues looking at the different publications and identifying ways in which coverage could help you.

Securing print coverage: national newspapers	
Tabloids – Dailies	*Mail, Mirror, Sun, Express,* and, in London, the *Evening Standard*
Tabloids – Sundays	*Mail on Sunday, Sunday Express, Sunday Mirror, News of the World,* the *People*
Broadsheets or 'Qualities' – Dailies	*Guardian, Telegraph, Independent, Times, Financial Times*
Broadsheets or 'Qualities' – Sundays	*Sunday Times, Sunday Telegraph, Independent on Sunday, Observer*

Magazines

6.64 There are a whole range of magazines. Heavyweight political week-lies like the *New Statesman,* the *Spectator,* the *Economist* or the Labour party's *Tribune,* may offer the opportunity for some well-targeted pub-licity that will reach 'elite' audiences (ie decision-makers or people with influence like ministers and parliamentarians). 'Softer' media, like women's magazines (eg *Cosmopolitan*) offer the opportunity to reach a much wider audience, which can be vital to build public sup-port for a campaign. Some magazines (eg *Marie Claire*) offer oppor-tunities for an interview or personal profile of a lawyer – which again can be a way to publicise a particular cause or campaign.

6.65 Your first point of contact will usually be the features editor who can signpost you on if necessary.

Tips:

6.66 • Remember that magazines have long lead-in times for stories and articles so you will need to check their timescales and plan ahead.

Specialist/trade press

6.67 There is a wealth of legal publications and websites, ranging from newsletters through to magazines and journals. Like any other publi-cation they will often combine news with comment, features and letters. They can be an extremely useful way to share information such as expe-riences or case studies with other lawyers; to publicise a key issue or cause or to establish a network of professionals to do some joint work.

Examples include *Counsel* (published on behalf of the Bar Council) and the *Law Society's Gazette, Lawyer, Legal Week* and the *New Law*

Journal. There are also numerous specialist publications: eg the *Criminal Law Review*, the *European Lawyer and Employers Law*. Publications from legal campaigns groups like Justice, Liberty and Legal Action Group are also useful.

Further information

6.68 • *Editors* is a series of directories which give full details of publications. The directory on 'Business and Professional Publications' has over 100 useful legal publications, some highly specialised, others of more general interest, like *Counsel* or the *Journal of the Bar of England and Wales*. *Editors* is published by Romeike and updated every 4 months.

• The *PMS Parliamentary Companion* lists basic contact details for the main national broadcast and print media (and some regional information).

• There are a number of sources of on-line legal publications (eg www.venables.co.uk).

Broadcast

6.69 There are a range of radio and television programmes (not only the news) that may provide opportunities for you to get your messages across. In addition to the traditional channels are a whole host of satellite, cable and digital channels. When you are proactively seeking coverage you will obviously need to think about the timing of any announcement or event. For example, judgment being handed down in a major case at 4 pm could result in some early evening broadcast coverage, whereas a story that is first reported on breakfast television may have died a death by lunchtime or early afternoon.

Radio

6.70 The radio is an excellent medium, giving the opportunity to speak directly to listeners and generally for longer periods than on television. There are numerous news bulletins and programmes throughout the day on national radio, both BBC and Independent Radio News (IRN). Political programmes include the *Today* programme, the *World at One* and *PM* (all on Radio 4).

6.71 Depending on your targets it's important not only to focus on the more heavyweight coverage. Radio Five Live, for example, is often looking for fairly informal pieces to fill up its *Breakfast* show (which often features lawyers), 'Drive time' or other slots. Remember that politicians are interested in the media their constituents read, watch and listen to and so a variety of media can be a way to influence them. In addition to news programmes there are legal 'factual' series, like Radio 4's *Unreliable Evidence* as well as one-off programmes dealing with an aspect of the legal system or the law. Radio 4's *Law in Action* has a practical focus, looking at how law impacts on people 'on the ground'. There are also programmes that often include the law in their remit (eg *Woman's Hour* has looked at a range of issues from closure of family courts through to the 'rule of thumb', the law that used to permit men to beat their wives). Discussion programmes may be looking for lawyers to contribute.

Tips:

6.72 • For proactive work, rather than issuing a news release, you can produce a short brief summarising the story, its topicality and details of available spokespersons.
 • You can talk initially to those responsible for planning, who can signpost you onto the right person. Or you can speak to a journalist directly.

Television

6.73 Proactive television coverage can be difficult to secure but if achieved can give access to millions of people. Lawyers who can provide context to a legal story are a valuable source of analysis, in particular to the 24-hour news channels looking for new interpretations and angles (eg BBC News 24, Sky and ITV), for consumer programmes and for a variety of national and regional news bulletins.

6.74 The main breakfast programmes are *BBC Breakfast* on BBC1 and *GMTV* on ITV. During the rest of the day and evening are: the 1 pm, 6 pm and 10 pm *BBC News*; the 12.30 pm *ITV Lunchtime News* and 6.30 pm *Evening News*; *Channel 4 News* at noon and at 7 pm; and *Channel Five News* at 11.30 am and 5.30 pm. BBC2's *Newsnight* and *ITV News* both start at 10.30 pm (although the timing of the latter varies). There are also current affairs programmes like *Tonight* with Trevor McDonald which have in-depth interviews but with a 'tabloidy' feel.

6.75 Discussion programmes like *Richard & Judy* on Channel 4 and *This Morning* on ITV, reach large numbers of people. In the run-up to the 2005 General Election the Labour party made extensive use of them.

Tips:

6.76 • Television channels will often run a story on the back of coverage in that day's newspapers or radio. For example, significant attention to a story on the *Today* programme may stimulate television coverage later that day.

• Those working on legal dramas often turn to lawyers to help them improve the programmes' authenticity!

Conducting media interviews

6.77 Most of the rules about media interviews are the same for print, broadcast and new media.

Print interviews

6.78 You should not embark on an interview unless you are sure why you are doing it; what you want to say and the status of the information you are willing to share. A print journalist will be taking notes or may be recording you. You therefore need to take responsibility for making clear what is 'on the record' (ie can be attributed to you) or 'off the record'. They are likely to offer their 'take' on what you have said as your quote, unless you disagree or offer an alternative. In all circumstances, unless you indicate otherwise, the journalist will assume that everything you are saying is on the record.

6.79 In most cases you will be giving the journalist the straightforward benefit of your knowledge and expertise and will be saying nothing that you would not share with anyone else. You still need to be clear about your objectives so that you can guide the journalist as to the 'real story' and be clear about what you would ideally like to be quoted as saying.

6.80 How do you approach creating the media attention? Sometimes people are happy to share information with a journalist but only as 'background' and on an unattributable basis – ie without the source being named. This sometimes appears as 'sources close to x said x' or 'a senior manager at x organisation said x'. The journalist may in addition seek to confirm and source the information from another party.

6.81 However, in some circumstances there may be limits on the information you would like to be publicly quoted or identified as having revealed. Here you will wish part or all of you what you say to be 'off the record'. You need to be quite sure that you and the journalist have a shared understanding of what is 'off the record'. Generally speaking you will use this when the conversation you are having is too sensitive for you to want it to be reported at all. However, the reporter is free to go away and get the information confirmed from another source.

Conducting television or radio interviews

6.82   Many of the same rules apply as with interviews for print media. An added word of warning – you should not say anything that you would not be happy to have recorded and broadcast – beware of feeling too relaxed before or after the 'official slot' and suddenly letting slip 'what you really think'. Many have fallen into this trap and regretted it. This applies both to 'pre-records' and live interviews. You should also expect to feel much more nervous about conducting a broadcast interview than speaking to a journalist over the phone or in person. Broadcast interviews carried out by lawyers are most likely to be reactive – often about a current high-profile case – but they may also be a result of some proactive work on a case or campaign in which you are involved.

6.83   If you deal effectively with a journalist and get your points across well, you are very likely to be asked back. It reflects badly on producers and journalists if the people they ask onto a programme fail to say anything intelligible or interesting. If you make a good impression, they will add you to their mental list of people who can be relied upon. Journalists tend to go back to the same people time and time again. So if you are tired of listening to or watching the same faces (a few are unkindly termed 'rent-a-quotes') try getting a chance to have your say.

Television interviews

6.84   Most lawyers don't receive any training before they are put in front of the cameras. Unsurprisingly they sometimes blind interviewers – and the public – with their tremendous grasp of the law. But in doing this they often fail to get across anything that will be understood – let alone remembered. Yet a lawyer who can convey clearly and in a few words what the problem is, what the law means and what needs to change can have much impact.

6.85   There are some basic questions that you should ask:

- Is the interview live or a 'pre-record'?
- When and where will it take place?
- If live, will you be on the sofa with the interviewer (eg for breakfast news) – or sitting next to the interviewer at a table?

- How long will the interview itself take and how long will they need you for altogether?
- What exactly are you going to be asked?
- What is the context – are there other interviewees and will the interview be part of a package (ie a series of clips with commentary)? It's very important to know this – from a producer's perspective good viewing is often about two people having passionately opposing views. Knowing who you are 'up against' will give you a clue as to their angle. If there is a package, sometimes you will get to see the package beforehand, or the producer should at least explain what is in it.
- Do you anticipate the interview being 'soft' (the interviewer basically being on your side and making it easy for you to get your information across) or 'hard' (the interviewer being keen to raise any controversy and to push you to respond to the other side)? It is best to prepare for both scenarios.

6.86   And finally a question for you. Are you the right person for the interview? Never be tempted to do an interview on a subject you are not equipped to talk about – it won't help anyone and could destroy your self-confidence for the next time.

6.87   You need to make sure that the programme researcher or interviewer runs over what they are looking for from the interview. They will probably be keen to talk through some of the background for the story (often referring to the press release if there is one) and will often be happy to share the first question – or even discuss what it should be. Sometimes they will run over other likely questions with you too. However, you should never rely on these being the ones that will actually be asked.

6.88   **Preparing your key messages:** Thinking about the questions is the wrong way to start. The most important task is to decide what you are going to say and practise saying it beforehand, ideally with a friend or colleague pretending to be the interviewer. A 2-minute interview only gives time to make three points at most – any more and none will be remembered. Remember that although you may have been asked along for a '3–5' minute interview you may only be given one or two minutes and a pre-record could then be edited down to a 10–15 second sound bite. What is the one message you want people to be left with? If you came out of court and a complete stranger asked you what 'that big case and all the cameras' is all about, what would be the simplest way to explain it?

6.89   The next part of the preparation is about how to deliver your messages. Think of different ways to say the same thing. Have a real life example or a story plus a startling fact or statistic – these are all quick ways to convey something and are more memorable than lengthy explanations. Use ordinary language that the person watching or listening will readily understand. A 'new criminal appeal mechanism' is 'a safety net for people who spend years in prison although they're no more guilty of a crime than you or I'. 'Anti-social behaviour' is about 'noisy neighbours, people who vandalise the playground on your estate, or bored kids who don't mean to be bad – they just need fun things to do'. Or 'anti-social behaviour orders are a sledgehammer to crack a nut. The courts will find them difficult to impose and impossible to enforce'. An interview about the government's plans to end trial by jury is not the time to explore the niceties of complex fraud trials. Better to say: 'These plans will send innocent people to prison whilst the guilty walk free'. Have a couple of 'sound bites' up your sleeve: 5–10 second punchy phrases that encapsulate the one thing you want to leave with your audience. 'Tough on crime, tough on the causes of crime' is a good example. Years old, it is perhaps still Tony Blair's best-known sound bite.

6.90 **Responding to the questions:** Thinking about the obvious – and less obvious – questions is the next part of preparing how to deliver your messages. Put yourself in the interviewer's shoes: what would you ask if you were them? The questions are essentially tools for you to deliver your message – however this doesn't mean you can ignore them altogether.

6.91 Most people interviewed on television fall into two common traps: ignoring the questions and saying what they want to say regardless (politicians are often accused of this) or fastidiously answering every single question the interviewer asks and utterly failing to get any of their points across. Lawyers sometimes fall into both traps – being rather politician-like in their disregard for what the interviewer says but then being over-keen to engage with the detail!

6.92 The most effective way to be is somewhere in between, always remembering that the questions are an opportunity for you to get your messages across. It's vital and only courteous to acknowledge the questions. After all if the interviewer was a friend, colleague or client you would be seeking to engage with rather than ignore them. But acknowledging a question does not mean being taken down the garden path and away from your agenda.

6.93 **Remember your 'ABC':** A common media training technique can help you prepare to say the things you want to! 'A, B, C' stands for 'Acknowledge, Bridge and Control'. You should never answer just 'Yes' or 'No', as this will be a missed opportunity to make a point. Try this technique out by playing 'devil's advocate' with yourself and thinking of lively questions – or better still phone a friend who has no knowledge of the issue and get them to question you.

The following example illustrates how 'ABC' can help you get your points across:

6.94   Imagine that you are being interviewed about a judgment of the House of Lords, which has interpreted EU law in such a way as to increase local authorities' duties to asylum-seekers to provide support and accommodation. Your key message could be that this will help asylum-seekers, including victims of torture, who will no longer have to sleep rough. Your secondary message could be that good local authorities are doing this anyway – the judgment will simply mean that everyone will be following their lead.

6.95   A first question might be: 'Isn't the real problem that Europe is dictating policy in relation to asylum-seekers – if we left the EU Britain could do what it liked and then local authorities could spend their money on other things?' You certainly don't want to be distracted into a major discussion about the nature of Britain's position in the EU. However the question needs acknowledgement. You could say something like:

6.96   'The question of British membership of the EU is a very big one (**acknowledgement**). But what the court was looking at today was something smaller and much closer to home (**bridge**) – the plight of just 1,000 asylum-seekers every year who find themselves sleeping rough – including many who are suffering from the effects of torture in their home country (**control** – you have managed to deliver your key message)'. Or 'the judgment in this case was about a challenge to a local authority's policy – and certainly not dictated by the EU – it's great that the judges saw fit to rubbish a policy which has led to torture victims sleeping rough and having no way of getting the treatment or care that could help them to recover from the trauma they have faced'.

6.97   News journalists and presenters are generalists – they have little more knowledge than any other member of the public and will often rely on you for a steer. A few minutes before the interview they will often run a first question by you or check some key facts. This can be a good chance to influence what they ask you – with seconds to go before a live interview on breakfast television about retirement ages a presenter asked me about state pension age (the two are commonly confused). I explained that state pension age wasn't the issue and diverted them back onto what I wanted to talk about. Thankfully the first question wasn't about state pension age, ensuring that I didn't have to waste valuable time on another issue rather than getting my key messages across.

6.98   You also need to check the latest news stories just before your interview; if a story is emerging that is relevant you are likely to be asked about it.

6.99   **Delivery:** You need to aim to be enthusiastic and 'slightly more than yourself'. Match your style and tone to the interviewer and context. Often the first question will be fairly open. You may have been involved in a case about private landlords' duties to asylum-seekers or to tenants more generally: 'What's this all about or what does today's judgment mean for homeless people/local authorities/asylum-seekers?'. This is a great opportunity to kick off with your most important point: 'It means that several hundred more people will be sleeping on the streets this winter than last – and that some of those will die from the cold'. A follow-up question might be: 'But surely private landlords can't be expected to shelter the burden of thousands of asylum-seekers deciding to turn up in a particular part of the country?'. To which a response might be: 'This is about the law offering protection to everyone – not only asylum-seekers – from a handful of unscrupulous landlords who fail in their most basic obligations to rent-paying tenants'. Don't save your most important point till last – the interviewer may have to cut things short so it's best to get it in first – and then repeat it – preferably in a slightly different way – if given an opportunity.

6.100   **Appearance:** Your appearance matters – not least because you may have only seconds to make an impression and you do not want anything to distract from that. It is best not to provide any additional distractions – such as untidy hair or garish jewellery. You should avoid checked or patterned suits (which look bad on television, think television interference), black and white which makes most people look washed out and red which does not work well with many studio backgrounds. A dark blue suit with a contrasting colour shirt or top underneath is ideal. Remember that the camera may show you from any angle – including from behind. You will usually be whisked off and quickly made up before you do a television interview. But this doesn't always happen so it is a good idea to do your own make up beforehand. 'Touché éclat', a cream used under foundation can help reduce the appearance of bags under your eyes, which cameras tend to illuminate.

6.101   Finally, don't forget that the camera may stay on you when the interview has stopped. Don't let your guard down until you are well away and sure you are no longer being recorded!

Securing coverage: what makes the difference?

Many organisations actively seek media coverage but some are more successful than others. How do they do it?

- Good spokespersons are vital: journalists will remember someone who was lively and impressive and request them in future. Never assume that someone will be a 'natural'; conducting interviews is different from other types of public speaking. You should always offer training and a run-through beforehand.
- By becoming a source of reliable information, intelligence and contacts. Journalists rely on sources and if you help them they will come back for more. Some organisations are known by journalists as a good source of factual information; others go one step further and seek to be more influential, eg by sharing political intelligence and analysis that can shape the way issues are covered.
- By being reliable and available, providing the information they promise, with clear contact details including mobile phone numbers.
- By thinking of new, creative events, activities and research that can be the basis for good stories.
- Some organisations run joint campaigns with a media partner, such as a national newspaper.
- As with any other influencing, by building good relations over a period of time and only approaching a journalist when they have something to offer them.
- By creating a series of stories on one issue over a period of time.

Radio interviews

6.102   Many of the same principles apply to radio as with television. You need to think more about your voice, as this will be the only part of you that the listener will be responding to. You may feel quite relaxed if you are lucky enough to be at home in your pyjamas doing an early morning radio interview, but it's important that you still remember to be enthusiastic and a 'bit more than yourself'.

6.103   **Preparation:** Most of the questions for television interviews will be relevant – eg will the interview be live or a 'pre-record'. An additional question should be asking whether the interview can be done 'down the line' – ie from your office or home (you will need to be on a landline rather than a mobile phone) or will they need you to go to a studio? Again, you need to find out about the context, likely angles and format including whether others are being interviewed and if it will form part of a package.

6.104   If you are doing a live interview you will be telephoned a few min-utes before your slot and will often hear the programme down the telephone line. Beware of being asked at the very last minute to com-ment on some other topic that you are not expecting – eg some other major legal case in the news – in addition to what you were asked beforehand. This is fine if you feel confident to do so but don't feel that you have to.

6.105   If the interview is pre-recorded you may have an opportunity at the end to re-do part of it if you feel that it didn't go well or missed a vital point – don't be afraid to ask to do this.

New media

6.106   Electronic or new media is simply an on-line channel – sometimes another site for the same stories as are being produced in print or broadcast, but sometimes with its own content. The *Guardian* and the BBC are unusual in having separate on-line journalists; most news organisations do not have separate cover. BBC On-line provides resources that are often used as background by journalists (eg briefings, links and previous stories on an issue).

News agencies

6.107   There are a number of news agencies who distribute stories to a whole variety of outlets and channels around the world. It is always worth sending news releases, comments, etc to the Press Association (PA) for inclusion as they will then distribute it to subscribers, who include numerous national and regional outlets who rely heavily on agencies as a source of stories. You can telephone and alert them to a story and email over news releases. See www.pa.press.net.

6.108-
6.116
Case study: what makes a good story?

Illustrates: The power of a legal case with strong human interest to attract sustained media coverage. The importance of lawyers involved in a case being 'media-savvy'.

The story: For a number of years, Gurkha soldiers and their families have challenged the discrimination they face when leaving the army (or dying in service). Their stories have attracted considerable media coverage over a sustained period which has helped prompt the government to act.

In 1999 the government finally agreed to end the discrimination in compensation given to the widows and families of Gurkhas killed in action. This was largely in response to media reports (national and international) about the disparity in compensation paid to the widow of a Nepali Gurkha, Balaram Rai, killed sweeping mines in Kosovo, compared with a British spouse. The Prime Minister Tony Blair chose to make a high-profile announcement at his weekly parliamentary question time. It was made clear that the new rules would be backdated, enabling the widow of Balaram Rai to benefit.

Three years later, in December 2002, the case of a Gurkha soldier who had spent years fighting against another injustice was finally resolved. Hari Thapa argued that his pay and, after discharge, his pension, were paid at a much lower rate than a British soldier. Although a review in 1997 had brought Gurkhas' pay largely into line with that of British soldiers, Mr Thapa had scarcely benefited, as he was discharged in early 1998. The review had failed to resolve the pensions issue. A settlement was reached, giving Mr Thapa 15 years of back pay that he had spent 5 years fighting for and leaving the way open for him to benefit from any future equalisation of pension arrangements.

The media coverage: Lawyers instructed by the Commission for Racial Equality (on behalf of the client) helped draft a press release at lightning speed highlighting the importance of the settlement both for their client and the wider cause. This attracted sympathetic national and regional coverage. A news hook was provided by the fact that just the week before the settlement an Employment Tribunal had ruled that they had no jurisdiction to hear the case (as most of his service was overseas) whilst sharply criticising the way in which the Ministry of Defence had conducted their internal review.

Around the same time, a group of cases was also taken on human rights grounds, again challenging unequal treatment as compared with British soldiers. Tabloids and broadsheets covered the cases at various legal stages including their eventual defeat in the High Court. Cherie Booth's role as the Gurkhas' barrister helped add to media interest.

The *Mirror* consistently covered these stories, and in spring 2003 also reported that the Ministry of Defence would not contest a further court decision in favour of three Gurkhas who had been excluded from a fund to help surviving British Prisoners of War who had suffered at the hands of the Japanese.[15]

In 2004–05, another group of challenges to Gurkhas' pay and pensions, supported by law firm Public Interest Lawyers also attracted media attention. The government's announcement (in autumn 2004) that immigration rules would be changed to allow Gurkhas to remain in the UK and become citizens provided a useful news hook for this story.

Analysis: These cases and the issues they raised had a number of elements likely to attract media interest.

- There was the strong human interest: Mr Thapa was married to a Welsh nurse and had spent years serving in the British Army. He was born in Britain and had a British passport.
- The catalogue of injustices provided a running story in which the media displayed sustained interest. When Balaram Rai was killed in Kosovo for example, the BBC reported the death as reviving 'an old feud between retired Gurkha soldiers and the UK Government'.
- Some of the cases contained controversial elements which added to media interest. For example, there had been some criticism from ex-servicemen's associations about Gurkhas being deployed in 'internal conflicts' such as Kosovo. The hazardous nature of the operations (and the fact that the British Army Gurkhas were among the first to arrive in Kosovo) helped to highlight the injustice of unequal treatment.

15 14 March 2003.

Scenarios – an introduction

6.117   At every stage a legal case offers the potential for publicity. At its inception an announcement can be made drawing attention to the case and
through it to the wider issue. The progress through court and the
defendant's reactions can provide a new story or hook. Each stage (eg
permission to appeal granted, or the lodging of papers) is likely to be
sufficiently far enough apart to create new interest. And there will be
drama and interest in the final decision – whether the defendant wins
or loses. Every stage has the potential for a strong human story, which
is exactly what journalists seek. However, you need to keep in mind your
wider objectives, when seeking to handle or to court publicity. The
following are some likely scenarios you may find yourself dealing with.

Scenario 1: Media-handling during a case

6.118   You need to bear in mind your professional and ethical responsibilities
as a lawyer as well as the several constraints of the law and court procedures. For the most up-to-date guidance, solicitors should refer to the
Law Society's website (www.lawsociety.org.uk) and in particular to
Practice Rule 2 of the Solicitors' Practice Rules 1990 and the Solicitors' Publicity Code.[16] A new Code of Conduct for solicitors, replacing
the Guide to Professional Conduct of Solicitors, is expected to come into
force in 2006. Barristers should refer to the section on rules and guidance on the Bar Council's website (www.barcouncil.org.uk). The Code
of Conduct prohibits barristers from expressing 'a personal opinion to
the press or other media or in any other public statement upon the
facts or issues' arising in 'anticipated or current proceedings or mediation in which he is briefed or expects to appear or has appeared as an
advocate'. See appendix 6 for details.

6.119   You should also be aware of journalists' responsibilities when
reporting cases. Essentially their reports must be 'accurate, balanced
and contemporaneous' in order to be protected from libel laws.[17]

6.120   Sometimes you will be involved in a case which is an integral part
of a wider campaign (or is stimulating interest in a wider cause or
campaign). You should plan ahead, thinking about the different stages
and opportunities they may offer for publicity. You should of course be
clear about how your client feels about publicity and whether or not they
would wish to speak about their experiences.

16   Solicitors' publicity code 2001, last amended 13 January 2003.
17   R Keeble, *The newspapers handbook*, 3rd edn, Routledge, 2000, p173.

6.121   News releases should include brief details of the upcoming hearing or judgment, with some brief legal commentary and key contact details.

6.122   Sometimes organisations take cases knowing that success is unlikely, but nonetheless hoping that it will make the case for change. For example, the Equal Opportunities Commission sought out and ran cases on pregnancy dismissal, specifically to raise the problems that women continued to face as an issue, without being confident that the cases would be won.[18] In this scenario it is important that everyone involved is crystal clear from the outset about the objectives and how media coverage could help achieve – or undermine them. You need to be very confident in the facts of the particular case, consider that the courts' approach may be unpredictable and feel sure that overall litigation will assist the wider cause.

6.123   Organisations and individuals also need to choose representatives carefully. A prominent or known 'campaigning lawyer' can in themselves add value, attracting media interest to a case they are involved in.

6.124   All lawyers are keenly aware of the unpredictability of the law. The most unlikely case can turn on an unexpected point; clients and judges alike may take you by surprise. Well-prepared lawyers also check *Who's* for background on the judges they appear before, or consult other colleagues who may have useful information.

6.125   Significant cases do not land on your desk neatly labelled 'Very important: I am a test case'. Instead, they emerge, sometimes unexpectedly from ordinary scenarios into unusual or new points of law. You need to be aware of the broader implications of a case: how it can become a *'cause célèbre'* or a national talking point for every taxi driver in the country.

6.126   If you are working with an organisation on a case (eg because they have instructed you) you need to make sure that the press office understands the key facts and implications for the wider cause before it starts to attract attention. A pre-briefing or short meeting can be very useful – and you need to make sure you are available and can respond quickly in the event of any calls from journalists.

Case study: Diane Pretty and voluntary euthanasia

Summary: Diane Pretty was suffering from Motor Neurone Disease and both she and her husband wanted him to be able to assist her to die at a time of her choosing. She took a legal case in pursuit of this right (represented by Liberty). The case did not

---

18   See www.eoc.org.uk for details of this campaign.

succeed but it attracted a great deal of publicity over a long period. When the legal case came to an end, a private peer's bill was introduced into Parliament (the Patient Assisted Dying Bill). This provided a range of other media 'hooks' to keep the story alive and make further progress.

Mr and Mrs Pretty, Liberty as Diane Pretty's legal representatives, the Voluntary Euthanasia Society (VES), and other groups, succeeded in generating media coverage, including through joint working (eg through joint press conferences held by the Prettys, Liberty and the VES). The following focuses on the work of the Voluntary Euthanasia Society. It is as an interesting example of an organisation who are not the legal representatives in a case using it to benefit a wider cause.

Media work: The Voluntary Euthanasia Society succeeded in creating sustained and positive media coverage, about Diane Pretty's case but also more generally. They were greatly assisted by Diane Pretty and her family's willingness to be open about her circumstances and share these through the media. Faced with significant opposition (eg from the Catholic Church) the organisation succeeded in putting other points of views, securing supporters and changing some people's minds. Particular wins included securing supportive editorials from the *Economist* and from the *Times* with an editorial acknowledging that the current law was not working and calling on Parliament to reconsider the issue. The tabloids and 'soft' media in general (coverage was secured on chat shows like *Kilroy*) were a crucial part of the strategy to foster greater understanding of the issues. The organisation highlighted the fact that less well-off people were likely to have fewer choices about their health care. This was important for attracting the interest of these sections of the media.

Critical success factors:
- The personal story was hugely compelling and attracted the interest of 'heavyweight' and 'lightweight' journalists alike.
- The family were both willing and very good at speaking to a range of media, as were many other individuals with equally powerful stories.
- Both the legal case and the private peer's bill that followed provided a string of hooks on which to peg new information and stories.

- Between July 2001 and March 2002 there were at least five major legal stages, from Liberty's letter to the Director of Public Prosecutions through to the final hearing of the European Court of Human Rights, all providing very public platforms to get across the key messages.
- Similarly the private peer's Bill provided not only every formal parliamentary stage, but also other opportunities, like the House of Lords select committee signalling a change of opinion among peers in a report issued in July 2004.
- The stories were run with a range of correspondents, including legal, political and social affairs, providing opportunities to give exclusives to different journalists at different times.
- The Voluntary Euthanasia Society provided reliable new information and content for journalists to keep them interested. Support by the Royal College of Nursing (Ethics Chair) was a great story run by the *Guardian* (and picked up by ITN) on the day that anti-euthanasia protesters were conducting a mass lobby of Parliament.
- The organisation maximised use of its limited resources, eg by making sure the Press Association had the information they needed to get copy out speedily, which was then picked up by a range of outlets. It also encouraged supporters to use the media, eg by writing letters to their local newspapers.

Outcomes: The law remains the same but the editorial policy of many news outlets changed as a result of the work of the Voluntary Euthanasia Society, Liberty and others. And the voices of many people, in situations like that of Diane Pretty, were heard directly by the public and decision-makers for the first time.

Scenario 2: You are asked to comment on some aspect of the law (not necessarily related to a specific case)

6.127 All the principles apply here from the sections on media handling and interviews. You may have been approached directly by a journalist or via an interested organisation. You need to clarify first of all why you are being asked to comment – what is the knowledge or specific expertise that has attracted the journalist's attention, and what angle are they pursuing? You need to think about your objectives – is there an opportunity here to comment on something you care about and/or could it raise your profile in a helpful way or attract some interest to your law centre, firm or chambers? Never feel under pressure to give an off the cuff comment; check the deadline and call back promptly. And try to ensure that your quote gets in – journalists are often happy to accept helpful background information but without rewarding their source with acknowledgement in the piece.

Scenario 3: You are involved in a campaign or lobbying activity, eg working on a Bill as it goes through Parliament and you would like to help secure positive media coverage

6.128   During the passage of a Bill, lawyers can add value by being able to explain simply what the draft proposals (or suggested amendments) would mean – or by highlighting points that others may not be aware of. For example, during the campaign on the 'ouster clause', lawyers pointed out the vast constitutional significance of the government seeking to remove asylum-seekers' rights to seek judicial review of key decisions.

6.129   Again, at the outset of the passage of a Bill you need to be very clear about your objectives – eg amendments that you are serious about seeing accepted and points that you want raised as matters of principle but with little hope that they will result in a change to the draft law. This will affect the media coverage that you will seek or the key message you put out reactively. Ministers are acutely aware of media coverage during the passage of an important Bill; all the more so if the Bill's passage could be under threat from opposition (eg when the governing party has a fairly small majority) and the media seems to be stoking this. Their departmental press teams will work hard to get positive stories out about their legislation but cannot guarantee these.

6.130   Although there is less straight reporting of Parliament's proceedings than there used to be, there is still a fair amount of coverage about debates on key Bills and not all confined to the politics sections of the broadsheets. Again, in order to influence politicians (who will be mindful of their constituents) it is just as important to be getting your messages across in the tabloids and 'lighter' broadcast outlets as in the more 'serious' media. Key targets will include lobby correspondents, other political journalists not in the lobby and those with a relevant specialist interest.

6.131   **Case example:** Age Concern used the passage of the Pension Credit Bill 2001 to highlight its opposition to pensioners having their benefits and pensions docked when in hospital for long periods. They built up support among parliamentarians and the public and managed to attract national and regional media coverage, including letters to the *Express* from writers angry that people were 'penalised for being ill'. The negative coverage appeared to help secure a concession from the government, who were no doubt concerned that attention was being drawn away from the potentially 'good news story' of the Bill: the introduction of a new benefit for pensioners.

Scenario 4: Turning the tide of negative media coverage

6.132 **You feel strongly that media coverage of an area you have knowledge of is flawed and you would like to influence it.**

6.133 Once an issue is being covered in a certain way, it can be difficult to shift the agenda. Conversely, if you are successful in changing the stance or coverage in one publication or outlet, you may see others follow suit. The government's policy on tuition fees is a good example. When first announced, the vast majority of national newspapers were vehemently opposed, as displayed in their leaders and other coverage. However, sustained efforts by the officials at the Department for Education and Skills resulted in a complete turn-around. By the time of the key parliamentary debates, the support of the majority of the nationals had been secured.

6.134 You are unlikely to have the resources of an entire government department at your disposal. However, if you join with other lawyers and the wider community you may be able to achieve a different kind of coverage in a tricky area and over time see movement in journalists' approach to an issue. You will need to think about reactive work – including regular rebuttal of negative stories as well as proactively trying to get across a different set of stories and key messages. It helps to be very targeted and probably not to start with the home of the most entrenched views. Which are the publications and programmes that matter – and of these where can you see some room for movement?

6.135-
6.138
Case study: immigration and asylum-seekers

The story so far: Immigration and asylum issues receive a huge amount of coverage, predominantly negative, scaremongering and with scant attention paid to the plight of individual immigrants, asylum-seekers and their families. Also largely missing is any analysis of the impact of the five major immigration and asylum

Acts passed in recent years. A rare exception has been the *Independent*, which has devoted front pages to individuals' stories and over a sustained period has run some thoughtful and sympathetic pieces. Predictably the *Guardian* has also run positive stories, such as a feature on Polish workers in the UK, following up on Poland's accession to the EU in May 2004. It pointed out that the Home Office's figures confirmed that only 21 of the 133,000 east European migrant workers had signed on the dole.[19]

Attempts at rebuttal: Media coverage of immigration and refugee issues is an area which is crying out for lawyers and others to co-operate. There is no doubt that the media has some influence on public attitudes in this area (how much is not known) and that without altering the media coverage it will be difficult to have a different kind of public debate about the issues. Some organisations and individuals have made valuable attempts to stop the onslaught, both through media monitoring and more proactive work. Mediawise (formerly Presswise), is a media ethics charity, set up by 'victims of media abuse' which provides advice, information, research and training on all aspects of media policy, practice and law (www.mediawise.org.uk). In 1999, Mediawise launched the Refugees, Asylum-seekers and the Media (RAM) project (www.ramproject.org.uk) which aims to promote best practice in media representation of refugee and asylum issues. It provides information, advice in rebutting inaccurate or unfair coverage and training in how to handle the media. Publications include a leaflet 'Reporting asylum and refugee issues', a 'good practice' guide for journalists.[20]

Many other lawyers and campaigners have also played a role, through specific cases and campaigns, in generating more positive coverage of migrants and asylum-seekers.

19 The *Guardian*, 9 March 2005.
20 Produced by Mediawise for the NUJ Ethics Council, with support from the United Nations High Commissioner for Refugees. See also the following publications: *The RAM Report: campaigning for fair and accurate coverage of refugees and asylum seekers*, 6 June 2005, edited by Rich Cookson and Mike Jempson; Article 19's report on media representation of asylum-seekers and refugees in the UK, *What's the story*, 2003; Information Centre about Asylum and Refugees in the UK (ICAR) paper *Media Image, Community Impact*, July 2004.

> **The way forward:** Many working in the field, including lawyers, advisers and medical professionals believe that a substantial shift in public opinion will be the only way to secure a less hysterical and more sympathetic hearing for immigrants and asylum-seekers. Media coverage will be a vital way to secure this and lawyers can help by doing more with the stories their clients share with them everyday – using them anonymously or as appropriate. They can help counter the diet of misinformation – by challenging media reports through letters to newspapers or taking part in radio phone-ins and seeking to have more positive stories placed. Reactive and proactive work is needed that responds to the sea of reports in newspapers that take a much more negative approach towards these groups. There are stories to tell that give a different perspectives and lawyers may well have access to information to help create these.

Scenario 5: You are facing negative publicity about your personal life or a case you are involved in

6.139   Occasionally you may be unlucky enough to be embroiled in negative publicity about your personal life or a case in which you are involved and be trying to limit the damage to your reputation, or that of your firm, chambers or organisation, and to put your side of the story. Many of the general tools and techniques described apply here as they do for the other scenarios. But for more information I have included a book by Nicholas Comfort in the list of further reading at the end of this chapter. Comfort's book focuses in particular on media management during these kinds of crises.

6.140   There is also the Press Complaints Commission, an independent body which deals with complaints from members of the public about the editorial content of newspapers and magazines. They receive a variety of complaints, about accuracy in reporting and many related to intrusion into privacy. All complaints are investigated under the editors' Code of Practice, which binds all national and regional newspapers and magazines. The Code – drawn up by editors themselves – covers the way in which news is gathered and reported. They can be an avenue for pursuing the inflammatory coverage on immigration, asylum and other issues. See www.pcc.org.uk for further information.

> **Case study: Good news, bad news: how much control do you have?**
>
> Remember that you only have limited control when handling the media.
>
> A Muslim woman working as a Crown Prosecutor in Bradford was accused of making inflammatory remarks about the attacks on America (such as 'it was all the fault of the Jews'), which took place on 11 September 2001. She was suspended from work as a result of a security guard reporting the alleged remarks. Halima Aziz said she had joked 'oh yes as if I am a friend of Osama Bin Laden' in response to the security guard saying 'here comes a security risk'. She denied making any anti-Semitic remarks, or as her managers alleged, clapping and cheering in court when the attacks happened. She said her only comment had been along the lines of 'Arabs don't like America because of its relationship with Israel'. Aziz's barrister opened the case with a plea to the journalists present to report the case sensitively. Although the reporter adhered to this, a picture of Osama Bin Laden accompanied the piece, next to a photo of the defendant. This is a neat illustration of a key principle: that it is only management and not total control that can be achieved, often in spite of your best efforts. (Halima Aziz won her claim against the CPS for race discrimination. However, in July 2005 there were ongoing appeals in the case.)

Changing the media agenda

6.141   If you are keen to make more strategic use of the media you could do the following:

6.142   • Organise media monitoring in a key area of interest. This can be done informally – sharing the load with a few colleagues and identifying the type and amount of coverage on an issue. Or you can buy into a specialist service. Some organisations including many charities carry out regular media monitoring and may have some useful information to share.

• Create a media network for your specialist area of law that feeds case studies into campaign groups – or input into existing media monitoring outfits.

- Build up a network of friendly journalists. It can be useful to have contacts who will give you tips about how to get stories in or the kind of information you should be looking to collect.
- Co-ordinate a regular legal bulletin that provides key points from recent cases that will be of interest to campaigners and help them in their media work.
- Interact with the media as a citizen – taking part in radio phone-ins, writing letters, etc.
- If you want to be able to keep on top of stories without wading through lots of publications you can sign up to a weekly on-line digest.
- Run a training session for the lawyers you work with – in your firm, chambers or specialist area. You could pool together to buy in a trainer for a couple of hours or longer. Or invite a media officer in from an organisation you work closely with to help with a session. Use real cases that you are likely to have to do media work on to make it most useful. Most trainers will ask for a press release or briefing on an issue beforehand so that they can prepare some questions for a mock interview.
- Don't forget to look out for relevant local stories. A local newspaper article prompted law firm Scott-Moncrieff Harbour & Sinclair to take up the case of a woman with multiple sclerosis who, despite having sufficiently significant needs to be given funding for daytime care was being denied the funding that she required for care during the night. Lucy Scott-Moncrieff, managing partner of the firm, contacted the woman via the journalist and eventually secured her the funding she needed after negotiations with the local authority. This alerted them to the potential number of other people in similar situations who are being denied the money they need for vital services. From one case they were prompted to work with others to try to change the unfair way in which people are assessed for entitlement to free continuing care.

Further information

6.143
- Andrew Marr, *My trade: a short history of British journalism*, Macmillan, 2004.
- Richard Keeble, *The newspapers handbook*, 3rd edn, Routledge, 2001.
- Nicholas Comfort, *How to handle the media*, Politicos, 2003.
- David Randall, *The universal journalist*, 2nd edn, Pluto Press, 2000.
- Sue Stapley, *Media relations for lawyers*, 2nd edn, The Law Society, 2003.

- Andrew Nicol QC and Geoffrey Robertson QC, *Media Law,* Sweet & Maxwell and Penguin, 2002.
- M Fletcher-Brown, *The media handbook: a guide to better media relations,* Reputation, 2003.

CHAPTER 7

Forging links: working in partnership to deliver social change

- The benefits of building relationships with other lawyers and organisations
- How organisations can make use of lawyers' skills and knowledge
- Maximising your impact on existing and new laws and campaigning for legal reform
- Running test cases: the benefits of the 'bigger picture'
- Campaigns checklists: ideas to use in everyday practice

Introduction

7.1 Lawyers are quick to acknowledge the benefits of partnership working – within their profession and outside. But they also point to the difficulties of making it happen. Solicitors in particular say that in spite of working closely with an organisation on a particular case involvement often ceases – until the next big legal challenge. Others point to 'referral mentality' as another barrier. This limited view sees organisations as a source of clients, rather than acknowledging their information provision and policy expertise. Many also emphasise the growing pressure of the 'contract culture' which demands a large 'throughput' of casework in few hours, leaving little time for more strategic work. Balancing money making with 'civil campaigning' is a real issue for many lawyers. To combat this, one public lawyer spoke of the need to 'incorporate campaigns into casework, to make it part and parcel of what you do'.[1]

7.2 A lawyer's 'day job' is focused on an individual – or perhaps a handful of individuals in any one week. Their work can have a real impact – for good or ill – on those people. But to effect more major or lasting change to structures and systems (not forgetting that a court victory can be overturned by a change to the law through Parliament) requires an engagement with the 'bigger picture', whether that be a knowledge of the wider social context that may impact on a judge; the involvement of campaign groups to shore up a test case victory with public support, thus dissuading the government from reversing its effects; or the support of other lawyers to identify a group of cases to challenge a pernicious policy. Working alongside other lawyers, individuals and organisations maximises information, ideas and ultimately your powers of influence.

---

1 Interview with public lawyer Karen Ashton.

What is this chapter about?

7.3 This chapter is about the different ways in which lawyers can work together as well as with organisations to achieve greater impact, not only in their own cases, but in wider social causes and campaigns. It is divided into three sections:

(1) the opportunities for lawyers to link up – eg in practitioners' associations, charities or alliances;

(2) how to effect change – via existing law (test cases); the introduction of new laws (through awareness-raising, training and capacity-building) and by pressing for law reform; and

(3) campaigns checklists for you to use as individuals or organisations.

Opportunities for working in partnership

7.4 **Summary:** There are dozens of ways in which lawyers can use their skills and knowledge – beyond their own caseload. You can make a difference as an individual lawyer within your own specialism or by forging links across disciplines; as a member of a practitioners' association or trade body; by joining up with a legal or non-legal organisation – or through informal networks or alliances. You could help build an organisation's capacity to make better use of the law in its daily work or assist them with a specific project such as a draft Bill.

Working in partnership: opportunities in the legal world

Practitioners' organisations, associations and groups

7.5 Many lawyers are involved with practitioners' groups (either permanent or one-off groups set up to deal with a particular issue or proposed law). These committees and groups do extremely valuable work – sharing information; identifying new legal challenges, as well as examining the potential effects of new legislation; and providing advice and training for their peers. Bringing together the experts in an area can provide matchless expertise that if co-ordinated can be a powerful way to identify and combat unfair policies and practice. But they also provide opportunities to broaden lawyers' knowledge of other fields. Community care lawyer Richard Gordon QC is passionate about the need to cultivate multi-disciplinary awareness. He says that important points are often missed in community care cases because of over-specialisation by lawyers, citing the case of Pamela Coughlan as an example where health and community care issues were intertwined and points in particular to the failure to pick up on crucial human rights aspects of community care cases. This case raised a question of whether a chronically disabled patient should receive nursing care as a social service from her local authority, for which she would be means tested for payment, or whether the care should be provided free of charge by the NHS.[2]

7.6   There are practitioners' groups in most areas in which publicly funded lawyers practice. Examples of particularly active groups are the Housing Law Practitioners' Association (HLPA) which holds regular meetings and also convenes an annual conference and the Immigration Law Practitioners' Association (ILPA) which carries out a range of research, policy and campaigning activities and has taken particular responsibility for co-ordinating practitioners' lobbying on the numerous immigration and asylum bills in recent years (see chapter 3 for more about this). A good example of co-operation across disciplines is the Housing and Immigration Group (HIG). An informal network of lawyers, advisers and campaigners, it brings together those who work for immigrants in the fields of housing and other social assistance. It meets regularly to exchange information, develop policy and identify potential test cases. Another notable example is the Human Rights Lawyers' Association which aims to share knowledge and ideas about human rights law, in particular between specialists in different areas. Its activities include seminars, lectures, publications and training and consultancy.

7.7   Criminal law is an area in which co-operation is essential, given the weight and coherence of the state machine as compared with hundreds of defence lawyers, all operating as individuals. Without co-operation between this group of lawyers, they and their clients will be 'at a perpetual disadvantage'.[3] Defence lawyers have to bear in mind that the police, Crown Prosecution Service and others will all be listened carefully to by the Home Office. It is vital therefore that the defence point of view is also conveyed – and this must entail lawyers sharing experiences and ideas in order to pinpoint the real effects of policies on the system. Vera Baird QC MP talks of the need to act 'if you come

---

2   *R v North and East Devon Health Authority, ex p Coughlan and Secretary of State for Health and Royal College of Nursing* [1999] 2 CCLR 285.

3   Interview with Vera Baird QC MP.

away from a case feeling that your client is the victim of systemic injustice'. She advocates the publicising of injustices, using in-house magazines, and all other tools open to practitioners' associations and other professional bodies. Key groups include the Criminal Bar Association which seeks to represent the views of members of the independent criminal bar throughout England and Wales. This association submits responses (sometimes in its own right, sometimes on behalf of the Bar Council) to major inquiries and reviews of the criminal justice system. There is also a Criminal Law Solicitors' Association which represents criminal practitioners throughout England and Wales.

7.8   There are often general issues connected with the justice system or legal profession as a whole which cry out for an integrated approach. Access to Justice Alliance is a coalition formed in 2004 bringing together a variety of organisations including Citizens Advice, Justice, Advice Services Alliance, Legal Aid Practitioners' Group and Legal Action Group in protest against cuts to legal aid. By working together the organisations hope to stave off further cuts to civil legal aid and in particular protect it from rising expenditure in criminal legal aid.

7.9   Plans to set up a newly integrated equality and human rights body for Britain (the Commission for Equality and Human Rights) in 2007 are also certain to benefit from a co-ordinated approach among lawyers. With discrimination on grounds of gender, race, age, sexual orientation, religion and belief, and disability being brought together with human rights in one body, there will be important information to share among discrimination and human rights lawyers and in particular lessons for areas with new legal protection (eg age) to be learned from areas with long-established laws.

7.10   Practitioners' groups vary in terms of their formality/membership arrangements but all are easy to get involved with.

See appendix 7 for a list of networks, groups and organisations organised by field (eg housing, immigration, etc).

Case study: accession to the European Union

Illustrates: The power of lawyers working together on an urgent legal challenge

Summary: With little notice, on 1 May 2004 housing and other support from the National Asylum Support Service (NASS) were withdrawn from asylum-seekers already in the UK who were from the countries about to enter the European Union (around 2,500 people). Lawyers identified the cases that were needed to mount effective challenges. A list of factors was drawn up which included people who were working and families with ill or disabled children. The caseload was shared out and expedited hearings requested. The first success was when the judge summoned the Treasury Solicitors and an undertaking was given that there would be no evictions pending a hearing. On 4 May 2004 the High Court gave permission for a full judicial review of NASS's decision to withdraw support. The government gave assurances that no one in this category would be evicted or have support withdrawn. With undertakings from NASS that a full human rights assessment would be carried out of each case, the case was settled. However, permission was not granted in relation to a broader challenge to the regulations which argued that they were incompatible with the EU Treaty, and an appeal against refusal of permission also failed.

Trade bodies and associations

For law centre advisers and workers

7.11   The Law Centres Federation is the co-ordinating body for law centres in England, Wales and Northern Ireland. It works closely with other legal NGOs and seeks to encourage the development of publicly funded legal services for the most disadvantaged. It is upfront about its campaigning role, stating that from its inception 'the Law Centre's movement has believed that the most effective use of the law to fight poverty and social exclusion is through a combination of casework and strategic work ...' Policy and campaigning activities include giving evidence to government and parliamentary reviews and inquiries (eg on access to legal aid) and playing an instrumental role in coalitions (eg on the challenge to the removal of support from asylum-seekers brought in by s55 of the Nationality, Immigration and Asylum Act 2002). See www.lawcentres.org.uk for further information.

7.12 The Advice Services Alliance is the umbrella body for independent advice services in the UK. Members are national networks of not-for-profit organisations providing advice and help on the law, access to services and related issues. Their role includes policy development, including responding to government initiatives and consultations that relate to advice services. See www.asauk.org.uk for further information.

For solicitors

7.13 The Law Society's work includes external influencing – both publicly and behind the scenes. It engages in parliamentary lobbying on current legislation and works on possible future law reform. It has a largely formal, committee-based structure which provides opportunities for members to become involved in policy development and influencing work. Committee members may alert solicitors to legal or political developments in which they can have their say, eg in calls for evidence from parliamentary committees. It is therefore worth identifying the committee members of committees you have an interest in. Advisory committees are served by policy advisers, who it is also worth making contact with.

7.14 Each committee will agree a set of priorities – for example, the Mental Health and Disability Law Committee for some time focused on new mental health and disability laws as they made their way through Parliament (and beforehand). On major Bills practitioners will come together to discuss key issues and the organisation may also hold informal seminars with officials, in part to look at practical problems with a draft law. Sharing examples from their practice about how the law is working on the ground is one of the most valuable ways that members can have some influence and the organisation will often make sure that practitioners can attend important meetings (eg with officials) to share these. As well as commenting on proposed new laws they try to be proactive and put forward ideas for law reform as well.

7.15 There are also groups representing special interests that are recognised by the Law Society but independent of it (eg Young Solicitors Group, the Group for Solicitors with Disabilities) and Law Society Sections offering practice-specific advice and guidance to practitioners in selected areas (eg Property Section). See www.lawsociety.org.uk for further information.

For barristers

7.16 Like the Law Society the Bar Council is actively engaged in seeking to influence law and policy. Its activities include meetings with ministers and parliamentarians, drawing up responses to government consultations and making its views known about upcoming new policies and draft legislation through the media and other channels. The Bar Council has a range of committees on issues including human rights, European affairs, law reform and legal services, all offering members an opportunity to get involved with the policy and influencing part of the Bar Council's work. Issues it engages with relate to the legal system (eg in 2004 it responded to proposals for a single civil court) as well as to specific areas of law (in the same year it responded to proposals for a new law on corporate manslaughter). The Chairman's annual report (on the website) gives a good flavour of the variety of issues and methods used in influencing and campaigns during the course of a year. See www.barcouncil.org.uk for further information.

The Law Commission

7.17   The Law Commission is a permanent body, principally tasked with working on law reform for England and Wales but which also works on consolidation of existing statutes and statute law revision. It comes within the remit of the Department for Constitutional Affairs. It works in a number of teams (including one on public law) and on around 20 projects at any one time. It has recently sought to increase its involvement of external groups. It consults and publishes its work programmes well in advance, making it easy both to make suggestions for work topics but also to input views. Criteria for new projects include the following: the issues must be 'important in themselves', demonstrate 'real need for reform', and be 'suitable for consideration by the Commission'.

7.18   A typical approach to a project will involve a study of the area of law in question and an attempt to identify its defects. A consultation paper will follow, setting out key findings and options. It is circulated widely, including to practising lawyers and academics. After consultation the Commission recommends a preferred option to the government, which almost always includes a change to the law (and a draft Bill to achieve this). See www.lawcom.gov.uk for further information.

Organisations

7.19   There are many organisations lawyers could or should be involved with. They do not fall into neat categories, but will include non-governmental organisations, charities, pressure groups, interest groups, trade unions and others. There are many that fall into more than one category; indeed some of the best-known effective pressure or campaigns groups are charities. Definitions vary again according to whether organisations are national or international. My focus here is those UK-based organisations that campaigning lawyers will be keen to engage with.

Organisations: some key definitions

- There is no generally accepted definition of a non-governmental organisation (NGO). However, they are usually independent from the government; non-profit-making and peaceful in their methods and may operate at local, national or international level. They tend to 'depend, in whole or in part, on charitable donations and voluntary service'. Although the NGO sector has become increasingly professionalised principles of altruism and voluntarism remain key defining characteristics.
- Voluntary organisations is a term not confined to bodies solely run by volunteers; it is often used for organisations with a mixture of paid and unpaid staff.
- Interest group is used most often for companies, trade unions and groups that have members or a constituency with a clearly defined 'self-interest'.
- The term pressure group is also used, often for environmentalists and human rights groups, who are pursuing goals that do not directly benefit themselves. The terms interest group, pressure group, lobby and private voluntary organization could all be applied legitimately to most NGOs.
- Charity is the short form for charitable trust, a charitable foundation, or a corporation set up entirely for charitable purposes. These are set up for specific causes. There are strict rules governing the kinds of purposes and activities that charities can undertake.

7.20   Although an increasing number of lawyers have experience of working in or with the not-for-profit sector, they may not all be familiar with the focus and operation of NGOs, charities, interest groups, etc in the early twenty-first century.

7.21   Non-governmental organisations (NGOs) do not divide neatly into categories: their most obvious characteristic is their diversity, including their difference in scale. An easy way to think of them is as primarily service-providers, campaigning organisations or those which do both.

For lawyers an additional question is their approach to the law as a tool for effecting social change. Do they see litigation as something to be avoided at all costs or are they an organisation that sees test cases as another tool in the toolkit to achieve their corporate goals? Do they focus heavily on calling for law reform, but less on using existing law to communicate their main issues?

7.22   There continues to be a tradition of direct service provision by charities to the public, often relying heavily on volunteers although increasingly managed by paid staff. Befrienders, respite for carers, or excursions for disabled children are just three examples of common charitable services. Often they have sprung from one person's experience who found that the service they needed did not exist and so went onto create it for others. They come in all shapes and sizes, operating at local, regional and national level, some more centralised and streamlined than others. Many of the oldest charities have adapted their services for a modern world while sometimes finding it hard to convey this to the public. Barnardo's for example worked with the BBC on a series of documentaries to help communicate their current projects with children and young people in need and seeking to dispel the myth that they still run homes for orphans.

7.23   Many NGOs have a political (although usually not partisan) or campaigning role although some do not describe it as such. This contrasts, according to Geoff Mulgan and Charles Landry, with the intentions of the sixteenth-century drafters of the original charity law, who would have seen charity as a personal and religious act. They argue that people are not satisfied by 'paternalistic giving or self-help. Whether the field is housing or AIDS, animal welfare or education, it is hard not to engage with the larger, politically influenced systems of provision'. As a result many organisations have added a public policy-making and lobbying role to their more traditional charity functions.[4] The Charity Commission provides guidance for charities on their campaigning activities (www.charity-commission.gov.uk).

7.24   Some NGOs confine themselves to an explicit campaigning role. Amnesty International is perhaps the best-known example in this category. Other organisations, like The World Development Movement are similarly campaigns-focused (working on campaigns for fairer world trade and cancelling Third World debt).

7.25   Many effectively combine the two roles, using their experiences of delivering services to the public as a foundation to add credibility to their

4   *The other invisible hand: remaking charity for the 21st century,* Demos, 1995, pp58–59.

influencing activities. In turn, effective influencing can open up opportunities to deliver more or different services. With a growing emphasis from the government and political parties on 'evidence-based policy making' NGOs' influence increasingly relies on an evidential rather than an ideological base for creating new policy. Service delivery helps provide this foundation, whether providing evidence of a policy not working out on the ground (for example, groups working with lone parents collecting examples of the services received from the Child Support Agency) or of a gap in services (eg Citizens Advice identifying the need for more debt advice).

NGOs: key developments

7.26   There have been three important developments in recent years.

7.27   First, organisations' service delivery role has grown on a scale unrealised by many and alternately praised (for giving value for money and being innovative) or criticised (on the basis that this should remain the responsibility of the state). This attracts controversy, with concerns that charities are taking on a role that should be performed by the state. However, others argue that voluntary bodies can provide a more effective service that is tailored to local and individuals' needs and are more trusted by users than the state. Few people realise that Age Concern is the largest provider of services to older people in the UK outside the National Health Service; or that Citizens Advice gives free information and advice from 3,200 locations and relies on 20,000 trained volunteers.

7.28   These and other changes in the sector led to the adoption in November 1998 of a 'Compact', a written understanding between the government and the voluntary sector, setting out a framework for their relationship. In July 2005 over 90 per cent of local areas in England were covered by, or were developing, a Local Compact and the government was consulting on plans for a revised Compact to meet changing needs. See www.ncvo-vol.org.uk for further details.

7.29   Second, NGOs have become increasingly professionalised, developing expertise in relevant policy areas but also becoming specialists in functions such as outreach and training, lobbying or media work. The development of policy specialists within NGOs is especially relevant for lawyers. They can be key partners, able to identify emerging issues, share information with lawyers and work together to influence policy or come up with new policy ideas. Lawyers seeking to have influence can learn a lot from public affairs specialists with expertise in persuading officials, ministers and parliamentarians to take note of their concerns.

7.30   Third, and related to this, NGOs have strengthened their influencing role with tangible changes to policy and law to show for it. Indeed Mulgan and Landry highlight the greater numbers willing to sign up to NGOs, as contrasted with dwindling membership of the political parties. Governments have grown to expect calls to action from a whole host of groups – indeed they rely on being lobbied so that they can argue the cause more effectively within government and then can claim credit for having listened and responded.

7.31   Size may be an obvious factor in the amount of services an organisation can deliver but does it matter when it comes to the clout to have influence? Stonewall, a lobby group formed in 1989 has had a major impact on the treatment of lesbians, gay men and bisexuals (in particular securing legislative changes including the Civil Partnership Act 2004 and to the age of consent). Heralded as a model in how to lobby, they have managed to achieve these changes and others with a handful of dedicated staff.

7.32   Since 1997 NGOs have been able to capitalise on a marked shift in the government's willingness to engage with voluntary organisations, listening to their views and relying on their expertise to help develop policy and practice. Some organisations have welcomed this; others complain of 'consultation fatigue' or of the government engaging but failing to take real account of NGOs' views.

NGOs' approach to the law

7.33   Organisations vary widely in terms of the quantity or type of legal work that they carry out. For some their legal work is primarily internally focused, eg drafting contracts for services and ensuring that their organisation complies with the law. For others it may include provision of legal services (either directly to individuals or to advisers/lawyers or other organisations) and/or supporting individuals in cases deemed sufficiently important. For organisations which do choose to use the law, it is a powerful weapon to empower people to enforce their rights or to challenge injustices. It can help put pressure on the government or companies to change their policies or practices. The spotlight that a case can throw on a social issue can help raise public awareness, prompt outrage and in turn promote change. There is wide variation in the extent to which NGOs have a legal 'arm' or activities and also how strategic their approach to the law is – ie linked to the organisation's overall priorities and plans. An organisation's support for a major test case can have an impact (and indeed some important cases would not be taken without such support), but an organisation can also do much through its support for 'ordinary cases' and legal services.

7.34   Organisations like Liberty, Justice or Legal Action Group (LAG) are clearly 'legal NGOs', with their concentration on law reform and cross-cutting legal issues such as access to justice and human rights. Included in this category could also be those with a focus on a specific area of the law or legal practice: Inquest for example works on coroners' inquests, supporting families and lobbying for changes to this archaic area.

7.35   The Child Poverty Action Group (CPAG) has a sustained history of using the law to promote social change and delivers a range of legal services alongside (and feeding into) policy and lobbying activities. It has a specific 'arm' to deliver its legal work: the 'Citizens' Rights Office' (CRO) and focuses on social security benefits that will have an impact on children in poverty. Its success and credibility as a test case organisation is due in part to this focus (with just one government department to target!). The organisation provides advice, training and information (including well-established and regularly updated benefits guides) to frontline advisers and lawyers and pursues test cases on identified issues. It also uses evidence from cases to inform its influencing work and campaigns and uses its expertise to analyse proposed legislation. It has adapted its focus from individuals to advisers and through its publications and training has built credibility with advisers. This means that it is often approached for assistance with strategically important cases. CPAG is seeking further to integrate its casework and test cases with its campaigns, for example its campaign for free school meals could have been supported by a legal case examining the need for nutritional standards. The CRO's Legal Director Stuart Wright suggests that their 'best case scenario' would be to 'mesh together all the elements', taking an organisational view on a policy area; having lawyers identify strategic test cases; using parliamentary tools and techniques to inform the legal case or to pursue the issues afterwards.

7.36   Other organisations have a remit that includes legal services and a track record of running test cases (Shelter, MIND) but have a focus that goes well beyond the law and strictly legal issues.

7.37   Many of the largest national NGOs (eg Citizens Advice) have a network of advice givers at local level that includes some legal advice and/or representation, but do not necessarily run a full 'test case' unit at national level, instead referring cases on or leaving them to be picked up by lawyers. Citizens Advice does however feed casework directly into their policy and campaigns, ensuring that issues are picked up from local bureaux and used in the selection and pursuit of policy and campaigns development.

7.38　Trade unions similarly provide legal advice and sometimes representation, sometimes taking major cases that will impact on thousands or millions of people – beyond their own members.

7.39　A useful distinction is between organisations who confine their activities to a few well-chosen test cases (and associated policy development and campaigns) and those who also provide legal services (eg information and advice to the public or to advisers). However, in recent years, organisations such as the Public Law Project which set out to be a 'test case and policy organisation' have developed an advice-giving 'arm', providing telephone advice on the Human Rights Act 1998. Opportunities from the Legal Services Commission to provide second tier advice (to lawyers and advisers) provide an important source of funding for such organisations (helping to pay for more strategic work). But they also offer contact with a range of lawyers with a through-put of cases. This trend is welcomed by many lawyers who believe that the links are vital for ensuring that organisations identify the most important issues and pursue them in a strategic fashion.

7.40　Non-statutory bodies like the Equal Opportunities Commission have legal work as a core part of their role. They give information and advice to individuals who then represent themselves; fund a small number of key cases; conduct formal investigations; do 'strategic legal follow-up' – for example having revision of a company's policy or other input written into the judgment of a case; and interventions. Services for individuals include 'self-help' resources and a helpline. There is a detailed website for advisers. The proposed new Commission for Equality and Human Rights will have a similar legal remit but in relation to a number of areas of discrimination as well as human rights.[5]

Getting involved

7.41　There are lots of opportunities for lawyers to involve themselves, not only in 'legal NGOs' or groups where they will be on familiar territory, but also in the broader not-for-profit sector.

5　The government plans to set up the new body in 2007. See www.dti.gov.uk for further details.

7.42   The involvement of external lawyers in NGOs is variable. Many organisations have in-house lawyers and legal advisers, making them operate fairly self-sufficiently in terms of taking forward cases and policy issues. However, others continue to rely on links with lawyers in practice both for referrals of test cases; for keeping on top of the emerging legal issues as well as for the financial and other support of lawyer members.

7.43   **Formal involvement:** Lawyers are in demand for management committees or trustee boards of charities - not only for their specialist knowledge, for example as housing or immigration practitioners, but also for other core areas such as employment law which can be invaluable for organisations seeking to follow appropriate practice in terms of recruitment, retention and other staffing issues. Lawyers' general skills and in particular their oral and written communications can also be useful to organisations seeking to manage a range of activities – complying with the legal requirements governing charities; selling themselves to funders and producing written evaluations of projects. Their contacts can also be useful – barristers' chambers and solicitors' firms can be a source of funding or additional expertise for an organisation. For casework organisations it is extremely valuable to have lawyers who can help with audits and quality control of case files, etc. All organisations, whether or not they are delivering legal services or activities, have a legal framework to comply with and lawyers can help them do this. There are some good schemes that help introduce lawyers and organisations, either with a view to helping with a specific project or a longer-term involvement. Examples include the Solicitors Pro Bono Group which provides free business law advice to not-for-profit community groups through a network of volunteer lawyers. See www.probonogroup.org.uk.

7.44   Aside from the main management committee or trustee board, which involves a formal commitment for a certain period, some organisations have separate legal advisory committees, networks or panels to help advise them on legal matters, for example, equality bodies such as the Equal Opportunities Commission and the Disability Rights Commission have various mechanisms for harnessing lawyers' skills – including formal, legal advisory networks or panels as well as groups they work with less formally. Or some organisations may retain individual lawyers for a set number of days per year – calling on them for a range of advice and other inputs – for example identifying current issues emerging from a helpline that could usefully form the focus of legal challenges.

7.45   For lawyers or advisers seeking to move into the not-for-profit sector, voluntary experience on a committee or Board can be invaluable

– providing an insight into how the not-for-profit sector works and an opportunity to get involved in the charity's campaigns.

7.46   Membership can also offer opportunities for involvement, through specialist committees or informal contact with other members. Some organisations have specific lawyers' sections or groups.

7.47   **Informal involvement:** Informal relationships with an organisation are also useful. Many lawyers build up relations with the relevant policy expert (in larger organisations there will be policy units or teams with specialisms, eg housing, social security or employment, in smaller organisations there may be one person responsible for policy (and a number of other functions as well!)). Those working in information provision (particularly in an organisation with a local or regional infrastructure) are also worth making contact with as they may be able to advise on the kind of issues coming up from call centres or other contact with individuals. In turn you may be able to help them look at this information with a legal eye, identifying legal principles or issues that could be tested. Similarly, some organisations run surveys, asking people to share their experiences, as jobseekers for example or in claiming a particular benefit. Lawyers can provide added value to these, again by examining them from a legal perspective and identifying potential challenges or areas worthy of further exploration.

7.48   Lawyers can also work with NGOs on applications to charitable foundations and trusts to carry out research and policy work.

7.49–
7.51

Case study: bail for immigration detainees

Illustrates: The involvement of lawyers in many different ways in a charity.

Background: Legal advisers, lawyers, church activists and refugee support groups were instrumental in setting up Bail for Immigration Detainees (BID), a unique charity which seeks to secure people's release from immigration detention in the UK and campaign against arbitrary detention more generally. Tim Baster, a caseworker from the Refugee Legal Centre, with the support of a group of immigration lawyers and others, set up BID in 1998. Since then the organisation has delivered a free bail service (information, advice and representation) to detained asylum-seekers and migrants. From individual cases it identifies and pursues broader issues, using its evidence base to put pressure on the Immigration Service, the judiciary and the Home Office to change their policies.

A key role for lawyers: From its inception, the organisation has relied on barristers acting pro bono to go into court, often at short notice, and run bail applications, prepared mainly by a team of volunteers working with legal officers. Immigration and human rights lawyers serve as trustees, sharing legal expertise and employment lawyers have helped the organisation with human resources issues. Lawyers have worked with staff to run external training courses, aimed at encouraging and equipping lawyers to take on bail cases. A developing element to BID's work: an outreach project delivering sessions in detention centres and prisons that equip detainees to represent themselves (or to work more effectively with their legal representatives) relies on lawyers to provide legal bulletins for detainees.

Law students and interns are among the active volunteers helping to conduct research and prepare cases and the organisation has built up relationships with pro bono units and law firms.

Academics

7.52   There is a gulf between practising lawyers and academics, which is extraordinary given the obvious benefits from linking up around common areas of interest. Virtually all journals are either for practitioners or academics and there are few examples of joint projects. However, there are real benefits in a more joined up approach. Academics have access to research budgets and, if funded, the time to carry out substantial projects that can lend real weight to a campaign for law reform. In addition to research (which can be useful for court cases as well as wider campaigns) they can also be a useful place to site work on a controversial area as they are seen as impartial researchers or observers.

7.53   A great example of this is a project which took shape after a decade of fighting a losing battle in the courts in relation to the rights of Gypsies and Travellers. Lawyers who had been involved in the cases worked with Gypsies and Travellers' groups to devise a 3-year project based at Cardiff University. After years of rejection and often hostility by the courts, this was the successful formation of a major new campaign for law reform. See chapter 4 for details.

7.54   Law students and law student organisations carry out valuable pro bono work, eg through the Solicitors Pro Bono Group, the Bar Pro Bono Unit and the Free Representation Unit (FRU). This can be an excellent way for students to develop skills but also could be a way for lawyers to engage with academic institutions.

Political parties

7.55   The main political parties have lawyers' associations (eg the Society of Labour Lawyers, Society of Conservative Lawyers and Society of Liberal Democrat Lawyers). There are also groups independent of any of the political parties, like the Haldane Society of Socialist Lawyers which provides a forum for discussion and analysis of law and the legal system, nationally and internationally, from a socialist perspective.

Think-tanks

7.56   Think-tanks are neglected by most lawyers, yet they are increasingly influential and generally open to outside ideas and engagement. They are on the up, with 72 outfits officially recognised by the National Institute for Research Advancement and half of these founded less than 15 years ago. As one springs up and occupies a certain positioning or niche on the political spectrum, others follow in reaction. Some are formally attached to a political party; others informally aligned or associated with one party more than others and some seek to maintain complete independence. All of them research and develop policy on issues of interest to lawyers. A few move from outsider to insider status. Mathew Taylor, for example, Director of the Institute for Public Policy Research (IPPR) was seconded to Number Ten in 2003, to develop and advise on policy from within government.

7.57   It is well worth engaging with a relevant think-tank. They are usually very receptive to ideas for research – from individuals as well as organisations. You need to bear in mind that their funding needs mean that they can often only carry out research or develop projects for which they can attract specific funding. Indeed many subsidise projects aimed at influencing government by undertaking consultancies for corporate clients.

7.58   Some think-tanks sit squarely within one of the main political parties, set up by a group of members, whilst others profess independence but have values and aims shared much more with one party than any other. Others are genuinely independent, acting more as consultancies to a range of organisations (including government). Most are categorised, rightly or wrongly, on a spectrum ranging from left wing to right wing, despite many think-tanks' best efforts to move debate away from these traditional divisions! Sometimes their ideas are initially rejected, only to be used or 'recycled' some years later when the political or social climate has changed and they seem to have become a 'good idea'. Along with the IPPR, some of the best-known think-tanks include Demos and the Fabian Society and at the other end of the political spectrum the Adam Smith Institute and the Institute of Eco-nomic Affairs. Perhaps their greatest value is to stimulate discussion about the 'unthinkable' – the topics that political parties will leave well alone, for fear that the public will take against them as well as to take a longer term approach, something that all governments, with their eye on the next election, seem to find it impossible to do. A new develop-ment is the interest some are now taking in 'doing' rather than merely 'thinking'. Civitas: the Institute for the Study of Civil Society, a right-leaning charity set up in 2000 which aims for a 'better division of responsibilities between government and civil society', is setting up its own school in west London.

Maximising your impact

Existing laws/test cases and public interest litigation

7.59   There are four main reasons as to why lawyers should work with each other and more broadly on test cases (or public interest litigation): (i) to help identify cases; (ii) to make good decisions about a case; (iii) to involve the right people with the necessary expertise; and (iv) to max-imise the impact of a case by tying it in with a wider campaign.

7.60   In theory a test case can be run in isolation – like any other case the product of a decision made by the client with the lawyer's advice. Indeed some test cases are run like this, without too much thought for the bigger picture or the full implications of the case. But in practice test cases should and do entail partnership working – their very nature involving a knock on effect on many more individuals than the client in question and often beyond the specific field of law into other areas.

Identifying the 'right' cases

7.61   The term 'test case' is used loosely; at its most basic it means a case that aims to test an aspect of existing law with a view to achieving a change that will have an impact far beyond the one case. Successful legal chal-lenges depend on finding the right case with the right facts. However, test cases do not land on solicitors' desks neatly labelled as such; often their importance is not immediately clear or only becomes so in ret-rospect and they therefore need to be analysed with reference to clear criteria. They sometimes turn into a different creature from that orig-inally envisaged – a case about urgent payments to miners during the strikes of the 1980s became authority for a fast-track appeal scheme.

7.62   Chance plays a large role in defining the cases that are pursued. A lawyer's awareness of an issue may come from an article in a magazine or journal, a meeting with fellow practitioners or a conversation with a colleague. An issue or case may emerge from a specialist advice line such as those funded by the Legal Services Commission and administered by different firms and chambers.

7.63   Firms with a specialism are well placed to take important cases forward. Scott Moncrieff, Harbour & Sinclair have a substantial mental health case-load and as a result have been well placed to pursue a number of significant legal challenges. A number of cases which started in the Mental Health Review Tribunal have been successfully challenged in higher courts (including at European level). Lucy Scott Moncrieff, one of the firm's partners, talks of the importance of a culture that enables lawyers to develop instincts for something not being 'quite right'. It is this which leads them to look at a case and explore the possibility of it being taken forward and use it to challenge the underlying legal principles.

7.64   Clarifying the issues that lawyers or organisations want to test and then being proactive in seeking them is a strategic approach to the identification of test cases. This is often reliant on joint working between lawyers and organisations. MIND is one of many organisations that develops casework selection criteria to help them focus on key cases. They consulted with users and then compared findings with their organisation's 5-year plan. Their concerns were examined alongside public lawyers' 'issues of the moment' – like the issue of conditional discharges being given but no resources to accompany this policy.

7.65   Lawyers' groups can be very effective in identifying the key issues and alerting colleagues in the same field to look out for cases that could progress these. However the net needs to be cast as wide as possible in order to maximise the chances of cases emerging that not only involve the relevant legal issue but also have strong enough facts. Public lawyer Karen Ashton thinks that traditionally legal aid practitioners have 'seen voluntary organisations as useful sources of referrals, but the value of their expertise in identifying and informing public interest casework has gone largely untapped'.[6]

7.66   In fact, groups and organisations in day-to-day contact with people with potential challenges have a vital role to play – especially for those organisations, eg some legal NGOs that do not provide any great

---

6   K Ashton, 'Public interest litigation realising the potential', *Legal Action* 4, July 2001.

volume of direct legal services, and therefore do not have access to a pool of potential cases. National bodies with regional and local infrastructure can encourage workers at all levels to help spot potential challenges, ensuring that call-centre workers are briefed on important issues and that people are passed on for more specialist help as appropriate. The Equal Opportunities Commission prioritises certain areas at any one time (eg pregnancy dismissals) and makes sure that employees at all levels – and crucially those taking calls from advisers or members of the public – are aware of these. The Child Poverty Action Group is another good example which advertises 'test cases needed' on their website and due to its recognised track record and expertise in social security often has cases referred to it by solicitors.

7.67　Listening to policy advisers in NGOs is also essential – they may well be picking up on issues that could be the subject of legal challenges and will welcome lawyers' input into how these could be pursued.

Case study: unfair charging of mental health patients

The issue: Some local authorities were charging some mental health patients for aftercare services on leaving hospital following a period of detention for treatment whilst others were not.

The law: The legal challenge involved s117 of the Mental Health Act 1983 under which there was no provision to charge for after care services. Guidance had not made this clear, although most local authorities did not charge for aftercare services provided in the person's own home. In contrast, s21 of the National Assistance Act 1948 did make provision for charging for care in a care home. On discharge from hospital, some local authorities were choosing to place people under the latter provision, as a way to charge them for services.

Although this had been the situation since the Mental Health Act came into force in 1983, it took years for a legal challenge to emerge, perhaps because it was particularly difficult for mental health patients to be able to identify that they were being wrongly treated.

Organisations' activities: Before any legal challenges had emerged, Age Concern had been raising its concerns with the Department of Health asking for clearer guidance. At the same time it also helped a complainant take a case up with the Ombudsman, securing £60,000 compensation for the person involved.

Age Concern's public information about local authority charging recommended checking the position where a person was detained in hospital for treatment. The organisation suggested checking that the detention was under the relevant section and whether s117 applied for aftercare. The organisation's fact sheets are widely available, and helped to alert people to the problem. And whilst the Ombudsman's case was being investigated a number of people started court proceedings, with the Public Law Project and other solicitors as their legal representatives.

With three other cases local authorities' practices were challenged in court and the cases were won at every level, including the House of Lords.[7] The courts found that local authorities had no power to charge for aftercare services provided to former patients under s117 of the Mental Health Act 1983.

Partnership working: This proved to be crucial, with charities and solicitors sharing information and valuable evidence. There were important considerations to share about the impact of the legal challenges on people who were not being charged (local authorities' practices were found to vary).

The impact: In early 2000, following the High Court decision, a government circular was issued to local authorities and health authorities in England drawing attention to the judgment. Local authorities still charging for services provided as part of aftercare under s117 of the Mental Health Act 1983 were advised that they should immediately cease to do so. However, many local authorities were not prepared to refund money to individuals until after the House of Lords considered the matter.

Follow up: The Ombudsman issued a special report in July 2003 following on from the cases they had dealt with. They expressed concerns that not all local authorities were paying back the money owed.

---

7   *R v London Borough of Richmond ex p Watson* (HSC 2000/2003: LAC (2000/03); *R v Manchester City Council ex p Stennett* (2002) 3 WLR 584; (2002) 4 All ER 124; (2002) UKHL 34.

Case study: Human rights and older people in care homes

Summary: No one can quite put their finger on why the Human Rights Act has been scarcely used by older citizens to challenge some of the worst abuses found in society: malnutrition, physical and mental abuse and other incidents in residential care homes which are clearly about people's dignity, a concept now emerging in the UK courts as a principle underlying human rights law. One reason may be the understandable reluctance of often frail, older people to challenge abuses – as well as the practical barriers in doing so. Another is likely to be the fact that human rights have yet to take firm hold in our society and to be recognised by ordinary people as tools to be used in their everyday lives. But another reason is likely to be that lawyers and organisations have not yet joined forces to publicise and seek out these cases or to find other ways to 'fill the gap'.

The challenge: A gap has been created by a restrictive, court-made definition of 'public authority' which bars many people in independent residential care homes from protection by the Human Rights Act, on the grounds that the care home is not a 'public authority' and therefore not covered.[8] Everyone, the government included, acknowledges that action is needed to clarify the situation. This was borne out in June 2005 when the government published guidance for public authorities to ensure that contracts with private organisations for the provision of public services impart the obligation to protect Convention rights.

Working in partnership: what can lawyers do?

- A case is needed to clarify the law in relation to 'public authority', enabling the protection of all older people in care homes, whether or not they or the local authority is funding their care. This is an obvious case where co-operation is needed, between individual lawyers and advisers, legal organisations with expertise in human rights and organisations delivering services to older people in order to identify a person who might be willing to take a case that could help thousands of others and to make sure that the 'right case' is taken. The government has registered its keenness to intervene in a

---

8 *R v Leonard Cheshire Foundation* [2002] HRLR 30.

> case, with the hope that the judges will take a very different approach than in *Leonard Cheshire*.
> * However, the weakness of the test case option is the length of time that might elapse before the 'right case' emerges. So a number of organisations and lawyers are also working on other law reform options (including seeking to amend other legislation, such as the Equality Bill 2005). To persuade the government that action is needed, organisations are also working to raise awareness of the gravity of the issue for some of the most vulnerable people in society. Lawyers' involvement is invaluable in advising on how the law could be reformed in a workable manner to achieve the desired goal.

Making the 'right' decisions

7.68   There are as many opinions as there are lawyers about the approach to deciding to pursue a test case. Most lawyers would feel that they cannot hang on for ever, awaiting the case with the perfect facts relevant to the specific point of law. But they are alive to the risks of taking a case. All lawyers would agree that discussion across different fields of law as well as with clients and interested organisations can help them give decent advice about a case.

7.69   Richard Gordon QC makes a plea for lawyers to take the 'right cases' to court and 'in an appropriate manner'. He advocates a gradualist approach, citing a judge who said that he could be pushed in new directions '10% but not too much more'. He argues that lawyers must understand how judges' minds work and that they are as mesmerised by new 'fads as anyone else'. He is critical of lawyers who bring bad cases 'either through ignorance or a desire to campaign' that make bad law for everyone else.[9]

7.70   However, others argue that it is essential to take cases that have no hope of (legal) victory even if this is 'campaigning through the courts'. Luke Clements a lawyer who spent over 10 years representing Gypsies and Travellers says that although there was no hope of winning the cases, it was important to 'flush out judges' prejudices'. Many say that the impossibility of predicting the outcome of a case mean that is wrong to make early judgments about the risks of making 'bad law'.

---

9 Speech to Legal Action Group Community Care Conference 2004.

7.71   Diane Pretty, represented by Liberty, fought a legal battle to allow her husband to help her commit suicide, fearing the choking and asphyxia that might afflict her, a sufferer in the late stages of motor neurone disease. It was widely predicted that she would lose her case and indeed she did at every stage – up to and including the European Court of Human Rights. In spite of the case effecting no legal change, it passed the 'taxi driver test' in that it got the nation talking about fundamental issues like the right to live or die. Some argue that for this alone it was a resounding success, and that the Human Rights Act gave a voice to someone in a situation with which many could sympathise; others argue that it irresponsibly sent out entirely the wrong message about disabled people and the quality of their lives. Whatever view you take, there is no doubt that cases such as Diane Pretty's play a major role in promoting discussion and to altering opinions (although this is hard to measure) of both the public and of judges.

Involving key partners

7.72   An important decision in a test case is the involvement of experts that can help inform the court and add weight to certain arguments. This has come to the fore with human rights cases (or cases involving Human Rights Act points) which make greater demands on judges to look at the 'bigger picture' so as to carry out the balancing exercise between the rights of the individual and society-wide considerations such as national security, public safety or 'the protection of health and morals'.[10]

7.73   One way for lawyers to involve experts is for an external organisation to intervene in a case. Judges appear to be taking an increasingly relaxed approach towards third party interventions, allowing them in effect to give expert evidence in relation to a general issue of principle that may not be raised if matters are left to the parties or to give factual information relevant to the main issues. Liberty Director Shami Chakrabarti calls them an 'alternative analysis of the public interest' – vital where it would otherwise be for an unpopular victim to make these points. As a result, interventions are developing not only as a way for organisations to influence a particular case but to raise their profile and the wider social issues that they care about. They are a relatively cost-effective option (compared with test cases) for an organisation, as they will generally only involve paying a barrister's fees for a half-day or day and in some cases lawyers will act pro bono.

10   Human Rights Act 1998.

7.74   Nuala Mole from the AIRE (Advice on Individual Rights in Europe) Centre advises caution when considering whether to intervene, in case lawyers have a good reason for avoiding certain issues. She advises always consulting the lawyers about a possible intervention. Roger Smith, Director of Justice, also argues in general for caution: 'interventions should be made only when there is a point that will not otherwise be made' although acknowledges that sometimes they may be useful to reinforce evidence or an argument.

7.75   Lawyers have an important role to play in identifying potential intervenors and if necessary encouraging or assisting them. Sometimes potential intervenors may feel that the lawyers running the case are missing important points in which case an intervention may help to add expertise. Many organisations are not aware of the potential for making an intervention but have policy expertise and a broad evidence base which they could contribute. Small as well as large organisations can successfully intervene: what counts is their expertise. It is vital that organisations co-operate, and bear in mind the overall goals, rather than competing to make an intervention.

Case study: *A and Others, X and Y v Secretary of State for the Home Department*

Background

In 2001 the government announced its intention to derogate from Article 5 (right to liberty and security) of the European Convention on Human Rights so that it could legislate to detain those it suspected of terrorist involvement in the wake of the attacks in the US on 11 September 2001. It had to introduce new legislation because the European Court of Human Rights had made plain that a terror suspect could not be deported if they were at risk of torture abroad (Article 3 is absolute and allows no derogation) and that overly long detention was a breach of Article 5.

The government was able to do this by using the provision under the Human Rights Act 1998 that allows a 'derogation order' from Article 5 in certain circumstances and to legislate to detain people under immigration rather than under criminal legislation (which offered more safeguards for those detained). As soon as the government announced its intention to derogate from Article 5, Liberty instructed David Pannick QC, a lawyer who frequently acts for the government, to advise on the legality of the derogation. His advice was: (i) that there was no public emergency of the scale or type envisaged by the drafters of the Convention; and (ii) that the measures were not 'strictly necessary' but were disproportionate. The opinion was drafted in sufficiently brief form and in plain English to be a useful campaigns tool and was shared with parliamentarians.

This sowed the seeds for a future intervention which was to bear fruit 3 years later, when the Law Lords overwhelmingly rejected the government's derogation, finding by a majority of 8:1 that whilst there may have been a state of emergency, the government's response to this was disproportionate and discriminatory. Mr Justice Collins described this as a good example of the value of a third party intervention. He pointed to the arguments about the discrimination put forward by Rabinder Singh QC (instructed by Liberty) that undoubtedly persuaded the House of Lords to find against the government. Several of the Law Lords referred to the unequal treatment meted out to the detainees, pointing out that the measures did not apply to British terror suspects thought to pose similar risks. Lady Hale asked what legitimate aim could be served by only having power to lock up 'some of the people who present that threat'. Would it be 'justifiable to take power to lock up that group but not the "white", "able-bodied", "male", or "straight" suspected international terrorist. The answer is clear'.

The ruling attracted widespread media coverage which included the intervention itself.

The government reacted by passing legislation at the eleventh hour (hours before the powers to detain people were about to run out) and narrowly succeeded in passing the Prevention of Terrorism Act 2005, a law that would allow 'control orders' (in effect house arrest) in certain cases.

Tying cases in with a broader cause or campaign

7.76   It is important for lawyers to have in mind the potential for test cases either to support an existing campaign or sometimes to spark a new campaign. Likewise, organisations should be aware of the usefulness of a legal case to give impetus and profile to an issue. The following are just three examples of cases which have linked with a broader cause or campaign.

7.77   **Milk tokens for asylum-seekers:** CPAG used the law to challenge the Home Office's refusal to provide milk tokens for an asylum-seeker mother with HIV. The High Court ruled that the Home Secretary had ignored the risk that the mother, who could not afford to buy formula milk, could pass the HIV virus on to her baby through breastfeeding and ordered the Home Secretary to reconsider his decision.[11] This case was part of a wider campaign led by CPAG (working with Neil Gerrard MP) to give asylum-seekers milk tokens. It succeeded in changing the government's policy and in March 2003 regulations were brought into force, giving additional support for pregnant women and children under 3 who are supported by National Asylum Support Service (NASS).

7.78   The legal cases of men and women challenging their dismissal from the armed forces gave profile to and ultimately stimulated changes to the policy governing their treatment in the military. Although the case of former RAF nurse Jeanette Smith and three ex-servicemen was dismissed in 1995 by the Court of Appeal, the judges' acknowledgement that their arguments had weight was seen as an important landmark, as was the earlier hearing at the High Court which warned that the 'tide of history' was flowing against the Ministry of Defence. Eventually, in 1999, the European Court of Human Rights found that there had been arbitrary discrimination and that the servicemen and women's right to respect in their private lives had been violated by sacking them solely due to their sexual orientation.[12] Shortly afterwards, the government announced a lifting on the ban of employing homosexuals in the armed forces.

Working in partnership: the introduction of new laws

7.79   Lawyers may typically think that their work starts when a new law comes into force and clients emerge. In fact their expertise is needed before this stage.

7.80   First, organisations often need help in assessing the likely impact of new law. Where will their clients go for advice, support and representation? Will there be unmet need and if so how much? How many and what kind of cases might be expected in the first year? Should the organisation adapt its services or look to others to meet the need? Will funding be available for short-term needs or to build capacity? Lawyers can help by offering this kind of advice based on their experience of the impact of other, relevant laws. For example, the experience of those

11   29 July 2002.
12   *Smith and Grady v United Kingdom* [1999] 29 EHRR 493.

involved in advising on disability discrimination rights when they were first introduced, will be instructive for those seeking to predict the kinds of demand when new anti-ageism laws come into force towards the end of 2006.

7.81   Second, publicity about a new law is vital. Without it take up of new rights will be low. Government publicity about a new law is important but generally not enough and tends not to attract the trust that independent organisations such as charities do. Lawyers have an especially important role to play in this which becomes even more important as national organisations are likely to have limited resources to publicise and alert potential claimants to new law (and in some areas there may not be any organisations at all). Lawyers can help, for example, by providing training for other lawyers, advisers and community organisations on any new rights.

7.82   Third, there is value in lawyers and organisations thinking early on about the key issues that should be challenged so as to ensure that the law develops in the right way. It is important to keep an open mind when thinking about early challenges. The rights of a man with schizophrenia to be employed by the Patent Office may not have sounded the most promising case to be taken under the Disability Discrimination Act 1995, but it turned out to be a crucial tribunal decision that not only established that schizophrenia clearly came within the definition of disability for the purposes of the Act; it also provided useful guidance for future cases. The Employment Tribunal dismissed the case, finding that Dr Goodwin failed to come within the definition of disabled. However, the Employment Appeal Tribunal rejected this and said 'it seemed to us most surprising that any tribunal could conclude that a person admittedly diagnosed as suffering from paranoid schizophrenia and who had been dismissed partly because of what one might call bizarre behaviour, consistent with that diagnosis, fell outside the definition ...'[13]

7.83   Some laws are carefully introduced when a government judges that society is ready for them: seatbelt laws are an often cited example, the argument being that when they were introduced most people thought that wearing a seatbelt was the right thing to do, which obviously helped compliance rates. Others are an attempt to lead society in a certain direction; they may be ahead of majority public opinion or create new language and punishments for a problem (eg anti-social behaviour orders).

13   *Goodwin v The Patent Office*, [1999] IRLR 4 (EAT).

7.84   Laws that introduce new protections and rights often require a shift in thinking, on the part of individuals, businesses and public bodies. Institutions may need to change their policies and practices (to protect themselves from unwanted legal actions) whilst citizens need to be encouraged to make use of a new law that could help them with a problem. For this type of law, work may be needed to deliver a fundamental change in culture. The Human Rights Act is a good example of this.

Case study: The Human Rights Act 1998

The Human Rights Act was a triumph for lawyers and others who had campaigned for it for many years. It achieved the transposition of new rights into UK law, giving citizens direct recourse to the domestic courts in suspected cases of human rights breaches. There are many cases in which citizens have been directly and positively assisted. However, it has certainly not led to the flood of cases that some predicted. Research indicates that the Act has not increased significantly the number of judicial review cases pursued and that Human Rights Act points are most often being used to supplement conventional public law grounds.[14] In some areas in particular (abuses of older people in residential care homes) the Human Rights Act has been underused, despite significant potential breaches.

At the time of its introduction there was some awareness-raising but not enough to publicise the positive benefits for individuals (especially given the hostile media coverage, eg about 'prisoners' rights to televisions') or how advisers or public service providers might use it in their everyday work to raise standards of service. It was important for a whole range of workers and public bodies to understand what the underlying intentions of the legislation were. For example, some professional carers were concerned that the Act's provisions would be used in a negative way against them, rather than as a tool to secure better treatment of those in their care. And it was the clear intention of the government that the HRA had the potential to be used as a tool to raise standards of public service, by providing a 'bottom-line', a 'floor beneath which standards will not be allowed to fall'.[15]

---

14   Public Law Project research; J Halford, *Legal Action*, March 2004, p21.
15   Home Secretary Jack Straw MP HC Debs Col 767, 16 February 1998.

This is clearly an area where more joint working (including training) is needed between lawyers and outside groups to help translate the laws into practical, everyday tools to be used to protect people from harm and improve the services they receive. Advisers and organisations need assistance in spotting a human rights 'point' or angle that can help them with a case. At a local level they need to be confident in using the Human Rights Act. The right references to the HRA in a letter to the local authority about an older person being moved from one care home to another can serve to remind the authority of its obligations and have a positive effect – removing the need for any more formal legal action to be pursued. The creation of the Commission for Equality and Human Rights should provide another opportunity to publicise the HRA and how it can be used in everyday life.

Case study: Campaign against cuts to support for asylum-seekers (introduced by section 55 of the Nationality, Immigration and Asylum Act 2002)

Illustrates: the power of lawyers and organisations working together pursuing legal and other routes.

Summary: The Act, which came into force on 8 January 2003, aimed to further restrict housing and other support for asylum-seekers. Asylum had to be claimed 'as soon as reasonably practicable' after the person's arrival into the UK. The rigid way in which officials interpreted this led to hundreds of asylum-seekers becoming homeless and destitute. Victims included pregnant women and those who had suffered torture. After a year of legal challenges, the government conceded that the provision was unworkable and said that claims made within 72 hours of arrival would be deemed 'as soon as reasonably practicable'. Further changes were subsequently secured through the courts.

Background: The Act did not define 'as soon as reasonably practicable', but in practice officials interpreted it as being no later than at the port of entry. The discretion to provide support if it appeared that an individual's human rights might be breached was scarcely used.

Activities: Once in force, lawyers quickly became aware of the impact of the new law. Many judicial review applications were lodged (1,100 by September 2003), in an attempt to secure at least interim relief for clients denied shelter and other support and in the hope that they would secure permanent change to the policy.

Strategy: By summer 2003 in spite of the heavy case-load on the Administrative Court (principally emergency and out-of-hours applications) there was no sign of a change of heart from the government and no sign of a consistent approach by judges. Lawyers agreed that they needed to continue to take cases, putting pressure on the courts for a resolution. In the summer the different agencies came together to discuss tactics, which resulted in cases continuing to be taken to the Administrative Court. However, it was felt that if the higher courts did not respond as hoped for, that cases would then need to be taken to Europe. Key practitioners' groups (including the Housing and Immigration Group and the Immigration Law Practitioners' Association) also discussed other ways of changing the legislation or decision-making process (eg via lobbying/parliamentary activity).

Partnership working: An exceptional number and range of lawyers and organisations came together to oppose the new policy. Whilst there were a large number of organisations involved, one of the problems was the small pool of lawyers willing to do section 55 cases. Regular meetings took place, involving people from all levels of the process: the initial referrers (eg the Refugee Council), medical workers, lawyers and NGOs including both homelessness and refugee/asylum-seekers' groups.

Media: The campaign attracted media coverage, including on *Newsnight* and the *Today* programme.

Turning points: About 95 per cent of the cases were successful in obtaining interim support and eventually, in December 2003, the Home Secretary David Blunkett announced (during the first debate on the Asylum and Immigration (Treatment of Claimants etc) Bill 2003) that claims made within 72 hours of arrival would be deemed to be 'reasonably practicable'.

However, problems remained, as officials would often dispute the date of arrival and continued to refuse support on this basis. In addition, there was still no clear guidance emerging from the courts.

Legal challenges: In an early case in February 2003 Mr Justice Collins held that the section 55 interview process was unlawful and that destitution itself was contrary to Article 3 (prohibition of torture) of the European Convention on Human Rights, incorporated into domestic law by the Human Rights Act 1998. However, on appeal by the Home Office, the Court of Appeal considered that an individual had to suffer the degrading effects of destitution before a human rights claim could be made.[16]

In the summer three individuals' claims that their Article 3 rights had been breached were upheld. However, the Court of Appeal overturned this decision (two cases settled prior to hearing), finding that cases could not be brought until people had reached or were 'verging on' the inhuman or degrading.[17] The court said that it could not establish a simple test that would work in every case, leaving the High Court no clearer on the correct approach. The toll that the cases were taking on the court was recognised when a number of cases were then listed before Mr Justice Maurice Kay for guidance. However, subsequent cases continued to reflect very different approaches. In a case heard in January 2004 and relying heavily on evidence from NASS about the alleged availability of charitable support for asylum-seekers, Mr Justice Newman held that being destitute for weeks did not necessarily establish a breach of Article 3.[18]

In contrast, a month later, Mr Justice Collins found that the government's plans to make people destitute 'removed the law of humanity' and were incompatible with Article 3.[19] Two further cases succeeded when other judges took a similar approach.[20] The Court of Appeal then had an opportunity to give definitive guidance, when the Home Office appealed all three cases to the Court of Appeal.

---

16 *R (Q) v Secretary of State for the Home Department* [2003] EWCA Civ 364.
17 *R (S, D and T) v Secretary of State for the Home Department* [2003] EWCA Civ 1285.
18 *R (Zardhast v Secretary of State for the Home Department* [2004] EWHC 91 (Admin).
19 *R (Limbuela) v Secretary of State for the Home Department* [2004] EWHC 219 (Admin).
20 *R (Tesema) v Secretary of State for the Home Department* [2004] EWHC 295 (Admin) and *R (Adam) v Secretary of State for the Home Department* [2004] EWHC 354 (Admin) Charles J.

On 21 May 2004 the Court of Appeal found in favour of the asylum-seekers, ruling that the policy breached Article 3. As a result of the ruling, the Home Office had to review asylum support and issue guidance on the implementation of section 55 to avoid further human rights breaches and the continued cost of decisions being tested in the courts. The impact of this decision was two-fold. The number of section 55 cases being taken to court almost ceased, as the decision-making process improved and due to clearer guidance. On the other hand, it left a significant number of cases outstanding in the Administrative Court. The tactic of the Home Office was to appeal to the House of Lords, effectively leaving the case 'hanging'. As a result the majority of cases in the Administrative Court are dismissed, as individuals' asylum claims come to an end and they no longer have the jurisdiction to continue their claim under section 55 as they are not asylum-seekers eligible for NASS support. (The Home Office can then avoid paying costs on these cases.) It is thought unlikely that the Home Office will go ahead with their appeal (in *Limbuela*, etc) to the House of Lords.

Tactics: Expert evidence from non-legal agencies was invaluable. Liberty and the Joint Council for the Welfare of Immigrants presented expert evidence to the Court of Appeal in an earlier group of cases. In one Court of Appeal case over 20 agencies from a variety of sources (eg the Refugee Arrivals Project, community associations and groups) gave evidence.[21] This evidence was also used in other cases including *Limbuela*. Shelter was given permission to intervene in *Limbuela* and Lord Justice Jacob cited its evidence extensively (eg about the increase in homelessness that the government's policy was causing) as well as referring to evidence from the Refugee Council about the lack of capacity in shelters for asylum-seekers. Such evidence clearly had an impact on the judges' assessment on whether an Article 3 breach should be found.

---

21   *R (T) v Secretary of State for the Home Department* [2003] EWCA Civ 1285.

Outcomes: The Home Secretary's announcement and the initial decisions in *Limbuela* (and guidance which followed) helped to reduce the number of refusals of support under section 55. The number of cases has plummeted and in relation to section 55(5) both the policy and procedure appear to be substantially better.

Principles: Lawyers appear to have been unprepared for the full force of section 55 until it came on-stream. This was perhaps unsurprising given that it received little publicity and that section 55 was debated for a total of 15 minutes when the Bill was going through the Commons. In addition, when the provisions were mentioned during the Bill's passage the Minister David Blunkett said that section 55 would only apply to people who had been in the country for a considerable period of time.[22] However, there may be a lesson here in the importance of monitoring and then sharing information about new legislation as it goes through Parliament.

- Lawyers' efforts to make the most from the legal routes and organisations' contributions (especially their policy expertise and the wider evidence they supplied, in and out of court) made for a powerful combination.
- The extreme conditions that asylum-seekers were faced with (destitution) helped to win support for the campaign. The 'wait and see' (if an asylum-seeker's circumstances fall below an Article 3 threshold) approach was so harsh that it drew judges to comment on it.
- 'Piling cases high' helped to bring about legal will for change. The system became unworkable, and the Court of Appeal judges pointed out that dealing with this via the courts was not tenable.

22 Hansard HC Debates col 199, 5 November 2002.

Case example – joint working between lawyers, NGOs, etc

In 2005 a team of solicitors at Fisher Meredith and barristers from Hardwicke Chambers set up a forum for lawyers, NGOs and others to work together on a range of issues relating to individuals' rights regarding public services. Years of experience in acting for vulnerable individuals faced with a variety of different public bodies (eg NHS trusts, schools and government departments) showed a clear need for lawyers and organisations working with and for vulnerable people to be more effective in exchanging information and co-ordinating their work. The Choice and Access to Public Services Group (CAPS) will look at a variety of issues, primarily involving community care and health (eg the impact of the Mental Capacity Act 2004, access to care, etc). Its activities will include speaker meetings, articles and sharing information (eg via their website: www.capsgroup.co.uk).

Working in partnership: law reform

7.85–
7.93

Case study: Mental capacity and mental health legislation: the importance of joint working

Illustrates: the influence that a wide range of individuals and organisations can have when working in partnership.

The legislation: The Mental Capacity Act 2004 and the Mental Health Bill.

Joint working: There are two notable coalitions operating in this area that have been playing a significant role in influencing the government's legislative agenda.

The Making Decisions Alliance (MDA): This was created in 2002, and brought together national older and disabled people's organisations who were keen to make sure that the Labour government did not forget its promise on taking office in 1997 of a new law on mental capacity.

Activities: The MDA ran a positive campaign in support of the Mental Capacity Bill 2004. In addition to having successfully lobbied during pre-legislative scrutiny (see chapter 3), the coalition also sought to improve it in certain areas when the Bill was going through Parliament. The Bill passed fairly quietly through its first stages in the Commons, the government resisting attempts to amend it. However, by its final stages, MPs were being lobbied vociferously by groups claiming it would let 'euthanasia in by the backdoor' and a number of Labour MPs rebelled against the government. (Unusually for this type of law, Labour MPs were 'whipped', however Conservatives and Liberal Democrats were given a 'free vote' to act according to their conscience.) There was also confusion during the final debate in the Commons with an embarrassed minister, David Lammy MP, appearing to be unaware of all the negotiations that had taken place. The government was forced onto the back foot as the debate became dominated by the issue of living wills, and promised to introduce safeguards around advance directives. During the Lords debate, the MDA secured important concessions around advance statements and the provisions on advocates.

Outcomes: The Bill made it through the Lords and onto the statute book just before the 2005 General Election was called.[23]

The Mental Health Alliance (MHA): This is a larger and more diverse coalition than the MDA whose membership it overlaps with. It brings together user groups, professionals, voluntary organisations and others (eg the Mental Health Foundation, the Royal College of Psychiatrists). The Law Society's Mental Health and Disability committee is an active associate member. In the context of an adversarial legal system in which professionals are often pitched against the individual and their lawyers, it provides a forum for individuals and groups to be exposed to each others' points of view.

Activities: It was set up in January 2000 to provide a focus for campaigning on reform of the Mental Health Act 1983. Their aim is new legislation that provides a legal right to assessment, care and treatment to help reduce the use of compulsory powers. It has been engaged in a difficult and protracted process of

23 The Mental Capacity Act became law in April 2005 and will come into force in 2007.

opposing the government's initial plans for reform which have focused on extending compulsory powers of detention.

Outcomes: The MHA hoped that the government would listen to concerns and produce a very different creature from a previous draft (see para 3.50 for details) which was roundly criticised by the Joint Committee tasked with examining it. However, the government confirmed that the Bill, which was included in the 2005 Queen's Speech, would include measures to compel people to be treated in the community and to detain some with personality disorders before any crime had been committed.

Critical success factors

Making Decisions Alliance

7.94
- MDA members agree that the degree of collaboration allowed them to influence the process, leading the government to reconsider its options and introduce a better quality of law.
- A core group of members met frequently. Their close working enabled them to establish common positions, eg when negotiating with the government. This united group helped to 'keep the show on the road' when faced with lobby groups (eg the Society for the Protection of Unborn Children) that were vigorously opposing the legislation.
- Ministers relied on the MDA and others to help ensure the parliamentary and public support the Bill needed. At times, it suited the government to have one coalition to deal with.

Mental Health Alliance

7.95   The unique make-up of the coalition and especially its combination of users and professionals has been acknowledged as helpful not only in the process of influencing current legislative plans, but more generally.

- The MHA has put resources into local events, consultations and other activities aimed at stimulating debate around the country. This has also helped to raise awareness but also an opportunity to hear users' views about their experiences and priorities.

Campaigns checklists

For organisations

7.96   This checklist can be used wherever you work – in a solicitors' firm, barristers' chambers, law centre or elsewhere. It is aimed at stimulating people to think about how to increase their influence and link their legal work with the wider political processes. If you already think of yourself as a 'campaigning lawyer', you could use this audit to encourage colleagues to do more of this important work. Or if you would like to put your skills to wider use, then you could use it to kick-start this process.

Information gathering

7.97   How does your organisation get information about new proposals, consultations and laws being floated or currently going through Parliament? You need to be looking out for proposals at the earliest possible stage, ideally when a European directive is being considered or at consultation stage rather than when legislation is being considered by Parliament.

Tips:

7.98   • If you rely on one or two interested individuals and sometimes miss important new laws until they've got royal assent, you could identify a more systematic approach. Many campaigning organisations hold a meeting shortly after the Queen's Speech. They run over all the Bills and identify those that are priorities they are going to actively seek to influence through briefings, etc; those they will monitor with a view to doing some more limited work; and those they will keep a 'watching brief' on – for information rather than actively to influence. You could do the same at your first meeting after the Queen's Speech – which (election years aside) usually coincides with the beginning of the festive season.
    • The most comprehensive source of what is going on in Parliament is the *Weekly Information Bulletin* published by the House of Commons Information Office and available at www.parliament.uk in the Parliamentary Publications and Archives section.
    • Campaigning organisations often use a government and parliamentary monitoring service that provides frequent updates and information with a choice of topics to be monitored.

- There are numerous free emails (from NGOs, law firms, etc) that you can sign up to that will keep you up to date with political developments and what's going on in Parliament, etc.
- Government department websites have details of current consultations.

Increasing your knowledge and experience of campaigns and influencing

7.99   Many lawyers build up their experience of influencing and campaigns over time, through involvement with specific projects such as working on a Bill.

Tips:

7.100 • Do you have contacts with campaigners or influencing experience that you could make use of? For example, through contacts with a campaigning organisation you may know a campaigner or lobbyist who you could ask in for a presentation or to run a training session on campaign tactics or on parliamentary procedures. Or you may want to recruit someone to your management committee or trustee board with this type of experience.
- You could identify an emerging legal issue (eg from a group of lawyers in your field) and organise a seminar or informal meeting for them and a wider group (eg practising lawyers, academics, campaigners, policy experts, etc). You could seek input from the campaigners and non-lawyers on how the issue might be shaped as a campaign.

Building relationships with other organisations

7.101 Lots of lawyers work with organisations but it can sometimes be on an ad hoc basis rather than building up relations over the long term.

Tips:

- Does your organisation have links with the key campaigns organisations working in your main areas of interest? There are often paid or unpaid opportunities to give legal advice or, less formally, simply to share ideas about emerging legal issues and this can help stimulate a fruitful relationship.

- Within your firm or team you could carry out an audit of relevant organisations, discussing whether you would like to build a more strategic relationship with one or two of them.
- A secondment to the legal or policy team of a large organisation could provide real insight into their workings and a chance to influence a specific project.
- You could identify a policy or campaigns person from an organisation and invite them in as a guest speaker.
- Many organisations publish bulletins or email newsletters which will give you ideas for linking up with their campaigns and provide opportunities to share information – eg for lawyers' groups looking for particular cases.
- You could consider joint projects you could be running with an organisation – eg as a new law emerges you could help to devise and deliver training for local groups.
- Do you have a charitable fund that helps external organisations? Donations, especially unrestricted and that can be spent on the charity's running costs, are obviously useful, especially if a sum is pledged for a number of years. But even more valuable could be advice or support in fundraising from other firms or chambers.
- You could think of new partnerships that bring together a wide range of experts and users. These need not be in traditional legal areas like employment and family but could be more cross-cutting (eg Choice and Access to Public Services, see p322).
- Is there a bank of anonymised case studies in your area that are readily available when needed for media or parliamentary work or could there be a way to share these more effectively?

For individuals

7.102 If you are interested in campaigning, why not approach an organisation in which you have an interest? Find out about any existing contact or involvement of lawyers in their work. Identify what you have to offer, eg specialism in employment or family law or links with a relevant practitioners' association.

Tips:

- Research the organisations to identify those of most interest to you and where your skills will be of most use.

- What kind of organisation is it – does it deliver services, focus on campaigns or both?
- What is the organisation's approach to law and lawyers? You could identify an organisation that does not currently make good strategic use of the law or external links with lawyers and think of useful input you might be able to give. Or you could input into an organisation that already has a well-developed and strategic legal 'arm'.
- Identify the key people in the organisation who can give you more information – eg the campaigns department or a specific policy officer.
- Look out for specific campaigns that your legal expertise has a link with.
- Be clear about what you have to offer – including time – and what you wish to gain from the experience.
- Don't overlook the value of your general legal skills to an organisation, in particular communications and analysis.

APPENDICES

Example second reading briefing

THE CATS BILL 2005

PARLIAMENTARY BRIEFING

House of Commons

Second Reading Tuesday 18 January 2005

PURPOSE OF THE BILL

The Cats Bill will take forward some of the issues covered in the government's green paper, 'Animal welfare in the 21st century' by identifying ways to protect cats who become strays, either because of deliberate abandonment by their owners or due to other circumstances (eg when the owner dies). The Bill's provisions include:

- The establishment of a Cats Welfare Protection Fund to provide protection to cats whose owners die or reject them
- A new obligation on local authorities to find homes for stray cats in their area

  Etc ...

GENERAL VIEW

X organisation warmly welcomes the Cats Bill, which at last recognises the need to tackle the growing numbers of stray cats including those who become strays when their owners die. We are pleased that the government listened to our concerns during their consultation on the Animal Welfare Green Paper and have strengthened the proposals for the new Cats Welfare Protection Fund. However, we remain concerned that unless there are sufficient resources made available, this will still leave many cats without protection and the opportunity of a home.

Etc ...

For further information please contact x on x number or by email: x. For general information about our work please go to our website: x.

CATS BILL: BRIEFING FOR SECOND READING DEBATE

Specific points

RESOURCES

X believes it is unacceptable that hundreds of cats become strays each year and that many go on to suffer and/or die prematurely as a result. Whilst we accept that the government cannot be held responsible for individuals' irresponsible actions, we do believe that local authorities should take responsibility once a cat has become stray. We would like to see local authorities penalised if they fail to find homes for all strays in their area and rewarded for positive actions. Related to this, we believe the new Protection Fund must be adequately resourced so that there will be enough money to go round all the local authorities and/or voluntary cat shelters who apply to it for assistance for stray cats. Our research indicates that an average charitable cat shelter spends approximately £300 per week per animal and we would like to see this taken into account when resource allocation is considered.

Joint working

We would like to see the government encouraging local authorities to work closely with a range of voluntary animal welfare organisations in its area to ensure that stray cats are identified quickly, so as to minimise the time they spend without a home. Our 10 years' experience of housing cats has shown us that the money that needs to be spent on a stray cat (eg on medical treatment) is substantially higher the longer the period they have spent living away from a home.

Etc ...

Summary: X is very supportive of the Cats Bill and welcomes all its proposals. However, we believe that the government must pay especial attention to the resources needed to make a success of the new scheme and in particular should take account of the actual costs of providing homes for stray cats.

Example briefing for an amendment to the Bill

Note:

- There are different types of amendment: eg to leave out parts of the text or to amend the long title. The House of Lords publishes 'A Guide to House of Lords Amendment Style' which gives details of the different types, examples and drafting tips (www.publications. parliament.uk).

- You should include each amendment and briefing on a separate page, to make it easier for parliamentarians to speak to them.

THE CATS BILL 2005

PARLIAMENTARY BRIEFING

House of Commons

Committee stage

Page 1, line 10, leave out 'temporary'

Summary

This amendment is aimed at clarifying the ways in which local authorities can discharge their new duty to provide accommodation for stray cats in their area.

Purpose

Clause 2 imposes a duty on local authorities to secure accommodation for stray cats. However, as currently drafted it only enables them to secure temporary accommodation (eg in a cat shelter). By leaving out the word 'temporary', this amendment would make it clear that in discharging their duty local authorities can either secure temporary or permanent shelter and accommodation (eg when a permanent offer of accommodation is made in a person's home). It would not impose any additional duties on them but would help clarify the range of options open to them in discharging their new legal duty.

Please contact x.

Example new clause briefing

PENSIONS BILL

HOUSE OF LORDS

Committee Stage – Commencing Tuesday 6 July

Parliamentary Briefing

Amendment

After Clause 282 insert the following new Clause –

'**Reduced contributions pensions**

(1) The Social Security (Widow's Benefit and Retirement Pensions) Regulations 1979 (SI 1979/642) is amended as follows.

(2) In Regulation 6(1), for "23" substitute "0".

(3) In Regulation 6(2), for "25" substitute "0".'

Aim of the new Clause

This new Clause will end the unfair 25% rule which means that people with fewer than 10 years' full NI contributions receive no pension at all in their own name.

Background to the Let's Make Pensions Work for Women campaign

Today in Britain, more single women pensioners live in poverty than male pensioners. The gender gap in retirement is so great that for every £1 that a man in a pensioner couple receives from a pension, a woman receives 32 pence. The government's own green paper on pensions described this issue as being one which will 'lag behind that of men for some years to come'. Older women face this situation for a number of different reasons such as: lower pay; more time spent out of the National Insurance (NI) system because of caring responsibilities; and anomalies in the pension system which means that paying into the system does not always mean getting anything in return.

Age Concern and the Fawcett Society have been actively campaigning on this issue for over a year as part of our *Let's Make*

Pensions Work for Women campaign. We have been working with political parties and the government to highlight this issue. At all stages of the campaign we have consulted government departments, such as the Department for Work and Pensions and the Treasury, to help us cost out our recommendations and assess the impact they would have. We believe it is crucial that the government addresses this issue. We feel that the Pensions Bill is an ideal time for the government to commit to taking action on this issue. We welcome the fact that the government has recognised the problems that women face with building up NI contributions. The government's paper *Working and saving for retirement – Action on occupational pensions* stated that: 'Many policy suggestions that emerged during the consultation [for the green paper on pensions] proposed ways in which National Insurance cover could be extended to include more women. We will examine these and other policy suggestions.' We welcome this commitment and look forward to being updated on these considerations.

Annual Report

We were particularly pleased that the government responded to a new clause tabled by Vera Baird MP during committee stage in the Commons and announced it would publish a report on women and pensions in 2005. This proposal was one which Age Concern England has been calling for. We hope that the report will go further than the chapter of the green paper on pensions which looked at women's pensions which only described the situation rather than coming up with concrete solutions. Our recent *One in Four* report built on the challenge set by the green paper by coming up with small step changes which could help to make the system work more effectively for women. We would like the government to comment on the recommendations, made in Age Concern England and the Fawcett Society's recent report and to offer solutions to the problems and milestones for change.

25% rule

One recommendation that we are making is to pay pensions to everyone who pays into the National Insurance system. We believe that all National Insurance contributions should count, yet tens of thousands of women pay their contributions – amounting to thousands of pounds – but receive no pension. Because they pay NI contributions for fewer than 10 years (because of the 25% pension entitlement rule) they are not eligible. The rule is patently unfair and should be scrapped. We supported a new clause tabled in the Commons to end this unfair ruling.

For further information, please contact x.

Practice Direction Hansard Extracts

15.7 Application – This Direction concerns both final and interlocutory hearings in which any party intends to refer to the reports of parliamentary proceedings as reported in the official reports of parliamentary proceedings as reported in the official reports of either House of Parliament, Hansard. No other report of parliamentary proceedings is to be cited.

15.8 Documents to be served – Any party intending to refer to any extract from *Hansard* in support of any such argument as was permitted by the decisions in *Pepper v Hart* [1993] AC 593; [1992]3 W.L.R. 1032, and *Pickstone v. Freemans plc* [1989] A.C. 66; [1988] CMLR 221, HL, or otherwise, must unless the judge otherwise directs, serve upon all other parties and the court copies of any such extract together with a brief summary of the argument intended to be based upon such report.

15.9 Time for Service – Unless the judge otherwise directs, service upon other parties to the proceedings and the court of the extract and summary of arguments referred to above is to be effected not less than five clear working days before the first day of the hearing. That applies whether or not there is a fixed date. Solicitors must keep themselves informed as to the state of the lists where no fixed date had been given.

15.10 Methods of service – Service on the court is to be effected by sending to the Court of Appeal, Civil Division, three copies to the Civil Appeals Office, Case Support Section, Room E307, Royal Courts of Justice, Strand, London WC2A 2LL.

15.11 Failure to serve – If any party fails to comply with this Practice Direction the court might make such order, relating to costs and otherwise, as is in all the circumstances appropriate.

Example news release

Media contact: 000

Telephone: 000

Out of hours: 000

Strictly embargoed until: 00.01 hours Saturday, 18 June 2005

EQUAL TREATMENT FOR WOMEN IS KEY TO PENSIONS SUCCESS warns Age Concern

The government will fail to deliver successful pension reform without putting the needs of women at the heart of the debate, warns Age Concern. New research[1] reveals overwhelming public support for a shake-up of the system to put carers on an equal footing with those in traditional paid employment.

As the government kicks off discussions to build a consensus on pensions, Age Concern's research sends a clear signal that the public is ready for radical reform:

- 75% want carers or those in part-time or low-paid work to have their contribution recognised in the same way as full-time employment[2]
- 61% believe that the government should reduce the number of years needed to qualify for a pension or introduce a pension based on residency
- Just 22% believe the current system is fair and shouldn't be changed

One in five single women pensioners in the UK now lives in poverty and just 16% of newly retired women qualify for a full basic state pension on their own contributions, compared to 78% of men.[4] Despite high divorce rates, the new figures reveal that a third of young women plan to rely on their partner for a pension.

The inequality between men and women has already been dubbed a national scandal by the government. But urgent action is needed if future generations of women – particularly carers, full-time mothers and low-paid or part-time workers – are to avoid the fate of their mothers and grandmothers.

Fundamental reform rather than incremental change is the only way to achieve a fair pension system that will meet the needs of an ageing population. Radical reform which tackles the scandal of pensioner poverty, gives women and carers a fair deal, and allows everybody the opportunity to build a decent retirement income is absolutely crucial.

Michelle Mitchell, head of public affairs at Age Concern said: 'Building a national consensus on pensions that will stand the test of time is critical. Unless the government puts gender equality at the heart of the debate it will fail to achieve a lasting settlement on pensions.

'The government must work towards introducing a pensions system that allows everybody, regardless of their working patterns or income, the chance to build up their own independent retirement income.'

-Ends-

Notes to editors

1　ICM research commissioned by Age Concern, June 2005.

2　The question asked was broken down into part-time, low-paid and carers: *for the purposes of building up a state pension, which, if any, of the following do you think should be recognised in the same way as full-time employment?*

   Part time employment – 79%

   Low-paid employment – 75%

   Staying at home to care for the family – 77%

4　Government, Principles for Reform, 2004

- ICM Research interviewed a random sample of 1010 adults aged 18+ by telephone between 10 and 12 June 2005. Interviews were conducted across the country and the results have been weighted to the profile of all adults. ICM is a member of the British Polling Council and abides by its rules. Further information at www.icmresearch.co.uk.

- Age Concern and the Fawcett Society have been jointly campaigning for the Government to tackle the scandal of female pensioner poverty since 2003. Two reports have been published 'One in Four' (February 2004) and 'A Blueprint for Reform' (April 2005) and are available from www.ageconcern.org.uk or by calling Helen or John on 020 8765 7514 or 7515.

- Case studies may be available on request.

- Radio producers: Age Concern has an ISDN line. Spokespeople are available for interview.

Extract from Bar Code of Conduct

MEDIA COMMENT

709.1 A barrister must not in relation to any anticipated or current proceedings or mediation[1] in which he is briefed or expects to appear or has appeared as an advocate express a personal opinion to the press or other media or in any other public statement upon the facts or issues arising in the proceedings.

709.2 Paragraph 709.1 shall not prevent the expression of such an opinion on an issue in an educational or academic context.

ADVERTISING AND PUBLICITY

710.1 Subject to paragraph 710.2 a barrister may engage in any advertising or promotion in connection with his practice which conforms to the British Codes of Advertising and Sales Promotion and such advertising or promotion may include:

(a) photographs or other illustrations of the barrister;

(b) statements of rates and methods of charging;

(c) statements about the nature and extent of the barrister's services;

(d) information about any case in which the barrister has appeared (including the name of any client for whom the barrister acted) where such information has already become publicly available or, where it has not already become publicly available, with the express prior written consent of the lay client.

710.2 Advertising or promotion must not:

(a) be inaccurate or likely to mislead;

(b) be likely to diminish public confidence in the legal profession or the administration of justice or otherwise bring the legal profession into disrepute;

(c) make direct comparisons in terms of quality with or criticisms of other identifiable persons (whether they be barristers or members of any other profession);

(d) include statements about the barrister's success rate;

(e) indicate or imply any willingness to accept instructions or any intention to restrict the persons from whom instructions may be accepted otherwise than in accordance with this Code;

(f) be so frequent or obtrusive as to cause annoyance to those to whom it is directed.

1   Amended 23 March 2005.
Source: Bar Council Website.

List of practitioners' associations

Community care
Solicitors for the Elderly
Julie Cameron
Solicitors for the Elderly
PO Box 257
Broxbourne
Hertfordshire
EN10 7YV
Tel: 01992 471568
Email: jcameron@solicitorsfortheelderly.com

Criminal practice
The Criminal Bar Association
289–293 High Holborn
London
WC1V 7HZ
Tel: 020 7242 1289
Email: Jbradley@barcouncil.org.uk

Criminal Law Solicitors' Association
Sue Johnson
CLSA Administrator
Suite 2 Level 6
New England House
New England Street
Brighton
BN14GH
Tel: 01273 676725
Fax: 01273 676231

London Criminal Courts Solicitors' Association
President: Robert Brown
Corker Binning Solicitors
12 Devereux Court
Strand
London
WC2R 3JJ
Tel: 020 7353 6000
Email: rb@corkerbinning.co.uk

Education law
Education Law Association
Registered Office Winterton House
Nixey Close
Slough
SL1 1ND
Email: elas@educationlawassociation.org.uk

Employment law
Employment Lawyers Association
PO Box 353
Uxbridge
UB10 0UN
Tel/fax: 01895 256972
Email: enquiries@elaweb.org.uk

Employment Law Bar Association
2nd Floor
2–3 Cursitor Street
London
EC4A1NE
Tel: 020 7242 1289
Fax: 020 7242 1107
Email: charris@barcouncil.org.uk

Family law
Association of Child Abuse Lawyers
ACAL
Suite 5
Claremont House
22–24 Claremont Road
Surbiton
KT6 4QU
Tel. 020 8390 4701
Fax 020 8399 1152
Email: info@childabuselawyers.com

Association of Lawyers for Children
ALC
PO Box 283
East Molesey
KT8 OWH
Tel/fax: 020 8224 7071
Email: admin@alc.org.uk

Family Law Bar Association
289–293 High Holborn
London
WC1V 7HZ
Tel: 020 7242 1289
Fax: 020 7831 7144
DX: 240 LDE
Email: charris@barcouncil.org.uk

Resolution (formerly the 'Solicitors Family Law Association')
PO Box 302
Orpington
Kent
BR6 8QX
Telephone: 01689 850227
Fax: 01689 855833
Email: info@resolution.org.uk

Housing law
Housing and Immigration Group
Email: hig@hflaw.org.uk

Housing Law Practitioners' Association
88 Old Street
London
EC1V 9HU
Tel: 020 7505 4693
Fax: 0207505 2168
Email: admin@hlpa.org.uk

Human rights
Human Rights Lawyers Association
2nd Floor
289–293 High Holborn
London
WC1V 7HZ
Tel: 020 7242 1289
Email: SMontgomery@barcouncil.org.uk

Immigration law
Immigration Law Practitioners Association
Lindsey House
40–42 Charterhouse Street
London
EC1 M 6JN
Tel: 020 7251 8383
Fax: 020 7251 8384
Email: info@ilpa.org.uk

Legal aid
Legal Aid Practitioners Group
Kate Comyn
10 Greycoat Place
London
SW1P 1SB
Tel: 020 7960 6068
Fax: 0207960 6168
Email: kate@lapg.co.uk

Mental health

Mental Health Lawyers Association
c/o Peter Lyle, David Turner & Co Solicitors
Suite 511
162–168 Regent Street
London
W1B 5TF
Tel: 020 7437 4439
Fax: 020 7038 3700
Email: dtplus@dircon.co.uk

Personal injury and clinical negligence

Association of Personal Injury Lawyers
11 Castle Quay
Nottingham
NG7 1FW
Tel: 01159 580585
Fax: 01159 580885
Email: sharon@apil.com

Medico-Legal Society
EMIS Professional Publishing
Fulford Grange
Micklefield Lane
Rawdon
Leeds
LS19 6BA
Tel: 08701 225525
Fax: 0113 3803423
Email: mls@emispp.com

Motor Accident Solicitors Society
54 Baldwin Street
Bristol
BS1 1QW
Tel: 0117 929 2560
Fax: 0117 904 7220
Email: office@mass.org.uk

Pan-European Organisation of Personal Injury Lawyers
Imperial House
31 Temple St
Birmingham B2 50B
Tel: 0121 643 4962
Email: admin@peopil.com

Personal Injuries Bar Association
3 Worthington Close
Henbury
Nr Macclesfield
SK11 9NS
Email: bridges4piba@hotmail.com

Pro bono

Bar Pro Bono Unit & Bar in the Community
289–293 High Holborn
London
WC1V 7HZ

Bar Pro Bono Unit
Tel: 020 7611 9500
Bar in the Community
Tel: 020 7611 9511
Fax: 020 7611 9505
Email: enquiries@barprobono.org.uk

Free Representation Unit
6th Floor
289–293 High Holborn
London
WC1V 7HZ
Tel: 020 7611 9555
Email: admin@freerepresentationunit.org.uk

Solicitors Pro Bono Group
10–13 Lovat Lane
London
EC3R 8DN
Tel: 020 7929 5601
Fax: 020 7929 5722
Email: info@probonogroup.org.uk

Public law

Bar Association for Local Government and the Public Service
Chairman c/o Birmingham City Council
Legal Services Office
Ingleby House
11–14 Cannon Street
Birmingham
B2 5EN
Email: Chairman@balgps.org.uk

Solicitors in Local Government
Stephanie Nunn
The Law Society
113 Chancery Lane
London
WC2A IPL
Tel: 020 7320 5801
Fax: 020 7831 0170
Email: stephanie. nunn@lawsociety.org.uk

Bibliography

TEXTBOOKS, ARTICLES AND GUIDES

The Civil Service Handbook.

Clerk of the House, 'Business of the House and its committees', January 2003.

Nicholas Comfort, *How to handle the media,* Politico's, 2003.

M Fletcher-Brown, *The media handbook: a guide to better media relations,* Reputation, 2003.

Paul Flynn MP, *Commons knowledge: how to be a backbencher,* Seren, 1997.

Carol Harlow and Richard Rawlings, *Pressure through law,* Routledge, 1992.

Peter Hennessey, *Whitehall,* 3rd edn, Pimlico, 2001.

Kavanagh and Seldon, *The powers behind the Prime Minister,* Harper Collins, 2000.

Richard Keeble, *The newspapers handbook,* 3rd edn, Routledge, 2001.

Andrew Marr, *My trade: a short history of British journalism,* Macmillan, 2004.

Andrew Nicol QC and Geoffrey Robertson QC, *Media law,* Sweet & Maxwell and Penguin, 2002.

John Pinder, *The European Union: a very short introduction,* OUP, 2001.

PMS parliamentary companion, PMS Publications.

David Randall, *The universal journalist,* 2nd edn, Pluto Press, 2000.

Scrutiny Committee, 'The European Union: Institutions and Legislation', www.parliament.uk.

Roger Smith, 'Test case strategies and the Human Rights Act', *Justice Journal,* 2004, Vol 1, No 1, p65.

Martin Stanley, *How to be a civil servant,* 2nd edn, Politico's, 2004.

Sue Stapley, *Media relations for lawyers,* 2nd edn, The Law Society, 2003.

'Test cases for the poor Legal techniques in the politics of social welfare', Child Poverty Action Group, September 1983.

Vacher's European companion, Vacher Dod Publishing Ltd.

Vacher's parliamentary companion, Vacher Dod Publishing Ltd.

WEBSITES

Acts of the UK Parliament
www.opsi.gov.uk/acts.htm
From 1988.

Bills before Parliament
www.parliament.uk/bills/bills.cfm

Britain and the EU
www.europe.gov.uk
Part of the Foreign and Commonwealth Office's website.

Directgov
www.direct.gov.uk
Has a wide range of information about government services,
how government works and useful links to other sites.

Euro Citizen Action Service
www.ecas.org
Aimed at NGOs.

European Commission
www.europa.eu.int/comm

European Court of Justice
www.curia.eu.int

European Information Service
www.lgib.gov.uk/eis
Published by the Local Government International Bureau.

European Parliament
www.europarl.eu.int

European Union
www.europa.eu.int

Factsheet (L11) on European Communities Legislation
www.parliament.uk/factsheets

A guide to House of Lords amendment style
www.publications.parliament.uk/pa/ld/ldamend.pdf
How to set out amendments to Bills when they are in the Lords.

House of Commons publications
www.publications.parliament.uk/pa/cm/cmpubns.htm

How to be a civil servant
www.civilservant.org.uk
Accompanies the book by Martin Stanley.

List of ministerial responsibilities
www.knowledgenetwork.gov.uk/elmr/minister.nsf
Includes agencies.

Parliament Live
www.parliamentlive.tv
Parliamentary sessions broadcast live over the Internet.

TheyWorkForYou
www.theyworkforyou.com
To check an MP's voting record.

UK Office of the European Parliament
www.europarl.org.uk

UK Parliament
www.parliament.uk
Vast array of information on all aspects of the workings of the UK Parliament.

UK Parliamentary Committees
www.parliament.uk/parliamentary_committees/
parliamentary_committees16.cfm

UK Statutory Instruments
www.opsi.gov.uk/stat.htm
Since 1987.

UKREP   www.ukrep.be

Weekly Information Bulletin
www.publications.parliament.uk/pa/cm/cmwib.htm
Full details of progress of each Bill, including Private Members' Bills.

Index

Malet Street, London WC1E 7HX
020-7631 6239
Items should be returned or renewed by the latest date stamped below.
Please pick up a Library guide or visit the Library website
http://www.bbk.ac.uk/lib/
for information about online renewals.

13/ 02/ 08

ONE WEEK LOAN